THE BUDDHIST PERSPECTIVES ON HUMAN RIGHTS

THE BUDDHIST
PERSPECTIVES ON
HUMAN RIGHTS

A N Das

MD PUBLICATIONS PVT LTD
NEW DELHI
www.mdppl.com

Published by :

MD Publications Pvt Ltd
"MD House", 11, Darya Ganj,
New Delhi-110 002
Phone : +91-11-45355555
E-mail : contact@mdppl.com
Website : www.mdppl.com

ISBN : 978-81-7533-292-8

Published and Printed by Mr. Pranav Gupta on behalf of
MD Publications Pvt Ltd at Printext, New Delhi.

PREFACE

Despite the grudging consensus, only a minority seem prepared to embrace Human Rights wholeheartedly within a Buddhist context. Others are deeply suspicious of the concept because they cannot find its germ in Buddhist teachings. Buddhist philosophy distinguishes between ultimate realities (dhamma), with which it is deeply concerned, and "concepts" (paññatti), with which it is not. Human Rights fall into the latter category. They are a man-made concept, developed within the specific context of modern Western culture. Yet within that culture, Human Rights are absolutely central to contemporary ethical thinking, so Buddhist thinkers must face the subject squarely if they are not to appear irrelevant or anachronistic.

Buddhism is a latecomer to the cause of human rights, and for most of its history has been preoccupied with other concerns. It might be suggested, in defense of Buddhism, that concern for human rights is a post-religious phenomenon which has more to do with secular ideologies and power-politics than religion, and it is therefore unreasonable to accuse Buddhism of neglect in this area. An intellectually dynamic tradition Buddhism is a lightweight in moral and political philosophy. A fig-leaf of a kind may be found in the suggestion that since much Buddhist literature remains untranslated there may be hidden treasures in these areas awaiting discovery. Such appeals to the unknown, however, lack credibility.

It might be said that in classical Buddhism the notion of rights is present in embryonic form although not yet born into history. Whether anything like the Western concept of rights has, or would, appear in the course of the historical evolution of Buddhism is a question for specialists in the various Buddhist cultures to ponder. In many respects the omens for this development were never good. Buddhism originated in a caste society, and the Asian societies where it has flourished have for the most part been hierarchically structured.

Political events in the course of this century, however, have forced the issue of human rights to the top of the agenda. The Chinese invasion of Tibet, the bitter ethnic conflict in Sri Lanka, and the experience of military dictatorship in countries such as Burma have all provided contemporary Buddhism with first-hand experience of the issues at stake. Another development which has done much to focus attention on social and political themes is the emergence of "socially engaged Buddhism," a movement whose very name implies a critique of the more traditional (presumably "disengaged") forms of Buddhism. It seems that the concept of a right may exist where a word for it does not. In Buddhism what is due in any situation is determined by reference to Dharma. Dharma determines what is right and just in all contexts and from all perspectives.

I am very grateful to Mr. Pranav Gupta, Director of MD Publications Pvt Ltd, New Delhi, for his kind cooperation and support for this book.

A N Das

CONTENTS

1

The Buddhist
Perspectives on Human Rights
An Introduction

It is incorrect to assume that the concept of human rights is readily identifiable in all societies of the world. The concept may perhaps be clear and distinct in legal quarters, but in actual practice it suffers greatly from lack of clarity and gray areas due to impositions by different cultures. This is especially true in Asia, where the two great civilizations of India and China have spawned such outstanding systems as Hinduism, Buddhism, Jainism, Yoga, Confucianism, Taoism and Chinese Buddhism.

These systems, together with other indigenous folk beliefs, attest to the cultural diversity at play that characterizes Asia proper. In focusing on the concept of human rights, however, we shall concentrate on Buddhism to bring out the common grounds of discourse. Alone among the great systems of Asia, Buddhism has successfully crossed geographical and ideological borders and spread in time throughout the whole length and breadth of known Asia. Its doctrines are so universal and profound that they captured the imagination of all the peoples they touched and thereby established a subtle bond with all.

What then is this bond? It must be something common to all systems of thought which opens up and allows spiritual discourse among them. In examining the metaphysical ground of all systems, one finds that there is a basic feeling for a larger reality in one's own experience, a kind of reaching out for a greater cosmic dimension of being, as it were. It is a deep sense for the total nature of things. All this may seem so simple and hardly merits elaborating, but it is a genuine feeling common among Asians in their quest for ultimate knowledge based on the proper relationship of one's self in the world. It is an affirmation of a reality that includes but at once goes beyond the confines of sense faculties.

A good illustration of this metaphysical grounding is seen in the Brahmanic world of Hinduism. In it, the occluded nature of the self (atman) constantly works to cleanse itself of defilements by yogic discipline in the hope of ultimately identifying with the larger reality which is Brahman. In the process, the grounding in the larger reality is always kept intact, regardless of whether the self is impure or not. In other words, in the quest for the purity of things a larger framework of experience is involved from the beginning such that the ordinary self (atman) transforms into the larger Self (Atman) and finally merges into the ultimate ontological Brahman.

A similar metaphysical grounding is found in Chinese thought. Confucianism, for example, with its great doctrine of humanity (jen), involves the ever-widening and ever-deepening human relationship that issues forth in the famous statement, "All men are brothers." In this sense, humanity is not a mere abstract concept but one that extends concretely throughout the whole of sentient existence.

Confucius once said that when he searched for jen, it is always close at hand. It means that humanity is not something external to a person but that it is constitutive of the person's experience, regardless of whether there is consciousness of it or not. It means moreover that in the relational nature of society, individual existence is always more than that which one assumes it to be. In this vein, all experiences must fit into the larger cosmological scheme normally spoken of in terms of heaven, earth and mankind. This triadic relationship is ever-present and ever-in-force, despite one's ignorance, negligence or outright intention to deny it. The concept that permeates and enlivens the triadic relationship is the Tao. The Tao is a seemingly catchall term, perhaps best translated as the natural way of life and the world. In its naturalness, it manifests all of existence; indeed, it is here, there and everywhere since it remains aloof from human contrivance and manipulation. In a paradoxical sense, it depicts action based on non action (wu-wei), the deepest state of being achievable. The following story illustrates this point.

A cook named Ting is alleged to have used the same carving knife for some 19 years without sharpening it at all. When asked how that is possible, he simply replied:

What I care about Is the way (Tao), which goes beyond skill. When I first began cutting up oxen, all I could see was the ox itself. After three years I no longer saw the whole ox. And now-now I go at it by spirit and don't look with my eyes. Perception and understanding have come to a stop and spirit moves where it wants. I go along with the natural makeup, strike in the big hollows, guide the knife through the big openings, and follow things as they are, so I never touch the smallest ligament or tendon, much less a main joint... I've had this knife of mine for nineteen years and I've cut up thousands of oxen with it, and yet the blade is as good as though it had just come from the grindstone.

Such then is the master craftsman at work, a master in harmonious triadic relationship based on the capture of the spirit of Tao where the function is not limited to a person and his or her use of a tool. And it is clear that such a spirit of Tao in craftsmanship is germane to all disciplined experiences we are capable of achieving in our daily activities.

Buddhism, too, has always directed our attention to the larger reality of existence. The original enlightenment of the historical Buddha told of a pure unencumbered experience which opened up all experiential doors in such a way that they touched everything sentient as well as insentient. A Zen story graphically illustrates this point. Once a master and a disciple were walking through a dense forest. Suddenly, they heard the clean chopping strokes of the woodcutter's axe. The disciple was elated and remarked, "What beautiful sounds in the quiet of the forest!" To which the master immediately responded, "you have got it all upside down. The sounds only make obvious the deep silence of the forest!"

The response by the Zen master sets in bold relief the Buddhist perception of reality. Although existential reality refers to the perception of the world as a singular unified whole, we ordinarily perceive it in fragmented ways because of our heavy reliance on the perceptual apparatus and its consequent understanding. That is to say, we perceive by a divisive and selective method which however glosses over much of reality and indeed misses its holistic nature. Certainly, the hewing sounds of the woodcutter's axe are clearly audible and delightful to the ears, but they are so at the expense of the basic silence of the forest (i.e., total reality).

Or, the forest in its silence constitutes the necessary background, indeed the basic source, from which all sounds (and all activities for that matter) originate. Put another way, sounds arising from the silence of the forest should in no way deprive nor intrude upon the very source of their own being. Only human beings make such intrusions by their crude discriminate habits of perception and, consequently, suffer a truncated form of existence, unknowingly for the most part. Now that we have seen Asian lives in general grounded in a holistic cosmological framework, we would have to raise the following question: How does this framework appear in the presence of human rights? Or, contrarily, how does human right function within this framework?

Admittedly, the concept of human rights is relatively new to Asians. From the very beginning, it did not sit well with their basic cosmological outlook. Indeed, the existence of such an outlook has prevented in profound ways a ready acceptance of foreign elements and has created tension and struggle between tradition and modernity. Yet, the key concept in the tension is that of human relationship. This is especially true in Buddhism, where the emphasis is not so much on the performative acts and individual rights as it is on the manner of manifestation of human nature itself.

The Buddhist always takes human nature as the basic context in which all ancillary concepts, such as human rights, are understood and take on any value. Moreover, the concept itself is in harmony with the extended experiential nature of things. And thus, where the Westerner is much more at home in treating legal matters detached from human nature as such and quite confident in forging ahead to establish human rights with a distinct emphasis on certain "rights," the Buddhist is much more reserved but open and seeks to understand the implications of human behavior, based on the fundamental nature of human beings, before turning his or her attention to the so called "rights" of individuals.

An apparent sharp rift seems to exist between the Western and Buddhist views, but this is not really so. Actually, it is a matter of perspectives and calls for a more comprehensive understanding of what takes place in ordinary human relationships. For the basic premise is still one that focused on human beings intimately living together in the selfsame world. A difference in perspectives does not mean non-communication or a simple rejection of another's view as there is still much more substance in the nature of conciliation, accommodation and absorption than what is initially thought of. Here we propose two contrasting but interlocking and complementary terms, namely, "hard relationship" and "soft relationship."

The Western view on human rights is generally based on a hard relationship. Persons are treated as separate and independent entities or even bodies, each having its own assumed identity or self-identity. It is a sheer "elemental" way of perceiving things due mainly to the strong influence by science and its methodology. As scientific methodology thrives on the dissective and analytic incursion into reality as such, this in turn has resulted in our perceiving and understanding things in terms of disparate realities.

Although it makes way for easy understanding, the question still remains: Do we really understand what these realities are in their own respective fullness of existence? Apparently not. And to make matters worse, the methodology unfortunately has been uncritically extended over to the human realm, into human nature and human relations. Witness its ready acceptance by the various descriptive and behavioral sciences, such as sociology, psychology and anthropology. On this matter, Cartesian dualism of mind and body has undoubtedly influenced our ordinary ways of thinking in such a manner that in our casual perception of things we habitually subscribe to the clear cut subject-object dichotomy.

This dualistic perspective has naturally filtered down into human relationships and has eventually crystallized into what we refer to as the nature of a hard relationship. Thus, a hard relationship is a mechanistic treatment of human beings where the emphasis is on beings as such regardless of their inner nature and function in the fullest sense; it is an atomistic analysis of beings where the premium is placed on what is relatable and manipulable without regard for their true potential for becoming. In a way it is externalization in the extreme, since the emphasis is heavily weighted on seizing the external character of beings themselves.

Very little attention, if any, is given to the total ambience, inclusive of inner contents and values, in which the beings are at full play. In this regard, it can be said that postmodern thought is now attempting to correct this seemingly lopsided dichotomous view created by our inattention to the total experiential nature of things. We believe this is a great step in the right direction. Meanwhile, we trudge along with a heavy burden on our backs, though unaware of it for the most part, by associating with people on the basis of hard relationships.

To amplify on the nature of hard relationships, let us turn to a few modern examples. First, Thomas Hobbes in his great work, *Leviathan* showed remarkable grasp of human psychology when he asserted that people are constantly at war with each other. Left in this "state of nature," people will never be able to live in peace and security The only way out of this conundrum is for all to establish a reciprocal relationship or mutual trust that would work, i.e., to strike up a covenant by selfish beings that guarantees mutual benefits and gains, one in which each relinquishes certain rights in order to gain or realize a personal as well as an overall state of peace and security. This was undoubtedly a brilliant scheme. But the scheme is weak in that it treats human beings by and large mechanically, albeit psychologically too, as entities in a give-and-take affair, and thus perpetuates the condition of hard relationships.

Another example can be offered by way of the British utilitarian movement which later was consummated in American pragmatism. Jeremy Bentham's hedonic calculus (e.g., intensity of pleasure or pain, duration of pleasure or pain, certain or uncertainty of pleasure or pain, purity or impurity of pleasure or pain, etc.) is a classic example of quantification of human experience. Although this is a most expedient or utilitarian way to treat and legislate behavior, we must remind ourselves that we are by no means mere quantifiable entities. John Stuart Mill introduced the element of quality in order to curb and tone down the excesses of the quantification process, but, in the final analysis, human nature and relationships are still set in hard relations. American pragmatism fares no better since actions by and large take place in a pluralistic world of realities and are framed within the scientific mode and therefore it is unable to relinquish the nature of hard relationships.

In contemporary times, the great work of John Rawls, A Theory of Justice, has given us yet another twist in pragmatic and social contract theories. His basic concept of justice as fairness is an example of the reciprocal principle in action, i.e., in terms of realizing mutual advantage and benefit for the strongest to the weakest or the most favored to the least favored in a society. Each person exercises basic liberty with offices for its implementation always open and excess available. It is moreover a highly intellectual or rational theory.

It thus works extremely well on the theoretical level but, in actual situations, it is not as practical and applicable as it seems since it still retains hard relationships on mutual bases. Such being the case, feelings and consciousness relative to injustice and inequality are not so readily spotted and corrected. That is to say, lacunae exist as a result of hard relationships and they keep on appearing until they are detected and finally remedied, but then the corrective process is painfully slow. Thus the theory's strongest point is its perpetually self-corrective nature which is so vital to the democratic process. Despite its shortcomings, however, Rawls' theory of justice is a singular contribution to contemporary legal and ethical thought.

By contrast, the Buddhist view of human rights is based on the assumption that human beings are primarily oriented in soft relationships; this relationship governs the understanding of the nature of human rights. Problems arise, on the other hand, when a hard relationship becomes the basis for treating human nature because it cannot delve deeply into that nature itself and functions purely on the peripheral aspects of things. It is another way of saying that a hard relationship causes rigid and stifling empirical conditions to arise and to which we become invariably attached.

A soft relationship has many facets. It is the Buddhist way to disclose a new dimension to human nature and behavior. It actually amounts to a novel perception or vision of reality. Though contrasted with a hard relationship, it is not in contention with it. If anything, it has an inclusive nature that "softens," if you will, all contacts and allows for the blending of any element that comes along, even incorporating the entities of hard relationships. This is not to say, however, that soft and hard relationships are equal or ultimately identical. For although the former could easily accommodate and absorb the latter, the reverse is not the case. Still, it must be noted that both belong to the same realm of experiential reality and in consequence ought to be conversive with each other.

The non-conversive aspect arises on the part of the "hard" side and is attributable to the locked-in character of empirical elements which are considered to be hard stubborn facts worth perpetuating. But at some point, there must be a break in the lock, as it were, and this is made possible by knowledge of and intimacy with the "soft" side of human endeavors. For the "soft" side has a passive nature characterized by openness, extensiveness, depth, flexibility, absorptiveness, freshness and creativity simply because it remains unencumbered by "hardened" empirical conditions.

What has been discussed so far can be seen in modern Thailand where tradition and change are in dynamic tension. Due to the onslaught of elements of modernity, Buddhism is being questioned and challenged. Buddhist Thailand, however, has taken up the challenge in the person of a leading monk named Buddhadasa who has led the country to keep a steady course on traditional values. The heart of Buddhadasa's teaching is that the Dhamma (Sanskrit, Dharma) or the truth of Buddhism is a universal truth. Dhamma is equated by Buddhadasa to the true nature of things It is everything and everywhere. The most appropriate term to denote the nature of Dhamma is sunnata (Sanskrit, sunyata) or the void. The ordinary man considers the void to mean nothing when, in reality, it means everything - everything, that is, without reference to the self.

We will return to the discussion of the nature of the void or sunnata later, but suffice it to say here that what constitutes the heart of Buddhist truth of existence is based on soft relationships where all forms and symbols are accommodated and allows for their universal usage. Robert N. Bellah has defined religion as a set of normative symbols institutionalized in a society or internalized in a personality. It is a rather good definition but does not go far enough when it comes to describing Buddhism, or Asian religions in general for that matter. To speak of symbols being institutionalized or internalized without the proper existential or ontological context seems to be a bit artificial and has strains of meanings oriented toward hard relationships.

Bellah, being a social scientist, probably neither could nor go beyond the strains of a hard relationship, for; otherwise, he would have ended in a non-descriptive realm. The only way out is to give more substance to the nature of religious doctrines themselves, as is the case in Buddhism. The Buddhist Dharma is one such doctrine which, if symbolized, must take on a wider and deeper meaning that strikes at the very heart of existence of the individual. In this respect, Donald Swearer is on the right track when he says:

The adaptation of symbols of Theravada Buddhism presupposes an underlying ontological structure. The symbol system of Buddhism then, is not to be seen only in relationship to its wider empirical context, but also in relationship to its ontological structure. This structure is denoted by such terms as Dhamma or absolute Truth, emptiness and non-attachment. These terms are denotative of what Dhiravamsa calls "dynamic being." They are symbolic, but in a universalistic rather than a particularistic sense. Swearer's reference to an underlying ontological structure is in complete harmony with our use of the term soft relationship. And only when this ontological structure or soft relationship is brought into the dynamic tension between tradition and modernity can we give full accounting to the nature of human experience and the attendant creativity and change within a society.

Let us return to a fuller treatment of soft relationships. In human experience, they manifest themselves in terms of the intangible human traits that we live by, such as patience, humility, tolerance, deference, non-action, humaneness, concern, pity, sympathy, altruism, sincerity, honesty, faith, responsibility, trust, respectfulness, reverence, love and compassion. Though potentially and pervasively present in any human relationship, they remain for the most part as silent but vibrant components in all experiences. Without them, human intercourse would be sapped of the human element and reduced to perfunctory activities. Indeed, this fact seems to constitute much of the order of the day where our passions are mainly directed to physical and materialistic matters.

The actualization and sustenance of these intangible human traits are basic to the Buddhist quest for an understanding of human nature and, by extension, the so-called rights of human beings. In order to derive a closer look at the nature of soft relationships, we shall focus on three characteristics, namely, mutuality, holism, and emptiness or void.

MUTUALITY

Our understanding of mutuality is generally limited to its abstract or theoretical nature. For example; it is defined in terms of a two-way action between two parts and where the action is invariably described with reference to elements of hard relationships. Except secondarily or deviously, nothing positive is mentioned about the substance of mutuality, such as the feelings of humility, trust and tolerance that transpire between the parties concerned. Although these feelings are present, unfortunately, they hardly ever surface in the relationship and almost always are overwhelmed by the physical aspect of things.

What is to be done? One must simply break away from the merely conceptual or theoretical understanding and fully engage oneself in the discipline that will bring the feelings of both parties to become vital components in the relationship. That is, both parties must equally sense the presence and value of these feelings and thus give substance and teeth to their actions.

Pursuing the notion of mutuality further, the Buddhist understands human experience as a totally open phenomenon, that persons should always be wide open in the living process. The phrase, "an open ontology," is used to describe the unclouded state of existence. The child is completely an open organism at birth. The senses are wide open and will absorb practically anything without prejudice. At this stage, also, the child will begin to imitate because its absorptive power is at the highest level. This open textured nature should continue on and on. In other words, if we are free and open, there should be no persistence in attaching ourselves to hard elements within the underlying context of a dynamic world of experience. The unfortunate thing, however, is that the open texture of our existence begins to blemish and fade away in time, being obstructed and overwhelmed by self-imposed fragmentation, narrowness and restriction, which gradually develop into a closed nature of existence and in this way, the hard relationship rules. But the nature of an open ontology leads us on to the next characteristic.

HOLISM

Holism of course refers to the whole, the total nature of individual existence and thus describes the unrestrictive nature of one's experience. Yet, the dualistic relationship we maintain by our crude habits of perception remains a stumbling block. This stunted form of perception is not conducive to holistic understanding and instead fosters nothing but fractured types of ontological knowledge-taking. Unconscious for the most part, an individual narrows his or her vision by indulging in dualism of all kinds, both mental and physical, and in so doing isolates the objects of perception from the total process to which they belong. In consequence, the singular unified reality of each perceptual moment is fragmented and, what is more, fragmentation once settled breeds further fragmentation.

The Buddhist will appeal to the fact that one's experience must always be open to the total ambience of any momentary situation. But here we must be exposed to a unique, if not paradoxical, insight of the Buddhist. It is that the nature of totality is not a clearly defined phenomenon. In a cryptic sense, however, it means that the totality of experience has no borders to speak of. It is an open border totality, which is the very nature of the earlier mentioned "open ontology." It is a non-circumscribable totality, like a circle sensed which does not have a rounded line, a seamless circle, if you will.

A strange phenomenon, indeed, but that is how the Buddhist sees the nature of individual existence as such. For the mystery of existence that haunts us is really the nature of one's own fullest momentary existence. Nothing else compares in profundity to this nature, so the Buddhist believes.

Now, the open framework in which experience takes place reveals that there is depth and substance in experience. But so long as one is caught up with the peripheral elements, so-called, of hard relationships one will be ensnared by them and will generate limitations on one understands accordingly. On the other hand, if openness is acknowledged as a fact of existence, then the way out of one's limitations will present itself. All sufferings (duhkha), from the Buddhist standpoint, are cases of limited ontological vision (avidya, ignorance) hindered by the attachment to all sorts of elements that obsess a person.

Holism is conversant with openness since an open experience means that all elements are fully and extensively involved. In many respects, holistic existence exhibits the fact that mutuality thrives only in unhindered openness. But there is still another vital characteristic to round out or complete momentary experience. For this we turn to the last characteristic.

EMPTINESS

Emptiness in Sanskrit is sunyata. Strictly speaking, the Sanskrit term, depicting zero or nothing, had been around prior to Buddhism, but it took the historical Buddha's supreme enlightenment (nirvana) to reveal an incomparable qualitative nature inherent to experience. Thus emptiness is not sheer voidness or nothingness in the nihilistic sense.

We ordinarily find it difficult to comprehend emptiness, much less to live a life grounded in it. Why? Again, we return to the nature of our crude habits of perception, which is laden with unwarranted forms. That is, our whole perceptual process is caught up in attachment to certain forms or elements which foster and turn into so-called empirical and cognitive biases. All of this is taking place in such minute and unknowing ways that we hardly, if ever, take notice of it until a crisis situation arises, such as the presence of certain obviously damaging prejudice or discrimination. Then and only then do we seriously wonder and search for the forms or elements that initially gave rise to those prejudicial or discriminatory forces.

Emptiness has two aspects. The first aspect alerts our perceptions to be always open and fluid, and to desist from attaching to any form or element. In this respect, emptiness technically functions as a force of "epistemic nullity," in the sense that it nullifies any reference to a form or element as preexisting perception or even post-existing for that matter. Second and more importantly, emptiness points at a positive content of our experience. It underscores the possibility of total experience in any given moment because there is now nothing attached to or persisted in. This latter point brings us right back to the other characteristics of holism and mutuality. Now, we must note that emptiness is that dimension of experience which makes it possible for the function of mutuality and holism in each experience, since there is absolutely nothing that binds, hinders or wants in our experience. Everything is as it is (tathata), under the aegis of emptiness; emptiness enables one to spread out one's experience at will in all directions, so to speak, in terms of "vertical" and "horizontal" dimensions of being.

As it is the key principle of enlightened existence, it makes everything both possible and impossible. Possible in the sense that all experiences function within the total empty nature, just as all writings are possible on a clean slate or, back to the zen story, where the sounds are possible in the silence (emptiness) of the forest. At the same time, impossible in the sense that all attachments to forms and elements are categorically denied in the ultimate fullness of experience. In this way, emptiness completes our experience of reality and, at the same time, provides the grounds for the function of all human traits to become manifest in soft relationships.

It can now be seen that all three characteristics involve each other in the selfsame momentary existence. Granted this, it should not be too difficult to accept the fact that the leading moral concept in Buddhism is compassion (karuna). Compassion literally means "passion for all" in an ontologically extensive sense. It covers the realm of all sentient beings, inclusive of non-sentient, for the doors of perception to total reality are always open. From the Buddhist viewpoint, then, all human beings are open entities with open feelings expressive of the highest form of humanity.

This is well expressed in the famous concept of bodhisattva (enlightened being) in Mahayana Buddhism who has deepest concern for all beings and sympathetically delays his entrance to nirvana as long as there is suffering (ignorant existence) among sentient creatures. It depicts the coterminous nature of all creatures and may be taken as a philosophic myth in that it underscores the ideality of existence which promotes the greatest unified form of humankind based on compassion. This ideal form of existence, needless to say, is the aim and goal of all Buddhists.

As human beings we need to keep the channels of existential dialogue open at all times. When an act of violence is in progress, for example, we need to constantly nourish the silent and passive nature of nonviolence inherent in all human relations. Though nonviolence cannot counter violence on the latter's terms, still, its nourished presence serves as a reminder of the brighter side of existence and may even open the violator's mind to common or normal human traits such as tolerance, kindness and non-injury (ahimsa). Paradoxically and most unfortunately, acts of violence only emphasize the fact that peace and tranquility are the normal course of human existence.

It can now be seen that the Buddhist view on human rights is dedicated to the understanding of persons in a parameter-free ambience, so to speak, where feelings that are extremely soft and tender, but nevertheless present and translated into human traits or virtues that we uphold, make up the very fiber of human relations. These relations, though their contents are largely intangible, precede any legal rights or justification accorded to human beings. In brief, human rights for the Buddhist are not only matters for legal deliberation and understanding, but they must be complemented by and based on something deeper and written in the very feelings of all sentient. The unique coexistent nature of rights and feelings constitutes the saving truth of humanistic existence.

In the autumn of 1993 the Parliament of the World's Religions met in Chicago to determine whether a consensus on basic moral teachings could be found among the religions of the world. The meeting was attended by representatives of the major world religions as well as ethnic and other minority groups. Representatives of many Buddhist schools, including Theravada, Mahayana, Vajrayana, and Zen were present and the main closing address was given by the Dalai Lama in Grant Park on September 4th.

One of the major fruits of this interfaith convention was a document known as the Declaration towards a Global Ethic.

The Global Ethic sets out the fundamental moral principles to which it is thought all religions subscribe. Many of these principles concern human rights, and the Global Ethic sees the universal recognition of human rights and dignity by the religions of the world as the cornerstone of a "new global order."

A related aim of the Global Ethic was to provide "the basis for an extensive process of discussion and acceptance which we hope will be sparked off in all religions." The present chapter is a contribution to this process from a Buddhist perspective. Its aims are limited to an exploration of some of the basic issues which must be addressed if a Buddhist philosophy of human rights is to develop. I say "develop" because Buddhism seems to lack such a philosophy at present. Buddhism is a latecomer to the cause of human rights, and for most of its history has been preoccupied with other concerns.

It might be suggested, in defense of Buddhism, that concern for human rights is a post religious phenomenon which has more to do with secular ideologies and power-politics than religion, and it is therefore unreasonable to accuse Buddhism of neglect in this area. I will suggest below that such an understanding of human rights is mistaken, but leaving the specific issue of human rights to one side there is no doubt that Buddhism lags far behind religions such as Christianity and Islam in developing the framework for a social gospel within which questions of this kind can be addressed.

For such an intellectually dynamic tradition Buddhism is a lightweight in moral and political philosophy. A fig-leaf of a kind may be found in the suggestion that since much Buddhist literature remains untranslated there may be hidden treasures in these areas awaiting discovery. Such appeals to the unknown, however, lack credibility. For one thing, it would be curious if only texts on these subjects had been lost to history while literature on all manner of other topics abounds. Nor can it be a coincidence that these subjects are absent from the traditional monastic curricula.

The absence of a discipline of philosophical ethics in Indian culture as a whole makes it much more likely that Buddhism simply invested little time in questions of these kinds. Political events in the course of this century, however, have forced the issue of human rights to the top of the agenda. The Chinese invasion of Tibet, the bitter ethnic conflict in Sri Lanka, and the experience of military dictatorship in countries such as Burma have all provided contemporary Buddhism with first-hand experience of the issues at stake. Another development which has done much to focus attention on social and political themes is the emergence of "socially engaged Buddhism," a movement whose very name implies a critique of the more traditional (presumably "disengaged") forms of Buddhism.

Leading Asian and Western Buddhists now routinely express their concern about social injustice in the Western vocabulary of human rights. What I wish to consider here is how appropriate this language is for Buddhism, and what grounds there are for supposing that Buddhism is committed to the cause of "human rights" or has any clear understanding of what the concept means. Given the lack of intellectual effort down the centuries in articulating, promoting and defending rights of the kind which the world (and especially the West) is now called upon to secure for oppressed groups like the Tibetans, the more cynical might suggest that this late conversion to the cause is born more of self-interest than a deep and long-standing commitment to social justice.

In calling for respect for human rights today, then, is Buddhism simply riding on the coat-tails of the West or is there, after all, a commitment to human rights in Buddhist teachings? The theme in this chapter may be summed up as the conceptual and doctrinal basis for human rights in Buddhism and concerned with the intellectual bridgework which must be put in place if expressions of concern about human rights are to be linked to Buddhist doctrine. There are many aspects to this problem, but three related issues will be considered here: the concept of rights, the concept of human rights, and the question of how human rights are to be grounded in Buddhist doctrine.

The essence of any doctrine of human rights is its unrestricted scope, and it would be as strange to have distinct "Theravada," "Tibetan" and "Zen" doctrines of human rights as it would be to have "Catholic," "Protestant" and "Eastern

Orthodox" ones. To insist on the priority of cultural and historical circumstances would be tantamount to denying the validity of human rights as a concept.

RIGHTS

The concept of a "right" has a long intellectual history in the West, and the contemporary notion of a right as an exercisable power vested in or held by an individual has its antecedents in a more impersonal understanding of what is objectively true or right. Etymologically, the English word "right" is derived from the Latin *rectus* meaning straight. *Rectus*, in turn, can be traced to the Greek orektos which means stretched out or upright. As Richard Dagger notes, "The pattern...is for the notion of straightness to be extended from the physical realm to the moral - from *rectus* to rectitude, as it were." In other words, the property of a physical object, namely that of being right, straight or upright, is applied metaphorically in a moral context. Dagger suggests:

By analogy with the physical sense, the primary moral sense of "right" was a standard or measure for conduct. Something was right - morally straight or true - if it met the standard of rectitude, or rightness...

Once the idea of "rightness" had been transferred to the moral domain, the next development was to view it as denoting a personal entitlement of some kind. Dagger continues:

From here the next step was to recognize that actions taken "with right" or "by right" are taken as a matter of right. The transition is from the belief that I may do something because it is right, in other words, to the belief that I may do something because I have a right to do it...Thus the concept of rights joins the concept of the right.

The metaphorical moral usage of terms such as "right," "straight" and "upright" (in opposition to "crooked," "twisted" and "bent") readily suggests itself to the mind. The rationale for the transition from the moral use of "right" to the notion of a right as a personal entitlement, however, is less obvious. Indeed, this development which took place in the West during the late Middle Ages, and which has been described as the "watershed" in the history of "right," may be a phenomenon which is culturally unique. The evolution of the concept in this direction occurs sometime between Aquinas in the thirteenth century and the jurists Suarez and Grotius in the seventeenth. The modern usage appears clearly in Hobbes, writing in the middle of the seventeenth century, and the idea of a right as a personal power occupies center stage in political theory from this time on.

As part of this evolution in the concept of a right the notion of natural rights comes to prominence towards the end of the seventeenth century, notably in the writings of John Locke. The belief that there are natural rights flows from the recognition of human equality, one of the great ideals of the Age of Revolution. Natural rights are inalienable: they are not conferred by any judicial or political process nor can they be removed by these or other means. These natural rights of the seventeenth and eighteenth centuries are the forerunner of the contemporary notion of human rights.

Two questions might be asked concerning the evolution of the doctrine of natural rights in the West. First, why did it take so long for the concept of natural rights to appear? The answer seems to lie in the fact that for much of Western history "rights" were closely tied to social status, and were essentially a function of position or role in society. A hierarchical social structure, such as was predominant in Roman and medieval society, is antithetical to the notion of natural rights. In these circumstances a person's duties and responsibilities are determined fundamentally by the office they hold (lord, citizen, slave), offices which are to a large extent hereditary. It was only when the hierarchical model was challenged and replaced by an egalitarian one that the idea of natural rights began to gain ground.

The second and more important question for our present purposes is: Does the part played by the unique cultural matrix of social political and intellectual developments in the Enlightenment mean that human rights are essentially a function of the historical process? This conclusion need not follow, for while it may be said that in the seventeenth and eighteenth centuries the notion of natural rights was "an idea whose time had come," the idea itself was not entirely new. The influence of Christian doctrine can be seen in several respects, such as the belief (ultimately derived from Judaism) of a "universal moral law rooted in the righteousness of God."

Since human beings are created in the image of God and loved by him as individuals each is worthy of dignity and respect. Furthermore, since each is a member of the human community under God, all other memberships (tribe, state, nation) are secondary. Apart from Christianity, ideas about the just treatment of individuals on the basis of their common humanity are found in a secular context in Stoicism and the writings of Cicero and Seneca. The philosophical justification for a doctrine of human rights has thus always been available, although the ground in which this seed might flourish - a particular combination of social, political and intellectual developments - has not.

So much for historical background. What of contemporary theories of rights? The concept of a right has been analyzed in a number of ways, as evidenced by the extensive interdisciplinary literature on the subject spanning diverse fields such as politics, law, philosophy and history. Within this discourse of rights there is no single definition of a right which commands universal assent. For our present purposes, however, a basic understanding of the concept will suffice. We noted above that a right is something personal to an individual: it may be thought of as something an individual has.

What the holder of a right has is a benefit or entitlement of some kind, and at the most general level this is an entitlement to justice. This entitlement may be analyzed into two main forms for which there are corresponding rights: rights which take the form of a claim (claim-rights), and rights which take the form of a liberty (liberty-rights). A claim-right is the benefit which A enjoys to impose upon B a positive or negative requirement. A liberty-right is the benefit which A enjoys of being immune from any such requirement being imposed by B. This basic understanding of a right may be summed up in the following working definition: a right is a benefit which confers upon its holder either a claim or a liberty.

One important feature of any right is that it provides a particular perspective on justice, in that the right-holder always stands in the position of beneficiary. This subjective aspect of the entitlement, which, as we have seen, appeared early in the history of the concept, remains crucial to the modern understanding of a right. This is brought out in the following definition by Finnis:

In short, the modern vocabulary and grammar of rights is a many-faceted instrument for reporting and asserting the requirements or other implications of a relationship of justice from the point of view of the person(s) who benefit(s) from that relationship. It provides a way of talking about "what is just" from a special angle: the viewpoint of the "other(s)" to whom something (including, *inter alia*, freedom of choice) is owed or due, and who would be wronged if denied that something.

The above brief review of the Western concept of a right was required as a preliminary to an assessment of its relevance to Buddhism. We are now in a position to ask whether the concept of a right is found in Buddhism. If it is, then talk of human rights in Buddhism seems legitimate. If it is not, there is a danger of anachronistically foisting onto the tradition a concept which is the product of an alien culture.

BUDDHISM AND RIGHTS

We took our cue for the discussion of rights in the West from etymology, and perhaps we can glean something further from this source. Above it was noted that the English word "right" is derived from the Latin *rectus* meaning straight. Both "right" and *rectus* themselves, however, have a more remote ancestor in the Sanskrit *ṛju* (straight or upright). The equivalent form in Pali is *uju* (or *ujju*) meaning "straight, direct; straightforward, honest, upright." It would therefore appear that both the objective sense ("straight") and the metaphorical moral sense ("rectitude") of the word "right" referred to earlier occur in

Buddhist as well as Western languages. Despite a common Indo-European etymology, however, there is no word in Sanskrit or Pali which conveys the idea of a "right" or "rights," understood as a subjective entitlement.

Does this mean that the concept of rights is alien to Buddhist thought? Not necessarily. Alan Gewirth has pointed out that cultures may possess the concept of rights without having a vocabulary which expresses it. He suggests that it is "important to distinguish between having or using a concept and the clear or explicit recognition and elucidation of it...Thus persons might have and use the concept of a right without explicitly having a single word for it." Gewirth claims that the concept of rights can be found in feudal thought, Roman law, Greek philosophy, the Old Testament, and in primitive societies. In connection with the last Finnis points out that anthropological studies of African tribal regimes of law have shown that "the English terms a 'right' and 'duty' are usually covered by a single word derived from the form normally translated as 'ought.'"

He suggests that the best English translation in these cases is "due" because "'due' looks both ways along a juridical relationship, both to what one is due to do, and to what is due to one." It seems, then, that the concept of a right may exist where a word for it does not. Could this be the case in Buddhism? In Buddhism what is due in any situation is determined by reference to Dharma. Dharma determines what is right and just in all contexts and from all perspectives. With respect to social justice the Rev. Vajiragnana explains:

Each one of us has a role to play in sustaining and promoting social justice and orderliness. The Buddha explained very clearly these roles as reciprocal duties existing between parents and children; teachers and pupils; husband and wife; friends, relatives and neighbors; employer and employee; clergy and laity...No one has been left out. The duties explained here are reciprocal and are considered as sacred duties, for - if observed - they can create a just, peaceful and harmonious society.©39

From this it would seem that Dharma determines not just "what one is due to do" but also "what is due to one." Thus through A's performance of his Dharmic duty B receives that which is his "due" or, we might say, that to which he is "entitled" in (under, through) Dharma. Since Dharma determines the duties of husbands and the duties of wives, it follows that the duties of one correspond to the entitlements or "rights" of the other. If the husband has a duty to support his wife, the wife has a "right" to support from her husband. If the wife has a duty to look after her husband's property, the husband has a "right" to the safe-keeping of his property by his wife. If under Dharma it is the duty of a king (or political authority) to dispense justice impartially, then subjects (citizens) may be said to have a "right" to just and impartial treatment before the law.

Should it be concluded, then, that the notion of a right is present in classical Buddhism? The answer depends on the criteria adopted for "having" a concept. Dagger sets out the options:

If one is willing to look primarily for the idea or the notion, however it may be expressed, then one can confidently say that the concept of rights is virtually as old as civilization itself.

On the other hand: If one insists that the form of expression is crucial...so that a concept cannot be said to exist unless there is a word or phrase that distinguishes it from other concepts, then one would have to say that the concept of rights has its origin in the middle ages.

I think our conclusion should be that the concept of rights is implicit in classical Buddhism in the normative understanding of what is "due" among and between individuals. Under Dharma, husbands and wives, kings and subjects, teachers and students, all have reciprocal obligations which can be analyzed into rights and duties. We must qualify this conclusion, however, by noting that the requirements of Dharma are expressed in the form of duties rather than rights.

In other words, Dharma states what is due in the form "A husband should support his wife" as opposed to "Wives have a right to be maintained by their husbands." Until rights as personal entitlements are recognized as a discrete but integral part of what is due under Dharma, the modern concept of rights cannot be said to be present. In this respect, however, Buddhism is far from unique, and a similar comment could be made about many other cultures and civilizations. Finnis points out with respect to Roman law:

It is salutary to bear in mind that the modern emphasis on the powers of the right-holder, and the consequent systematic bifurcation between "right"...and "duty", is something that sophisticated lawyers were able to do without for the whole life of classical Roman law.

He also suggests, rightly I think, that "there is no cause to take sides as between the older and the newer usages, as ways of expressing the implications of justice in a given context." A right is a useful concept which provides a particular perspective on justice. Its correlative, duty, provides another. These may be thought of as separate windows onto the common good which is justice or, in the context of Buddhism, Dharma. It would therefore be going too far to claim that the notion of rights is "alien" to Buddhism or that Buddhism denies that individuals have "rights."

In sum it might be said that in classical Buddhism the notion of rights is present in embryonic form although not yet born into history. Whether anything like the Western concept of rights has, or would, appear in the course of the historical evolution of Buddhism is a question for specialists in the various Buddhist cultures to ponder. In many respects the omens for this development were never good. Buddhism originated in a caste society, and the Asian societies where it has flourished have for the most part been hierarchically structured. MacIntyre, citing Gewirth, mentions that the concept of a right lacks any means of expression in Japanese "even as late as the mid-nineteenth century."

The preconditions for the emergence of the concept of rights would seem to be egalitarianism and democracy, neither of which have been notable features of Asian polity before the modern era. On the other hand, a justification for the rejection of hierarchical social structures is not hard to find in Buddhism - one need look only at the Buddha's critique of caste. Buddhism also holds, in the doctrine of no-self, that all individuals are equal in the most profound sense. Like the Christian doctrine that all men are created equal before God this would appear to be fertile ground for a doctrine of natural rights. What seems to have been lacking in both faiths, but perhaps more so in Buddhism, was the will to incarnate this theoretical vision of man in the flesh of historical institutions.

HUMAN RIGHTS

In the preceding section attention was focused on the concept of a right. Here we consider what it means to characterize certain rights as human rights, and pursue further the discussion initiated in the preceding section as to whether Western notions of human rights are compatible with Buddhism.

The point has already been made that what are today called human rights were originally spoken of as "natural" rights, in other words, rights which flow from human nature. In the seventeenth century philosophers and statesmen began to define these rights and enshrine them in early constitutions such as the "Fundamental Orders of Connecticut" as early as 1639. Documents of this kind inspired the publication of other declarations, charters and manifestos in a tradition which has continued into modern times. As an example of a modern charter of human rights we may take The Universal Declaration of Human Rights proclaimed by the General Assembly of the United Nations in December 1948. Since its promulgation this thirty-article code has been used as a model for many subsequent human rights charters.

What is the Buddhist position with respect to declarations of this kind? It may be useful to begin by asking whether Buddhism would endorse the Universal Declaration of Human Rights. The repeated calls by the Dalai Lama for respect for human rights give some reason to think that it would. The signing of the Global Ethic by many Buddhists also suggests that Buddhism has no reservations about subscribing to charters or manifestos which seek to secure universal human rights. Moreover, there seems to be nothing in any of the thirty articles to which Buddhism would take exception. Perera's commentary on each of the thirty articles of the Universal Declaration shows them to be in harmony with early Buddhist teachings both in letter and in spirit. In his Foreword to the commentary Ananda Guruge writes:

Professor Perera demonstrates that every single Article of the Universal Declaration of Human Rights - even the labour rights to fair wages, leisure and welfare - has been adumbrated, cogently upheld and meaningfully incorporated in an overall view of life and society by the Buddha.

But how are these rights to be justified with reference to Buddhist teachings? In asking this question I am not seeking justification by reference to textual passages which seem to support the rights claimed. There are many passages in the Pali Canon, as Perera has ably demonstrated, which support the view that early Buddhist teachings were in harmony with the spirit of the Declaration. The justification required at this point has more to do with the philosophical presuppositions underlying these passages and the overall Buddhist vision of individual and social good.

The various declarations on human rights themselves rarely offer a justification for the rights they proclaim. MacIntyre observes dryly how "In the United Nations declaration on human rights of 1949 [sic] what has since become the normal UN practice of not giving good reasons for any assertion whatsoever is followed with great rigor." A gesture towards justification is sometimes made in recital clauses by reference to the "inherent dignity...of all members of the human family" or some similar form of words. The Global Ethic, which provides a fuller statement than most, echoes the Universal Declaration in its call for "the full realization of the intrinsic dignity of the human person." It states: "We make a commitment to respect life and dignity, individuality and diversity, so that every person is treated humanely." This is amplified as follows:

This means that every human being without distinction of age, sex, race, skin, color, physical or mental ability, language, religion, political view, or national or social origin possesses an inalienable and untouchable dignity. And everyone, the individual as well as the state, is therefore obliged to honor this dignity and protect it.

Elsewhere, as part of his dialogue with world religions, Küng makes a constructive suggestion on this point that students of Buddhism might do well to pay heed to:

Should not Buddhist thinkers, as they critically assess their own and alien traditions, make a more direct effort to establish anthropology centered on human dignity (which the Buddha himself deeply respected)? Buddhists are fully aware that man can be adequately understood only as conditioned in every way, as a relational being within the totality of life and the cosmos. But should they not reflect more earnestly, especially in an ethical vein, on the problems of the unique, inviolable, non interchangeable human self, with its roots in the past and its future destiny?

It is by no means apparent, however, how human dignity is to be grounded in Buddhist doctrine. The very words "human dignity" sound as alien in a Buddhist context as talk of rights. One looks in vain to the Four Noble Truths for any explicit reference to human dignity, and doctrines such as no-self and impermanence may even be thought to undermine it. If human dignity is the basis of human rights Buddhism would seem to be in some difficulty when it comes to providing a justification for them. The theistic religions, on the other hand, seem much better equipped to provide an account of human dignity.

Christians, Muslims and Jews typically refer to the ultimate source of human dignity as divine. Article one (paragraph 1700) of the most recent Catechism of the Catholic Church, for instance, states: "The dignity of the human person is rooted in his creation in the image and likeness of God." Buddhism, clearly, would not wish to make such a claim. Küng notes how leading Buddhists at the Parliament of the World's Religions felt called upon to protest at calls for "a unity of religions under God," and at references to "God the Almighty" and "God the Creator" in invocations during the proceedings. He suggests, however, that these differences are reconcilable since the Buddhist concepts of "Nirvana, Shunyata and Dharmakaya...fulfill analogous functions to the concept of God" and can be regarded by Christians as "parallel terms for the Absolute."

It may or may not be the case that Mahayana schools recognize a transcendent reality which resembles the Christian concept of God as the Absolute, and there are those better qualified than myself to address such a question. Here I will make only three brief points regarding the problems which arise in regarding these things as the source of human dignity. The first is that since these concepts are understood differently by the main Mahayana schools they are unlikely to provide the common ground which is required as a foundation for human rights.

The second is that it is difficult to see how any of these things can be the source of human dignity in the way that God can, since no school of Buddhism believes that human beings are created by them. The third point is that even if some metaphysical ground of the above kind can be identified in Mahayana Buddhism it still leaves the problem of how human dignity is to be grounded where Theravada Buddhism is concerned. For the Theravada, Nirvana is not a transcendent Absolute, nor do the concepts of Sunyata and Dharmakâya have anything like the meaning or significance they attain later. No grounding for human rights can be truly satisfactory, I would suggest, unless it unambiguously forms part of the core teachings of classical Buddhism as a whole.

One suggestion as to how human rights can be grounded in Buddhist doctrine has been made by Kenneth Inada. In a discussion of "The Buddhist Perspective on Human Rights," Inada suggests "there is an intimate and vital relationship of the Buddhist norm or Dhamma with that of human rights." He explains the relationship as follows:

Human rights is indeed an important issue, but the Buddhist position is that it is ancillary to the larger or more basic issue of human nature. It can be asserted that the Buddhist sees the concept of human rights as a legal extension of human nature. It is crystallization, indeed formalization, of the mutual respect and concern of all persons, stemming from human nature. Thus, human nature is the ultimate source, the basis from which all other attributes or characteristics are to be delineated. They all have their respective raison d'etre in it. They are reflections and even byproducts of it.

The reason for assigning human nature the basic position is very simple. It is to give human relations a firm grounding in the truly existential nature of things: that is, the concrete and dynamic relational nature of persons in contact with each other, that which [sic] avoids being caught up in rhetorical or legalistic tangles. Few would disagree with the proposition that human rights are grounded in human nature. Towards the end of the extract, however, Inada seems to move away from his initial suggestion that human nature is the "ultimate source" of human rights towards the view that the ultimate ground is the "dynamic relational nature of persons in contact with each other." In other words, it is in the interrelatedness of persons rather than in the persons themselves that the justification for human rights is to be found. This is confirmed a little later:

Consequently, the Buddhist concern is focused on the experiential process of each individual, a process technically knows as relational origination (patòicca-samuppâda). It is the great doctrine of Buddhism, perhaps the greatest doctrine expounded by the historical Buddha. It means that, in any life-process, the arising of an experiential event is'a total, relational affair.

How is the link between dependent-origination and human rights to be forged? The argument reaches its conclusion in the following passage:

Like a storm which consumes everything in its wake, an experience in terms of relational origination involves everything within its purview. Hence, the involvement of elements and, in our case, human beings as entities should not be in terms of mere relationship but rather a creative relationship which originates from the individual locus of existence. In other words, each individual is responsible for the actualization of an "extensive concern" for everything that lies in his or her path of experience. So, we may say that the sum total of the "extensive concerns" can be referred to as a mutually constituted existential realm, and it thereby becomes a fact that there will be mutual respect of fellow beings. It is on this basis that we can speak of the rights of individuals. These rights are actually extensions of human qualities such as security, liberty, and life.

In simple language, the argument seems to be as follows. Human beings, like everything else, are part of the relational process described in the doctrine of dependent-origination; since no-one exists independently we should look out for one another; looking out for one another means respecting each other's rights; examples of the rights we should respect are security, liberty and life.

Although I have described this as an "argument" it is little more than a series of assertions. Working backwards, it is difficult to know what sense to give the concluding sentence: "These rights are actually extensions of human qualities such as security, liberty and life." It is unclear what is meant by "human qualities" here. In what sense is security a "human quality" (perhaps a "need")? Why is life described as a "quality" of a human being? Even granted that these things are "human qualities," what does it mean to say that rights are extensions of "human qualities?"

In the first extract quoted above, Inada suggests that "the Buddhist sees the concept of human rights as a legal extension of human nature." What is left unexplained, however, is how human nature (or "human qualities") become legal rights. Do all "human qualities" extend into rights or only some? If so, which and why? Finally, if "human qualities" are what give rise to rights, why invoke the doctrine of dependent-origination?

The derivation of human rights from the doctrine of dependent-origination is a conjuring trick. From the premise that we live in "a mutually constituted existential realm" (we all live together) it has "thereby become a fact" that there will be "mutual respect of fellow beings." In the twinkling of an eye, values have appeared from facts like a rabbit out of a hat. However, the fact that human beings live in relationship with one another is not a moral argument about how they ought to behave. By itself it offers no reason why a person should not routinely abuse the rights of others.

Inada's suggestion that human rights can be grounded in the doctrine of dependent-origination turns out to be little more than a recommendation that people should be nice to one another on the ground that we are "all in this together." The approach adopted by Perera is rather different. Perera's main concern is to demonstrate that the articles of the Universal Declaration are adumbrated in early Buddhist teachings, rather than explore their philosophical foundations. He acknowledges that "Buddhism credits the human personality with a dignity and moral responsibility" but does not explain fully whence this arises or how it provides a foundation for human rights.

In a number of places he suggests certain possibilities regarding the source of human dignity, not all of which seem to be compatible. At one point he defines "the ethical assumption on which the Buddhist concept of human rights is founded" as the "fundamental consideration that all life has a desire to safeguard itself and to make itself comfortable and happy." Basing rights on desires, however, is problematic. One reason is that certain people, for example those who seek to end their lives through suicide, seem to lack the desire in question. Nor is difficult to conceive of a justification for human rights abuses along the lines that the victims "no longer cared what happened to them."

If they themselves had no interest in their future, whose rights would have been violated? A deeper problem is that the mere existence of desires establishes nothing from a moral point of view. Desires are many and varied and can be met in manifold ways. Moral questions arise both at the level of whether a desire should be met and how it should be met. The identification of a desire may be a starting point for moral reflection, but it is certainly not its end.

On the preceding page Perera suggests an alternative foundation for human rights, one which links it to human dignity. He writes: "Buddhism posits, as Jean Jaques Rousseau did much later, that the essence of human dignity lies in the assumption of man's responsibility for his own governance."

No Buddhist sources are cited in support of this claim, and I believe it is unlikely that Buddhism would wish to link human dignity quite so closely to politics. Perhaps if this suggestion were developed a little further it would make reference to underlying human capacities such as reason and autonomy which enable men to constitute themselves into orderly societies, and then point to these as the underlying source of human dignity. While political institutions may be produced through the exercise of distinctively human capacities; however, it is unlikely that Buddhism would locate "the essence of human dignity" in their creation. According to the Aggaññasutta, the evolution of political societies is the consequence of depravity and decline, which makes them a dubious testament to human dignity.

Where then, should the foundations for a Buddhist doctrine of human rights be sought? The proper ground for a doctrine of human rights, I suggest, lies elsewhere than in the doctrine of dependent-origination, as suggested by Inada, or in either the desire for self-preservation or the acceptance of responsibility for self-government, as proposed by Perera. Perera, in fact, comes closest to what in my view is the true source of human rights in Buddhism in his commentary on Article 1. In discussing the first sentence of the Article ("All human beings are born free and equal in dignity and rights") he comments that "Buddhahood itself is within the reach of all human beings...and if all could attain Buddhahood what greater equality in dignity and rights can there be?" To focus attention upon the goal, I believe, is more promising than any of the other approaches considered thus far. Perera seems to grasp its significance in a remark towards the end of his commentary on Article 1. He writes:

It is from the point of view of its goal that Buddhism evaluates all action. Hence Buddhist thought is in accord with this and other Articles in the Universal Declaration of Human Rights to the extent to which they facilitate the advancement of human beings towards the Buddhist goal.

I believe the above statement provides the key to understanding human rights from a Buddhist perspective.

What is missing in Perera's commentary, however, is the explicit linkage between the goal and human dignity, and it is this which I will now try to establish. What I will suggest in general is that the source of human dignity should be sought not in the analysis of the human condition provided by the first and second noble truths (the area where Buddhist scholarship has myopically focused its attention) but in the evaluation of human good provided by the third and fourth. Human rights cannot be derived from any factual non-evaluative analysis of human nature, whether in terms of its psycho-physical constitution (the five "aggregates" which lack a self), its biological nature (needs, urges, drives), or the deep structure of interdependency (patòicca-samuppâda). Instead, the most promising approach will be one which locates human rights and dignity within a comprehensive account of human goodness, and which sees basic rights and freedoms as integrally related to human flourishing and self-realization. This is because the source of human dignity in Buddhism lies nowhere else than in the literally infinite capacity of human nature for participation in goodness.

The connection between human rights and human good can be illustrated by asking what the various declarations on human rights seek to secure. Documents which speak of human rights commonly announce a list of specific rights and freedoms and proclaim them to be inviolable. The rights proclaimed by the Universal Declaration include the right to life, liberty, security of person, equality before the law, privacy, marriage and protection of family life, social security, participation in government, work, protection against unemployment, rest and leisure, a minimum standard of living, and enjoyment of the arts.

The exercise of these rights is subject only to such general limitations as are necessary to secure due recognition and respect for the rights and freedoms of others and the requirements of morality, public order and general welfare (Article 29.2). Otherwise, the rights are expressed in categorical forms such as "Everyone has..." and "No-one shall..." For example, Article 3: "Everyone has the right to life, liberty and security of person." And Article 4: "No one shall be held in slavery or servitude; slavery and the slave trade shall be prohibited in all their forms."

The document thus understands the rights it proclaims as both "universal" and exceptionless. Using the terminology introduced earlier it can be seen that some of these rights are claim rights while others are liberty rights. Article 2 confirms this when it speaks of an entitlement to both the "rights and freedoms set forth in this Declaration." What do these rights and freedoms amount to? It might be said that they map the parameters of human "good-in-community." In other words, these rights and freedoms are what is required if human beings are to lead fulfilled lives in society.

Article 29.1 recognizes this when it observes "Everyone has duties to the community in which alone the free and full development of his personality is possible." In the absence of human rights the scope for human development and fulfillment through social interaction is drastically reduced. The rights specified define and facilitate aspects of human fulfillment. The right to life is clearly fundamental since it is the condition for the enjoyment of all other rights and freedoms. The right to "liberty and security of person" (Article 3) is also basic to any understanding of human good.

Without these minimum conditions the scope and opportunity for human fulfillment would be intolerably restricted. The same would apply in the case of slavery (Article 4), torture (Article 5), and the denial of rights before the law (Article 6). It can also be seen that many of the detailed rights identified are actually derived from more fundamental ones. Article 3, for example, "No one shall be held in slavery," is clearly implied in Article 2, "Everyone has the right to...liberty." It might thus be said that many of the thirty articles articulate the practical implications of a relatively small number of fundamental rights and freedoms which are the basis of the common good.

It may be noted that the Universal Declaration itself and modern charters like it do not offer a comprehensive vision of human good. This is not intended as a criticism, for the purpose of such charters is to secure only what might be termed the "minimum conditions" for human flourishing in a pluralistic milieu. The task of articulating a comprehensive vision of what is ultimately valuable in human life and how it is to be attained falls to the competing theories of human good found in religions, philosophies and ideologies.

Buddhism provides one view of human nature and its fulfillment, Christianity another, secular philosophies a third. To pursue any of these different paths, however, requires the substructure known as "human rights," a complex of fundamental rights and liberties which are the preconditions for the realization of the particular opportunities made available by the competing ideologies. If the aim of human rights declarations is understood in the way outlined above then human rights is fundamentally a moral issue.

Where there is no right to life, liberty and security of person, and where torture is routine, the opportunities for the realization of human good are greatly reduced. Freedom of religion (Article 18), for example, is vital to the Buddhist vision of individual and social good, and the consequences of the loss of these rights are all too obvious in Tibet. Human rights is thus an area in which religions have a legitimate and vital stake, and there is every reason why it would be proper for Buddhism both to endorse the Universal Declaration and call upon others to respect and implement it.

If religions have a legitimate stake in human rights, we might expect to find many of the rights and liberties spelled out in human rights charters present in either an express or implied form in their moral teachings. These typically include commandments or precepts forbidding killing, stealing, adultery, and lying, as do the first four of the Five Precepts. These evils are prohibited because it is immediately apparent that they are antithetical to human flourishing-in-community. The rationale for these prohibitions, I suggest, coincides to a large extent with that of the various human rights manifestos.

These manifestos, indeed, may be regarded as a translation of religious precepts into the language of rights.

The process of casuistry can be seen at work in both. Just as a limited number of moral precepts can be expanded to meet the needs of different social situations (many of the extensive Vinaya rules, for example, have their source in a handful of moral precepts), so the many articles in human rights charters are extrapolated from a comparatively small number of basic rights and freedoms.

It must be admitted there are grounds for skepticism towards the parallel which has just been suggested since it cannot be denied that the Buddhist precepts look and sound very different from contemporary declarations on human rights. The Buddhist precepts make no reference to "rights" at all, and are couched instead in the form of undertakings. Let us examine what these undertakings involve. On the basis of our earlier analysis it would seem that "taking the precepts" in Buddhism is actually the formal acknowledgment of a subsisting duty, a duty which arises from Dharma.

The person who takes the precepts is saying in effect "I hereby recognize my Dharmic duty not to do x,y, and z." Since duties have their correlative in rights, however, rights must also be implicit in the good the precepts seek to promote. We saw earlier that rights provide a way of talking about what is just and unjust from a special angle. We noted further that a person who has right has a benefit, a benefit which can be described as either a claim or a liberty. In the context of the precepts, then, the right-holder is the one who suffers from the breach of Dharmic duty when the precepts are broken.

In the case of the first precept this would be the person who was unjustly killed. The right the victim has may therefore be defined as a negative claim-right upon the aggressor, namely the right not to be killed. In simple terms we might say that the victim has a right to life which the aggressor has a duty to respect.

That the translation between precepts and rights is accurate, and that the agreement between the two formulations is more than superficial or accidental, is supported by the authenticity with which the Dalai Lama was able to affirm the Global Ethic. Kuschel comments as follows:

Something else seems decisive to me: authenticity and humanity. The reason why the Dalai Lama's speech was so convincing, and indeed seized people's hearts, so that it was often interrupted by spontaneous applause, was that this man simply wanted to be an authentic Buddhist. His plea for mutual respect, dialogue and collaboration, for understanding between peoples and respect for creation, was not an adaptation to Christian or Western values, but came from the depths of his own Buddhist spirituality.

Further evidence of the linkage between the Buddhist precepts and social justice is found in the Theravada tradition. Writing on the theme of "Justice in Buddhism" Vajiragnana states:

Man is responsible for society. It is he who makes it good or bad through his own actions. Buddhism, therefore, advocates a five-fold disciplinary code for man's training in order to maintain justice in society...These five...precepts are extremely important fundamental principles for promoting and perpetuating human welfare, peace and justice.

I suggest, then, that the apparent differences between the moral teachings of Buddhism and human rights charters are one of form rather than substance. Human rights can be extrapolated from Buddhist moral teachings in the manner described above using the logic of moral relationships to illumine what is due under Dharma. A direct translation of the first four precepts yields a right to life, a right not to have one's property stolen, a right to fidelity in marriage, and a right not to be lied to. Many other human rights, such as the rights to liberty and security can either be deduced from or are extant within the general corpus of Buddhist moral teachings.

A right not to be held in slavery, for example, is implicit in the canonical prohibition on trade in living beings. These rights are the extrapolation of what is due under Dharma; they have not been "imported" into Buddhism but were implicitly present. If modern conceptions of human rights and Buddhist moral teachings are related in the way I have suggested, certain conclusions follow for our understanding of the Buddhist precepts.

If there are universal and exceptionless rights, as human rights charters affirm, there must be universal and exceptionless duties. If human rights such as a "right to life" (by which I understand a right not to have one's life taken unjustly) are exceptionless, there must also be an exceptionless duty to abstain from unjustly depriving a human being of life. The First Precept in Buddhism, therefore, should be understood as an exceptionless duty or moral absolute.

Is this reverse translation, from absolute human rights to absolute moral duties, supported by textual sources? There is every reason to think that it is. Such an understanding of the precept is clearly evident in classical Buddhism, which tirelessly reiterates the principle of the sanctity of life found in the pan-Indian teachings on non-harming (ahimsa), and which gives no reason to suppose that its moral precepts are to be understood as anything other than exceptionless norms.

If, on the other hand, it is thought that the precepts are not to be understood as moral absolutes, then it is difficult to see what justification there can be for Buddhists to hold that there are universal and exceptionless human rights. It would be inconsistent to affirm the latter but deny the former. The above account of human rights in Buddhism has been given entirely within the context of an understanding of human good which has its apex in nirvâna in this life. Reference to the transcendent dimension of human good and its ground has been avoided for several reasons. The first is that no reference need be made to transcendent realities in order to ground human rights.

That this is so can be seen from the absence of any reference to such realities in contemporary human rights charters, and the fact that many atheists are vigorous defenders of human rights. Where Buddhism is concerned, the vision of human good set out in the third and fourth noble truths provides the necessary basis for a doctrine of human rights. Human rights turn out in essence to be what justice requires if human good is to be fulfilled. The second reason for avoiding reference to transcendent realities is that my aim has been to suggest a basis for human rights acceptable to classical Buddhism as a whole. Since all schools of Buddhism affirm the third and fourth noble truths and the vision of human good they proclaim, the required common ground for a pan-Buddhist doctrine of human rights is present.

The above should not be read as a denial that there can be a transcendent ground for human rights in Buddhism. Because the transcendent dimension of human good is left obscure in Buddhist teachings, however, the transcendent ground for human rights is also obscure. In terms of the account given here, the transcendent ground for human rights would be post-mortem nirvana, not in the sense of an absolute reality (as suggested by Küng) but as the universalization of human good on a transcendent plane. The twin axes of human good are knowledge (prajñâ) and moral concern (karuna) and on the graph defined by these axes can be plotted the soteriological coordinates of any individual.

Through participation in these twin categories of good, human nature progressively transcends its limitations and becomes saturated with nirvanic goodness. Eventually, in post-mortem nirvânòa, this goodness attains a magnitude which can no longer be charted. If a transcendent ground for human rights is desired, this is where it should be sought. To sum up: it is legitimate to speak of both rights and human rights in Buddhism. Modern doctrines of human rights are in harmony with the moral values of classical Buddhism in that they are an explication of what is "due" under Dharma.

The modern idea of human rights has a distinctive cultural origin, but its underlying preoccupation with human good makes it at bottom a moral issue in which Buddhism and other religions have a legitimate stake. The Global Ethic endorses the view that the principles it sets forth on human rights are neither new nor "Western" when it states: "We affirm that a common set of core values is found in the teachings of the religions, and that these form the basis of a global ethic."

A final thought. Above I have spoken only of human rights, and in the context of Buddhism this perspective may be unduly narrow in that it seems to preclude the universe of sentient non-human beings from any entitlement to rights. Buddhists may feel, therefore, that it is less prejudicial in discussions of this kind to revert to the older terminology of "natural" rights. Whether or not animals have rights, and whether these are the same rights as human beings, is a matter which requires separate discussion. If human rights flow from human nature, as suggested, it may be that rights of different kinds flow from natures of different kinds. Such would seem to be the understanding of classical Buddhism.

2

Resonances and Dissonances

In 1991 L.P.N. Perera, Professor of Pali and Buddhist Studies in Sri Lanka, published a Buddhist commentary on the Universal Declaration of Human Rights. In this commentary Perera tries to show that, in the Pali canon, i.e. the canonical scripture of Theravada Buddhism, for every single article of the Human Rights Declaration a substantial parallel or at least a statement with a similar tendency can be found. Indeed, says Perera, Article 1, which affirms the dignity and rights of all humans, "is in complete accord with Buddhist thought, and may be said to be nothing new to Buddhism in conception".

In contrast, the Buddhist Peter Junger, Professor of Law at the University of Cleveland, Ohio, judged in 1995 that though followers of Buddhist traditions do value most, if not all, of the interests underlying the rhetoric of human rights, they may not have much use for the label itself, which is, after all, a product of the traditions of Western Europe and the parochial histories of that region.

Junger goes on to say that "the concept of human rights is not likely to be useful in... following the Buddha Dharma". Thus Perera and Junger agree that the content of the various human rights is acceptable for Buddhists. However, they disagree strongly in their evaluation of the idea of human rights in itself. In this respect Damien Keown has rightly argued that the crucial question on 'Buddhism and Human Rights' is not so much whether Buddhism can accept any particular human right but rather whether the idea of human rights as such can find a philosophical justification within the "overall Buddhist vision of individual and social good".

It is this problem that I would like to pursue in this chapter. In the first part I will sketch some basic characteristics of the idea of human rights. In the second part I will point out what resonances this idea finds in Buddhism or by which Buddhist concepts the human rights idea can be justified. And finally, in the third part, I will deal with the question of potential dissonances between the idea of human rights and Buddhist concepts.

ON THE NATURE OF HUMAN RIGHTS

With the United Nations' Universal Declaration of Human Rights in 1948 and the various subsequent human rights conventions the rights of individuals were for the first time inscribed into international law, which had previously recognised only collectives as legal subjects. By formulating universal rights as valid for every individual human being regardless of race, colour, sex, religion, birth, etc. the Universal Declaration points to the most important feature of the idea of human rights: the protection of the individual or, to be more precise, the protection of the individual against powerful institutions of the state, society, religion or others.

It is individual self-determination and free agency that are protected through human rights. Human rights define the minimum of what is necessary in order to guarantee the freedom of individual agency and the freedom of self-determination. By the definition of inalienable rights, the idea of human rights sets limits to those collectives and institutions in which we usually live, limits which for the sake of the basic liberty of the individual are not to be transgressed. Michael Ignatieff summarises this understanding of human rights with the words: "rights exist to protect individuals", and "they are worth having only if they can be enforced against institutions like the family, the state, and the church". Therefore "moral individualism" is "the core of the Universal Declaration".

It is true that the further development of the human rights debate, particularly within the context of the United Nations, has led to an extension of the idea of human rights to collective rights and collective legal entities by including among human rights, for example, a nations' right to self-determination and the right to peace and the right to development. However, in my opinion it would be highly problematic to take this as relativising the understanding of human rights as protecting the rights of the individual.

Such collective human rights should be regarded rather as articulating wider settings and conditions for the protection of the individual in the sense that, for example, the right to a healthy economic development guaranteeing the satisfaction of the basic existential needs of a state's citizens, is necessary, because hunger does not restrict human agency any less than arbitrary imprisonment does.

If human rights are understood primarily as rights for the protection of individuals, then a further crucial aspect is that these rights hold for all individuals in an equal way and that therefore the claim of their validity is universal. It is the principle of equality through which the moral character of the human rights idea becomes particularly clear. For the principle of equality rests on the 'Golden Rule,' so that all others are to be protected against abuse in the same way that one would claim this for oneself. And from the principle of equality follows the claim to the universal validity of the idea of human rights, for the equal validity for all individuals entails universal validity.

Taken together, both point to a problem which has moved more and more to the centre of the current human rights debate: the question of how to justify the claim to universal validity of the human rights idea within the horizon of different cultures, religions, and ideologies. The view that human rights apply to all individuals equally, irrespective of any particulars of sex, race, colour, nationality, social position, etc., can also be expressed by saying that these rights have to be adjudicated to humans as humans, that is on the basis of their humanness alone, and that this is the reason why they are called human rights.

This seems to suggests that the universal validity of human rights needs to be derived from human nature or more precisely from the dignity of that nature. Although the 1948 Universal Declaration abstains consciously from giving any justification of human rights, it nevertheless indicates a close connection between human rights and human dignity by mentioning both in one breath in the preamble and in Article 1.

However, a justification of the universal validity of human rights by recourse to universal human dignity is not without problems. On the one hand, there is a variety of culturally rather diverse concepts of human dignity. And, on the other, there are some clear examples that the idea of human dignity does not only support equality before the law but also inequality. One has only to recall the numerous instances where a legally restricted status of women is justified by an alleged specific womanly dignity. Therefore, I would support Ignatieff's suggestion that within the context of justifying human rights, dignity should be restricted sharply to the dignity of free individual agency and self-determination.

Beyond that, it should be left precisely to this individual freedom as to how he or she wants to understand his/her dignity in more detail. Can the different cultures and religions agree on such a restriction? This question provides a kind of litmus test, for the freedom of men and women to decide for themselves on how they want to understand their own human dignity is a central implication of the human right to religious liberty.

Ignatieff concedes that the specific association of the idea of human rights with the idea of human dignity and the idea of free individual self-determination is of Western origin. But he rightly insists that the question of origin does not necessarily determine the range of validity. This takes us to the centre of the relativist critique of the idea of human rights, which has been summarised (but not approvingly) by Diane Orentlicher:

What we call 'universal' human rights are, in fact, an expression above all of Western values derived from the Enlightenment. Understood in this light, the human rights idea is at best misguided in its core claim that it embodies universal values-and at worst a blend of moral hubris and cultural imperialism.

In the discussion of the relativist critique two things are worth mentioning. First, in principle it is possible to base the human rights idea-even and particularly in its hard core of a 'moral individualism'-on more than just one foundation only. One can think of philosophical justifications coming from different cultural and religious origins but nevertheless concurring in their endorsement of the idea of human rights. Second, in the face of the relativist critique it should not be forgotten that opposition is exactly what has to be expected when it comes to the idea of human rights, precisely because its point is the protection of the individual agent against collectives, institutions, traditions, religions, etc. that are too powerful.

This in itself seems to be an intercultural universal. In the West the idea of human rights had to be pushed through against a fierce and persistent resistance coming from political and religious authorities. Pope Leo XIII, for instance, accuses human rights of being "unrestrained doctrines of liberty" and Pope Gregory XVI designated the idea of a right to religious liberty as "madness". Hence, one should not be surprised if the idea of human rights meets with comparable resistance in other civilisations.

Surprise would be rather appropriate if that did not occur, for then one should fear that the idea of human rights has become so wishy-washy that it no longer appears as something that is to be taken seriously by those powers against whom it is directed. Thus, when it comes to the universality of human rights what is at stake is also and in particular the universality of critical standards, which may have to be asserted against ancient traditions, whether of the Western or of any other civilisation. In this respect it is quite encouraging to see that the fourteenth Dalai Lama-despite being himself a high representative of an ancient tradition-acknowledges exactly this critical function of human rights:

Diversity and traditions can never justify the violations of human rights. Thus discrimination of persons from a different race, of women, and of weaker sections of society may be traditional in some regions, but if they are inconsistent with universally recognized human rights, these forms of behavior must change. The universal principles of equality of all human beings must take precedence.

RESONANCES

At least since the reign of emperor Ashoka (middle of the 3rd century BCE) Buddhism has presented itself as a politically and socially formative factor, and this was probably just about one hundred years after the Buddha's death. To my mind, this did not require a radical transformation of Buddhism, for contrary to a prejudice still widespread in the West, Buddhism was, right from the beginning, by no means a purely individualistic and escapist doctrine of salvation.

Rather, we find already in the Pali canon a number of ancient texts which demonstrate not only an obvious interest in questions of common ethics but also apply specific features of the Buddhist explanation of the origin and removal of suffering to the social and political sphere, that is, to war, social discord, crime, poverty, legal insecurity, etc. The traditional Buddhist answer to these issues revolves around the idea of a Buddhist monarchy, i.e. around the idea of a king ruling the country according to the moral principles of the Dharma:

The king, the ruler of the world, the dharmic Dharma-king (dhammiko dhammaraja) relies just on Dharma; honours Dharma, reveres Dharma, esteems Dharma; with Dharma as his standard, with Dharma as his banner, with Dharma as his mandate, he sets a Dharma watch and bar and ward for folk within his realm (...) for warrior and camp follower, for Brahman and for householder, for town and country folk, for recluse and for godly man, for beast and bird alike.

In this context the word 'dharma' has a fairly broad meaning. It is usually translated as 'law' but means much more than that. In the Buddhist context it signifies primarily the teaching of the Buddha which, however, is not regarded as the Buddha's invention but as something that the Buddha has rediscovered, like a forgotten city overgrown by the jungle. Accordingly, Buddha's teaching reflects a kind of cosmic law which describes the basic syntax of all life-suffering, its causes, its ultimate appeasing in Nirvana as well as the path leading to the removal of suffering and, as an integral part of this, morality and justice. While the Dharma has therefore transtemporal validity, this does not, in traditional Buddhist understanding, hold for monarchy itself.

According to an ancient myth, codified in the Pali canon, monarchy is based on a kind of social contract. In primordial times the idea of private property arose among human beings due to their greed. As a result of private property and greed, theft, lies, and violence became rife and so it was resolved to appoint a king. By the power conferred on him to dispense justice, the elected king should fight the evils that had arisen and should be paid for this by the citizens of his state.

However, the powers and duties of a king are not confined to this power. In correspondence with the basic Buddhist insight that painful phenomena are best removed by removing their causes, it also counts among the king's duties to provide financial aid for the poor and to make sensible economic investments in order to fight poverty as one of the major causes of all sorts of social evil. The Buddhist scriptures contain several catalogues of a king's virtues and duties, among them the particularly important scheme of the ten virtues of a Dharma king (dasa rajadhamma), which are: "generosity, morality, spirit of sacrifice, integrity, mildness, spiritual discipline, peaceableness, non-violence, forbearance, and non-offensiveness" (dana, sila, pariccaga, ajjava, maddava, tapas, akkodha, avihimsa, khanti, avirodhana).

In a symposium on "Buddhism and Human Rights" Damien Keown suggested that the Buddhist concept of duties and virtues of the king determined by the Dharma anticipates the modern idea of rights and human rights in an "embryonic form". Underlying Keown's suggestion is the argument that justice can be expressed both ways, by rights and by duties: someone's right expresses entitlement to be treated justly and someone's duty expresses the obligation to treat others justly. From this Keown concludes that rights and duties can be mutually deduced.

Therefore, even if the Buddhist Dharma does not speak of rights but of duties, rights can nevertheless be deduced from it by the following model: "If under Dharma it is the duty of a king (or political authority) to dispense justice impartially, then subjects (citizens) may be said to have a 'right' to just and impartial treatment before the law". Keown extends this argument to the whole of Buddhist morality, so that, in his view, different rights emerge from the various moral precepts of Buddhism: for example, the right to life from the precept not to kill, the right to property from the precept not to steal, etc.

In other words, the modern ideas of rights in general and of human rights in particular are not explicitly mentioned in the traditional Buddhist scriptures but can be extrapolated from the explicitly stated Dharma-related duties. Against Keown, Craig Ihara has argued that while it is true that from every right a corresponding duty can be deduced, the converse does not hold-that is, one cannot deduce from every duty the claim to a corresponding right. In my mind it is true that there are forms of responsibilities which go beyond that what can be described as satisfying or respecting a particular right.

Therefore, Ihara is correct in that it is not possible to deduce from every duty or responsibility someone else's legal claim or right to that. But, as Ihara himself admits, the converse is perfectly correct: legitimate rights lead to the moral duty of others to respect or not to violate these rights. This is of crucial importance for the idea of human rights, for stating particular human rights means making a serious appeal to the duty of the powerful not to violate these rights. Therefore, in the end, Keown is right insofar that at least some specific moral duties of kings, as stated in traditional Buddhism, may be understood as expressing an appeal that would in substance correspond to the idea of rights.

Regarding the Buddhist conviction that a king should rule in accordance with the Dharma, one may indeed assume that this is backed by the feeling that such a dharmic exercise of power is highly desirable, particularly from the perspective of the subjects. In any case, it is a familiar view of the early Buddhist texts that kings are among those things from which or whom one needs protection. For, in a frequently appearing standard formula kings are mentioned in one breath with fire and water, robbers and bad heirs. Hence, it does not seem to be totally misleading to assume that the demand for an exercise of power in accordance with the Dharma was also motivated by the intention to protect the subject from 'royal' catastrophes.

This is certainly not yet the same as the modern formulation of the idea of human rights. However, it is compatible with it or-more strongly-predisposed to it. One can hardly expect much more from texts which are more than 2,000 years old. But what about the question so central to the idea of human rights, the question of justifying the worth of individual self-determination and free agency? Does Buddhism have a solid and sound basis for human dignity in the sense of the dignity of the free individual that must be respected and protected? A number of Buddhist authors, including the Burmese Nobel Peace Prize Laureate Aung San Suu Kyi, have answered the question of how to justify human dignity in Buddhism by hinting at the specific status of human beings in respect to their potential for enlightenment and liberation.

One should recall first that in Buddhism human beings do not occupy an absolutely privileged position but are seen against the doctrine of rebirth as being continuous with all 'sentient beings,' that is, with all forms of existence in which rebirth can take place. Within the context of the human rights debate, Buddhists have therefore repeatedly pointed to an additional need for animal rights. However, the fact that the Buddhist understanding of human beings does not allocate to them an absolutely exceptional position entails by no means an indiscriminate levelling.

Rebirth as a human being is regarded as particularly precious because it carries the most favourable conditions for progress on the Buddhist path of salvation. Therefore it is usually assumed that enlightenment can be achieved only in human form. Subhuman forms of existence, i.e. as animals, ghosts, or beings in hell, leave no or too little room for free moral and spiritual action and the life of the gods is too pleasant for gaining full insight into the basically unsatisfactory character of samsaric existence. The Buddhist scriptures repeatedly praise existence in human form as particularly precious with regards to its specific prospects for enlightenment and salvation.

And this implies the specific worth of individual self-determination and free agency. Thus the Buddha admonished his disciples shortly before he died with the words: "Be islands unto yourselves! Be a refuge to yourselves; do not take to yourselves any other refuge. See Dharma as an island, see Dharma as a refuge. Do not take to yourselves any other refuge".

This does not imply any sort of inclination to postmodern or pre-modern arbitrariness. There is no doubt that the Dharma is objectively given and definitely proclaimed by the Buddha and is as such the "island" or "refuge." However, what is important for individual progress on the path of salvation is nothing but personal appropriation through one's own understanding and experience and in this sense everyone must be one's own "island" or "refuge." Accordingly, the Buddha says in his well known discourse to the Kalamas:

Be ye not misled by report or tradition or hearsay. Be not misled by proficiency in the collections [or scriptures], nor by mere logic or inference, nor after considering reasons, nor after reflection on and approval of some theory, nor because it fits becoming, nor out of respect for a recluse (who holds it). But, Kalamas, when you know for yourselves: these things are unprofitable, these things are blameworthy, these things are censured by the intelligent; these things, when performed and undertaken, conduce to loss and sorrow,-then indeed do ye reject them.... But if at any time you know of yourselves: These things are profitable, they are blameless, they are praised by the intelligent: these things, when performed and undertaken, conduce to profit and happiness, then Kalamas, do ye, having undertaken them, abide therein.

The personal responsibility of humans for their deeds and their consequences is also at the centre of the Buddhist teaching on karma and is emphasised by the standard formula: "I myself am responsible for my deed, I am the heir to my deed", meaning that a good or bad spiritual development is rooted in the direct responsibility of the individual. The accentuation of personal responsibility seems also be the key reason for the Buddhist critique of the caste system (one's deeds, rather than one's birth, show an individual's worth), for the affirmation of an (at least in principle) equal status of the sexes, for the critique of deterministic understandings of karma and deterministic versions of theism, as well as for the rejection of the materialistic idea that everything happens purely by chance.

Moreover, for Buddhism there is no contradiction between responsibility for oneself and responsibility for one's fellow humans or beings. Both are seen to belong closely together: "Protecting oneself, one protects others; protecting others, one protects oneself ". A central foundation for this is the so-called 'Golden Rule,' which is also well-known in Buddhism: "For a state that is not pleasant or delightful to me must be so to him also; and a state that is not pleasing or delightful to me, how could I inflict that upon another?" And this in turn is based on the fundamental insight that all beings "... yearn for happiness and recoil from pain".

Given the high value that traditional Buddhism attributes to the direct responsibility of the individual, it is not surprising that some Buddhists commit themselves to the protection of individual freedom, also on the level of legislation, that is, to an undivided validity of the human rights which are instrumental to this protection. An outstanding example of this is Bhimrao Ramji Ambedkar, the founder of Indian Neo-Buddhism and the father of the Indian constitution. The legal abolition of caste distinctions through the Indian constitution in 1949 and the constitutional guarantee of human rights are primarily Ambedkar's work and for him an expression of his Buddhist convictions.

The organisers of the symposium on "Buddhism and Human Rights," mentioned above, issued a "Declaration of Interdependence" which seems to be meant as a kind of draft Buddhist equivalent to the Universal Declaration of Human Rights. The first paragraph of the preamble summarises the Buddhist foundations for the idea of human rights in the following way:

Those who have the good fortune to have a "rare and precious human rebirth," with all its potential for awareness, sensitivity, and freedom, have a duty to not abuse the rights of others to partake of the possibilities of moral and spiritual flourishing offered by human existence. Such flourishing is only possible when certain conditions relating to physical existence and social freedom are maintained. Human beings, furthermore, have an obligation to treat other forms of life with the respect commensurate to their natures.

Despite the Buddhist potential for a positive affirmation of the idea of human rights, the relationship between Buddhism and this idea is not entirely free from tension.

DISSONANCES

In the thirteenth century the poet Ramacandra composed these verses after his conversion to Buddhism:

When the idea of an ego arises, it will also procreate egotism. Soon the latter will produce the greed for being, and that begets from moment to moment delusion. The root of suffering is this idea of an ego. Cut it off from me, o Jina, with the sword of your word.

In these verses Ramacandra summarises the Buddhist belief that the idea of an ego or 'I' is one of the main reasons for the human predicament. Some Buddhist authors have criticised the idea of human rights by the argument that it would promote this idea of an ego and the egotism so closely linked to it. Craig Ihara, for instance, says "... invoking rights has the inevitable effect of emphasizing individuals and their status, thereby strengthening the illusion of self. While Buddhism has a holistic view of life, the rights perspective is essentially atomistic". Therefore Ihara holds... that rights in the sense of subjective entitlements are conceptually incompatible with classical Buddhist ethics and their introduction would require a fundamental conceptual transformation.... The change to a modern concept of rights is one from conceptualizing duties and obligations as the role-responsibilities of persons in a cooperative scheme to seeing them as constraints on individuals in their interactions with other individuals all of whom are otherwise free to pursue their own objectives.

Ihara's view that the Buddhist Dharma and the associated ideal of the Dharma-king must not be understood in the sense of the idea of rights finds a vivid illustration or even radicalisation in the idea of a "Dictatorial Dhammic Socialism" from the eminent Thai Buddhist reformer, Bhikkhu Buddhadasa. For Buddhadasa the first priority of every political system must be the well-being of the community. To this the freedom of the individual must be unequivocally subordinate.

Moreover, the concept of freedom is, according to Buddhadasa, in itself highly ambiguous. From a Buddhist perspective, the individual is controlled by negative, selfish tendencies and it is precisely this with which liberalism's concept of freedom cannot effectively deal: "Liberalism cannot provide a basis for social utility because it promotes selfishness, individual benefits rather than social benefits". But a liberal concept of freedom is also the basis of liberal democracy-which therefore has to be rejected too. For Buddhadasa, true freedom consists in conquering all selfish tendencies. Socialism with dictatorial features, being opposed to the liberal ideal of individual freedom, is therefore more suitable for dealing adequately with the problem of selfishness than liberal democracy.

However, it is necessary that the socialist dictator follow the Dharma and manifests-in accordance with the ancient Buddhist ideal of the Dharma-king-the ten virtues of kingship: "If a good person is the ruler the dictatorial socialism will be good, but a bad person will produce an unacceptable type of socialism. A ruler who embodies the ten royal virtues will be the best kind of socialist dictator". Such an ideal Buddhist dictator, says Buddhadasa, will look after his people the way good parents look after their children.

Above all, he will "promote the common good" and "abolish the evil of private, selfish interest". But how is that to be achieved? Among Buddhadasa's disciples some illuminating suggestions have been made, such as: the removal of capitalism in favour of an "economic structure of... contentment... moderation... and self-reliance," oriented by the example of rural cultures; "healthy sexuality within healthy families;"

promotion of indigenous, local entertainment, songs, and dance; promotion of healthy and creative forms of sports and play; new ways of education which-in the long run-might even render schools and universities unnecessary; removal of rich and powerful religious institutions; removal of political parties; promotion of the awareness of "the need... to make sacrifices, let go of self, and give up selfish interests for the good of society"; installation of a general system of monitoring, including something like "moral ombudspersons," "empowered to... investigate, and sanction," etc.

Such views take us right into the intensive and partly heated debate which has become known as the controversy on 'Asian values.' During the 1990s political leaders of various Asian states, headed by Malaysia and Singapore and markedly supported by China, have repeatedly criticised the idea of human rights as being too Western and contended in particular that the individualism on which it is based is opposed to community-oriented 'Asian values'.

For some countries like China, Vietnam, Burma (or Myanmar) and others, it is only too obvious that this argument was used to distract attention from considerable violations of human rights within their own states or to escape international criticism. But underlying some of the Asian voices is clearly the genuine concern that a liberal individualistic ethos in conjunction with a legalistic, aggressive, and consumerist attitude does not meet traditional values of Asian societies, i.e. social harmony, respect for family and authorities and, in particular, emphasis on duty and responsibility rather than on rights that can be claimed.

Such concerns should not be easily dismissed. Bhikhu Parekh has rightly pointed out that, on the one hand, emphasising 'Asian values' "... is vulnerable to the collectivist danger and unlikely to create a culture conducive to the development of individuality and choice" but that, on the other hand, a one-sided liberal stress on rights is hardly able "to nurture the spirit of community and social responsibility".

This statement marks a good starting-point for understanding that both sides, the representatives of 'Asian values' and the defenders of 'Western Liberalism' could learn from each other and in a sense complement each other, although not on the same level exactly-i.e. not on the legal level of those minimal protective rights which are meant to guard the freedom of the individual from powerful communities and institutions. It is true that emphasizing such individual protective rights is not enough for promoting moral sensitivity and social responsibility.

Responsibility exceeds that which can be secured legally. Therefore, it makes a great deal of sense to identify, in addition to The Universal Declaration of Human Rights an intercultural and inter-religious basis for a Universal Declaration of Human Responsibilities as intended within the context of the "Global Ethic Project". Human responsibilities and human rights should complement rather than supersede each other. Emphasising social and moral responsibility must not lead to a removal of that basic intuition of human rights that seeks legal protection for the individual's freedom of self-determination. On the other hand this right cannot prevail without any limitations.

It finds its limits-as already stated in the 1948 Declaration-at the rights of others and "the just requirements of morality, public order and the general welfare." But it must not be crushed by the latter. This, however, seems to be the danger of concepts such as Buddhadasa's "Dictatorial Dhammic Socialism." The problem, which is here particularly obvious, consists in the intention to force the high ethos of Buddhist morality on a complete society. But, among other things, it is precisely a tutelage like this against which human rights ought to protect people. This is not a specific problem of Buddhism but a problem of religion and human rights in general.

The crucial challenge for religions is therefore to support the key intention of the idea of human rights, even and in particular if this entails restricting the power of the religious institutions. I think that in principle Buddhists could and should make this intention their own. Not only because-as the Thai Buddhist and scholar of politics, Saneh Chamarik, has rightly remarked-well-intentioned dictatorships can only too easily end up with horrendous subjugation but also because religious tutelage ultimately contradicts the Buddhist respect for the individual's own spiritual responsibility.

What happens if someone living under such a Dharma dictatorship does not share the high ideals of Buddhism and prefers rather to be selfish and greedy? What happens if someone likes to indulge in pleasures which, from a Buddhist perspective, are inferior or 'unhealthy' or enjoys different music and dances from folk music and folk dancing? What happens if someone would like to retain religious institutions, political parties and universities? Will methods of intensified education then be imposed? I think that Buddhadasa's and his disciples' suggestions are as naive as they are perilous.

Asia has had enough painful experiences with analogous visions from communists. Buddhists who accept the idea of human rights can support specific Buddhist values and ideals by the old means of preaching, the lived example and, of course, by all sorts of constructive social cooperation but not by dictatorial force. The spirit of human rights demands that Buddhists respect and try to protect the freedom of individuals even and in particular if they want to understand themselves other than in a Buddhist sense. That such ideas are not only modern and exclusively Western is perhaps illustrated by the following instructions from the Vinaya, the monastic rule, of the Mulasarvastivadins:

If-says the Vinaya-one has to carry out some building measure for the Buddha and if for this reason one has to cut a tree which is inhabited by a tree-deity, then one should present to this tree-deity incense, flowers and offerings and subsequently expound to the deity the wholesome forms of conduct and after that ask the deity to move into a different tree just because this tree is needed for the Buddha. If, however, the deity refuses to leave the tree then "one shall praise to the deity the advantages of generosity and explain the disadvantages of miserliness and greed." But if even that is of no use and the deity still refuses to leave its tree, then-says the instruction-"one is not allowed to cut it.

RELIGIOUS PLURALISM

The question of how the concept of human rights-so crucially important for the implementation of justice in a rapidly globalizing world-relates to the plurality of cultures and religions has still not been solved. Controversies such as those over land rights in Aboriginal Australia and Asian values in Southeast Asia have shown this repeatedly. In such cases, discussion eventually becomes focused on the universality of human rights, not just the global scope of the idea itself but the universal validity of catalogues of specific rights such as those contained in the United Nations' Universal Declaration of Human Rights (December 10, 1948).

There is something arbitrary and unsystematic about such charters, as is shown by the rather different emphases in the African and Islamic documents which were meant to correct the UN's lack of universality. But if, in attempting to explore this problem seriously, one appears to tamper with the principle of universality, one can easily be accused of diluting the ethical force of human rights by questioning their applicability to every human being without exception. Nothing could be further from my mind, so before explaining what I wish to do in this chapter I shall first set out some presuppositions that I take to be axiomatic:

1. Our starting point is the dignity of the human, the unique value of each individual human life as a world constituted by consciousness, an originating source of free acts, which is therefore an end in itself and must never be misused as a means to other people's ends. This principle is reflected in formulations such as dignitas humana in the social teaching of the Catholic Church, which goes back to the biblical doctrine of the creation of human beings in the image of God, or in the unique status of the human being in the Buddhist scale of existence, on which neither animals nor gods but only humans are in a position to grasp the reality of their situation and strive for definitive release from the chain of becoming; hence the severity of the prohibition on taking human life as the third of the four cardinal offences (parajika).

2. The concept of "human rights" is one way of acknowledging this unique moral status of human dignity, in that rights

accrue to the individual person simply by virtue of his or her being rational, autonomous, and free. To this extent human rights language belongs within the Western tradition of liberal discourse, which lies at the heart of Western democracies and was profoundly influenced by Christianity. Conceptions of what it is that makes the human uniquely valuable, however, are very differently constructed in different cultural and religious traditions.

3. What rights language tries to express in the conceptual framework provided by European culture has universal validity, although it is otherwise expressed in other cultures, for example, in terms of "duty," "obedience," "taboo," and so on. Problematic as it is in the context of postmodern discourse, the sameness in-difference of the human as the criterion for rights everywhere and without exception is a categorical imperative on which the effectiveness of human rights as an instrument of justice depends.

4. Conceptions of universality, however, may themselves be culturally determined and usually arise in contexts of domination: what is taken to be universally valid is often somebody's particular version of the truth of things which by virtue of a claim to universality is then imposed on others as "the" truth. Such conceptions are necessarily generalizations, whereas the moral impulse arises in the face-to-face encounter with the alien, unexpected and unwanted "other," as Levinas has shown.

5. Universality is thus not available a priori but remains implicit in the intersubjectivity of human interaction until it is realized through shared practice and the negotiation of meanings; this applies all the more to interactions between religions and across cultures.

6. Rights language, though a powerful instrument for the implementation of justice, is thus incomplete unless its Western (and Christian) conceptual presuppositions are complemented by the metaphors, stories, and ideas supplied by other cultures. Once this begins to happen, and in the light of growing ecological awareness, we realize that the concept of rights has to be expanded to include nature itself, not only all sentient beings but species as well, within the

scope of justice. Care for cultures-our own and those of others-and care for ecologies-both local and global-are seen to form part of one overarching ethical purpose.

Karl Popper used to say about scientific theories, when we think we have a good one we should not try to protect it from criticism and possible refutation-which is in fact what scholars, like scientists, mostly do-but to test it in every conceivable way, because it is in discovering how it could be falsified that we provide the best warrant for its provisional truth.

Something like this is my purpose here. Rights language, I have been assured by social activists in the Asia-Pacific, is the sharpest instrument they have for combating authoritarian regimes and economic injustice, but it is alien to many cultures in the region and its imposition can have the paradoxical effect of suggesting domination rather than liberation. Though it is somewhat over-simplified, the following schema sets out the terms in which I wish to discuss the problem:

This is not to suggest that individual rights are an exclusively Western notion, whereas less developed cultures are not content with community duties, nor that ecological care is characteristic only of indigenous peoples. In Thai Buddhism, to take one example, the dhammic democracy proposed by Phra Prayudh Payutto argues for individual freedoms, both political and economic, whereas the dhammic socialism of Buddhadasa Bhikkhu extols the ethical value of community responsibility.

Similarly, the social ethics proposed by the Christian ecumenical movement through the World Council of Churches has had to struggle to get beyond its somewhat individualistic base in liberal Protestantism, while the social teaching of the Catholic Church, though ever wary of anything that could be construed as socialism, has always taken its stand on the duties and obligations arising from the common good of all members of society and has articulated the principles of solidarity and subsidiarity. What I wish to suggest is that we must carry out three sets of mediations, indicated by the arrows in the diagram, if both the strengths and limitations of rights language are to be appreciated.

The relationship between individual and community might seem to be reciprocal, in that communities consist of individuals and individuals achieve individuality only within communities. We must remember, however, that in cultures like those of Pacific Islanders, though striking individual characters emerge (think of the Bikman of Melanesia), the sense in which they are individuals is quite different from that inculcated by Western education. The relationship between rights and duties is even less clearly complementary.

It is self-evident that, once rights are established, whether as claims to something that is due or as freedoms from something that is unjust, these entail duties on the part of others, whereas the inference does not necessarily hold the other way around: it is not evident that duties, obligations, or responsibilities in the context of community harmony and social cooperation entail rights on the part of those to whom these duties are owed. It has been argued, for instance, that there is not even an "embryonic" concept of rights in traditional Buddhism and that the social relevance of Buddhist compassion stands out all the more clearly in consequence.

Compassion is far more fundamental than rights, and it only becomes necessary to insist on rights when the practice of compassion declines. There is a certain affinity here with St Paul's insistence that justification-the state of being righteous-comes from faith, not law. The role of ecology in both Buddhist and Christian ethics and their human rights discourses is a larger topic that complicates matters still further. The potent combination of population growth and technological advancement is sufficient indication of both the human rights issues (family limitation, abortion) and the environmental devastation involved in, say, providing every family in China with an automobile and an air conditioner.

But in my view the ecological dimension could be crucial in bringing about the necessary mediations outlined in the diagram above. Buddhism, conceived entirely within the worldview defined by karman-samsara, the endless cycle of rebirth according to the residue of deeds in previous lives, sees human life as an integral part of this perpetual flux of life forms. Its relationship with the rest of sentient nature is thus one of constant recycling until radical release (moksha) is achieved in nirvana. For this reason the ancient Indian unwillingness to harm any sentient being (ahimsa) is an integral part of Buddhist ethics.

This does not mean that Buddhism has a ready-made ecological ethic for today, but it is a promising starting point. Christianity, on the other hand, was so preoccupied with human sin and redemption that it reduced nature to the exemplar of natural law as it applied to humans and lost sight of care for creation as an ethical goal, so that the idea that nature could have rights or that ecology could be a matter of justice now seems incomprehensible.

This is as much an indication of the limitations of rights language in expressing a universal ethic as it is of Christianity's tendency to be individualistic and anthropocentric. Both Buddhist and Christian traditions, I shall argue below, could benefit from their encounters with the primal traditions of indigenous peoples in developing new attitudes toward nature. When primal traditions, oral cultures without scriptures and philosophies but with close bonds to land and nature, are affected by progress, development, and globalization, the universality of rights language becomes dubious, because it is precisely the universality of Western norms that is invoked to justify such interventions.

The concept of universality demands more discussion than we can give it here, but it is closely bound up with the mind's capacity for abstraction and generalization. This is a powerful tool of science, but no matter how much it is refined it leads us further away from the ethical issues we wish to consider here, which are at one and the same time concrete and transcendent (in Levinas's terms: the "infinity" disclosed in the ethical encounter can never be reduced to "totality"). This observation becomes relevant when we turn to the purportedly universal religions.

It is important to realise that primal traditions are not simply outside the spheres of influence of the universal religions (unless they happen to be touched by them in missionary contexts). Rather, primal traditions form the social and cultural media through which the so-called world religions take on historical shape and articulate themselves in any context; conversely, there is a sense in which Aboriginal, Jewish, or Japanese religion, though ethnic and bound to land and place, are world religions. The problem is that, having achieved a distinctive historical identity in a few defining instances-the Theravada Buddhism of Southeast Asia and the Orthodox Christianity of Eastern Europe are striking examples-the Universalist religions tend to make these inculturations normative and claim timeless and universal validity for them.

We thus find the customs of the Himalayas, the Byzantine court or the Arabian desert being imposed as religious duties on Buddhists, Christians, and Muslims in markedly different contexts. These particular (sit venia verborum) "samsarisations," incarnations, or inscripturations of traditions that claim universal validity could have turned out otherwise, but their particularity is the indispensable accompaniment of historical existence. This realization further complicates the problem of the universality of rights discourse in interesting ways.

In order to systematize these differences somewhat I have found it helpful to speak in terms of at least two basic types of traditions. There are religions that might be called metacosmic, because they reckon in one way or another with a transcendence in the light of which the phenomenal world of perception and experience appears to be contingent at its core, whether the context be *creatio ex nihilo* or the dependent co-arising of all constituents of existence (paticca-samuppada).

At the other end of this scale there are the myriad traditions of indigenous peoples the world over, which might appropriately be called biocosmic in that they find whatever is of ultimate significance to them immanent within the natural rhythms of the cosmos and the physical processes by which life is propagated and sustained. The cultures of the Pacific Islands, particularly Melanesia, provide numerous examples. At various points in between we might locate traditions such as Daoism or Shinto, which derive wisdom for living from identification with the balance of cosmic forces (yin and yang in Chinese religion or the Three Principles represented by salt, water, and rice; star, moon, and sun; or sword, jewel, and mirror in Japan) and could therefore be called sapiential.

In the Hebrew Bible we can find examples of all of these types of religion; none of them is hard and fast, but all can interact and-the salient point for our present reflections-each can enrich and strengthen the others. The point is worth making, however, that metacosmic traditions such as Buddhism and Christianity are in danger of becoming abstract and absolutist unless they are continually grounded in the biocosmic traditions of primal religion. This process has happened over and over again in the course of their respective histories, but it can easily stagnate, leaving an inheritance of petrified rituals and institutions whose significance as expressions of the traditions' defining ideas is no longer reflected upon but whose universality is taken for granted.

The problem was classically formulated by Ernst Troeltsch as that of the relationship between norms and history: precisely as normative, ethical principles and religious doctrines demonstrate a certain a priori necessity that transcends the contingency of their historical origins; yet such norms are themselves the products of history, humanly constructed and subject to modification each time they are redefined in new cultural contexts and historical circumstances. The problem is merely compounded when divine revelation is invoked to legitimate such principles, as when *lex natura*, though intelligible to human reason, is corroborated by *lex divina* in traditional Catholic moral theology.

Human rights language is undeniably Western, unable to conceal its origins in the legal categories inherited from Greece and Rome. So conceived, it is an abstract universal that is logically independent of the myths and doctrines in which the various religions seek to found the unique worth of human nature. The concept of human rights, though at home in the Western liberal context of individual autonomy and political freedoms, is for this reason communicable to cultures that construct the human differently. The Dalai Lama, for example, has no problem endorsing human rights as a means of obtaining justice while insisting on the priority of wisdom and compassion, and, though they initially resisted human rights as 'liberal,' neither do the popes in their social teaching.

The question is, in what categories and under what conditions is the concept of human rights communicable across cultures? Certainly not those of the assumed superiority of Western ideas and values and their imposition on others by force as has happened often enough in the colonial and missionary past of Western Christianity. The recognition of differences in the mythical foundations of human dignity does not imply that the various stories are functionally equivalent and may be substituted for one another or combined at will to reinforce an account of the human that is already given a priori. It is the human itself that is differently constructed, and the Western construct is one among others.

Thus the powerful myth of creation by the Word of God and in the image of God, common to all three Abrahamic faiths, emphasizes the inalienable uniqueness of each human being and the irrevocable consequences of each and every act of free will. In the cosmic mythic complex of indigenous cultures such as those of Aboriginal Australia or Melanesia, by contrast, the human is an integral part of physical nature as represented in myths and rituals that stress belonging to the comprehensive metacommunity of kinship, ancestors, and nature spirits rather than individual uniqueness.

When Aboriginals become Christians, the prospect is opened up of an Aboriginal Christianity whose horizons are expanded by a universality that transcends ethnicity and locality yet which offers Western Christians the chance to confront their "Archaic other" (David Tracy) and rediscover what it means to cherish the land as the place that bestows identity and the earth as our common home. In India, the richly symbolic concept of dharma connotes the obligations arising from both social and cosmic status and is less amenable to the notion of rights (ius); it could be said to encompass a cosmocentric view of the world in which the cosmic is not necessarily subordinate to the human.

Buddhism, which appears to do away with the notion of an individual substantial self altogether (anatta, the teaching that every conceivable constituent of the individual is not-self), may seem to be inimical to the very idea of individualising human nature in order to provide a foundation for rights and freedoms. Yet the teaching on emptiness (sunyata) can be construed as a radical and original way of ensuring that ego-attachment does not hinder the universal scope of compassion, thereby giving free rein to the realization of good and the alleviation of suffering without the need for insisting on rights.

The Chinese, whose civilization was already deeply imbued with the Confucian sense of family duty when it was confronted with the Buddhist teachings and monastic institutions, eventually found ways to assimilate these to the subordination of the individual to nature in Daoist mysticism and the paradigmatic importance of family ties in Confucianism. When this Sinicized Buddhism reached Japan, it may be said to have assimilated so completely to the indigenous Way of the Kami (Shinto) as to have compromised its identity, for the Japanese regarded Shinto as merely the formalisation of the religion of Japaneseness (nihonjinron) and Buddhism as that dimension of indigenous religion that relates to death and the afterlife.

Each of these religious traditions, separately and in combination, gives rise to a conception of human dignity derived from a mythical account of human nature-but not necessarily emphasizing individuality or expressed in terms of rights. The Western story of the triumph of freedom and the pre-eminence of the individual is neither unique nor self-evidently superior to those of others, though it does predominate in a world shaped by Western technology and institutions. The doctrine of unrestricted free choice, though it is directly derived from the dignity of the human and makes democratic institutions possible, turns out to be pernicious when magnified by a global economy bent on profiteering, consumerism, and environmental destruction.

This is a hard lesson to learn for the West: that it is now being defined by others just as it once defined them. At the same time, however, it opens up the prospect that, although we must disabuse ourselves of the notion that one culture-ours-is transculturally superior to others; cross-culturally we are not only able to communicate but also morally obliged to do so for the sake of our own survival. But there are ethical issues involved in understanding and communication between cultures, and it is to these that I wish to turn in conclusion, because they are crucial to solving the problem of universal human rights in a situation of religious plurality.

Edward Said's concept of Orientalism, in its wider context of postcolonial theory, has made us aware that knowledge, even in the form of scientific research and literary expression, can be a function of domination, systematically distorting perceptions of difference by cloaking attitudes of superiority and contempt under a facade of fascination with the exotic. This is only one of the ways in which the Western liberal tradition-to which, we must never forget, we owe the freedoms we enjoy-has failed the test of acknowledging otherness in all its threatening strangeness, whether it be that of race, gender, culture, religion, or extra-human nature.

The principle of equality is noble but abstract; in practice, arguments could always be found to justify the powerful interests of commerce and security and the equally powerful instinct of prejudice in subordinating those who were different and exploiting their resources. This is still the case, as immigration policy, the so-called war on terrorism and the lip service paid to ecology in many countries show. Ironically, the destruction has been most ruthless where the protection of indigenous cultures coincides with the protection of the environment, in that these cultures have traditionally created balanced ecologies in which humans and nature alike can flourish.

There can be no question, however, of idealizing or romanticizing such cultures. These abuses are just as prevalent in Asia as in the West: India, China, and Japan are among the worst offenders against both human rights and nature's rights; Thailand's collusion with the corrupt regime in Myanmar is shameful; and Buddhism seems even more helpless than Christianity in the face of such abuses. But these are all arguments for intensifying inter-religious mutuality so that conceptions of the transcendent and conceptions of the human-in-nature can be mediated to one another.

I believe the argument can be made that the religions preserve denser accounts of how the rights of individuals, community responsibility, and care for the earth can reinforce one another than the relatively thin doctrines of individual liberty and religious pluralism inherited from the liberal tradition. One of the cornerstones of this tradition was the independence of ethics from religion and the exclusion of comprehensive doctrines of the kind propagated by religions from the public sphere of rational and pragmatic discussion. Ethics and religion are logically distinguishable and in this sense ethics may be rationally constructed without reference to religion. But there are pragmatic as well as formal logics; the logic by which a doctor arrives at a diagnosis or a judge at a decision is not the same as that of formal deduction.

The logic involved in moral decisions is a logic of self-involvement akin to that which structures religious commitment. Historically the insight into the transcendence that is intrinsic to ethical acts occurred in religious contexts (the Upanishads, the Book of Ezekiel, the New Testament, the Bhagavadgita), and the motivation to act morally was nourished by religious narratives. The normative dimension of moral decision making, experienced in the demands of conscience and expressed in the categorical imperative, is complemented by an element of vision which need not be explicitly religious but is typically so.

Even allowing for counterexamples such as godless cultures and atheistic philanthropists, it can be shown how ethics is contextualized in narratives of comprehensive liberation and fulfillment, whether these tell stories of the good life (the gutpela sindaun of Melanesian cultures), the peace that comes from the cooling of desire (nirvana), or a salvation that embraces humans and the cosmos.

Universality thus becomes a function of the "inter-" in terms such as "intersubjective," "intercultural," and "inter-religious"; equality takes full account of irreducible human differences while pinpointing the principle of mutual respect that transcends them;

rights are defined to counteract the manifest inequalities introduced by domination and exploitation; and pluralism can no longer be an excuse for limiting the applicability of rights and the values underlying them to exclusive groups. In such an expanded context human rights, while recognized as an indispensable instrument for achieving justice, are put in perspective alongside the much more fundamental values of love and wisdom, care and compassion.

In 1993 at the Second World Conference on Human Rights, national delegates from around the globe adopted the Vienna Declaration: "all human rights are universal, indivisible and interdependent and interrelated...." Like most rhetoric-in particular, rhetoric that surrounds human rights discourse-the Declaration's compelling language veils acute problems that emerge the moment one strives to bring its abstract claims to bear upon real world affairs and normative claims. But precisely this aspiration makes the human rights movement worthwhile. Should the discourse of human rights remain in theoretical limbo, solely the subject of armchair philosophy, then the very concept of human rights law becomes quixotic.

Only insofar as human rights discourse enacts, or maintains the potential to enact, concrete changes in the behavior of international actors does the human rights movement retain its value. Only insofar as one can articulate what claims this discourse supports can the movement begin to realize the lofty ideals that permeate its rhetoric. Many conceptual and practical difficulties confront universal human rights: Who has rights? Do individuals alone have rights or can groups-ethnic, religious, racial, or cultural-assert valid human rights claims, and can the claims of each be reconciled? Should civil and political rights remain primary, or do social, economic, and cultural rights warrant equivalent status? How should human rights be enforced? Which domestic and international arenas constitute the appropriate fora in which to press human rights claims?

This Article brackets these debates-except insofar as they are implicated tangentially-and proposes a new answer to-or, at least, a new way to think about-what arguably remains the most serious challenge to universal human rights: cultural relativism. Simply stated, cultural relativism insists that human rights cannot be universal because, as a matter of social fact, cultures maintain highly divergent mores and conceptualize human rights differently, or not at all, and these mores conflict in intractable ways that belie pretensions to "universality."

Cultural relativism, then, poses both theoretical and practical challenges. Theoretically, universal human rights imply, at a minimum, some set of "morally weighty" social norms that preempt, under all but the most exigent circumstances, other cultural value priorities. "Rights," as Jack Donnelly argues, "are `interests' that have been specially entrenched in a system of justifications and thereby substantially transformed, giving them priority, in ordinary circumstances, over, for example, utilitarian calculations, mere interests, or considerations of social policy... which otherwise would be not only appropriate, but decisive, reasons for public or private action." But how can one set of values-international human rights-warrant universal acknowledgment as peremptory norms when, as a matter of social fact, highly divergent practices, morals, goals, and value hierarchies deeply divide the world's multiple and diverse civilizations?

Practically, universal human rights must provide guidance about when and under what conditions international actors may intervene justifiably in the affairs of sovereign states to deter, terminate, or redress human rights violations. If, however, certain cultural traditions permit-perhaps even encourage-practices deemed morally abhorrent by other societies, by what criteria do we decide whether they violate "universal" standards that warrant international intervention?

For public international law, this question presents a serious difficulty. Traditional state sovereignty-the idea that what occurs exclusively within the territory of a state remains solely within its domestic competence-no longer constitutes the paramount principle of international law; it has been weakened, in fact, precisely by the post-World War II international human rights movement. But by no means has the primacy of state sovereignty been abandoned. The UN Charter affirms that "nothing contained in the present Charter shall authorize the United

Nations to intervene in matters which are essentially within the domestic jurisdiction of any state."

Furthermore, nations continue to object vociferously to international interference with, or even judgment of, their domestic affairs on the basis of alleged "universal" human rights standards. Those affairs, however, no longer remain wholly exempt from international scrutiny. Most nations acknowledge, at least in theory, that certain categories of state action are not "matters which are essentially within the domestic jurisdiction of any state"-international human rights violations. What counts as a human rights violation, then, assumes tremendous significance.

For to concede that some state practice violates universal human rights standards implies that the international community may justifiably interfere in the internal affairs of that state to deter, terminate, or redress the practice. States, therefore, maintain a significant stake in delimiting the scope of international human rights and, in particular, in ensuring that social, cultural, and political practices embedded in the fabric of the society or societies within their territory remain outside the class of universal norms that vindicate international interference.

This article pursues two related objectives. First, it does not seek to defend a conception of universal human rights that does not deny the empirical validity of cultural relativism-nor does it concede the normative assertions that many cultural relativists assume follow from this concession. Second, it argues that, given this conception of universality, most human rights critiques that rely upon relativism fail to establish their objective-in particular, they do not undermine the legitimacy of imposing certain human rights norms on states that purport to reject them for cultural relativist reasons.

It offers some historical background regarding the Western liberal traditions that relativist critiques often target, and it discusses the genesis of universal human rights-as manifested in the drafting of the Universal Declaration of Human Rights (UDHR)-in the aftermath of World War II. Finally, it sets forth several alternative grounds upon which the universality of human rights might plausibly be claimed. Each, for reasons elaborated below, is ultimately rejected. It remains to determine, however, what normative consequences this concession compels.

In particular, it appears to suggest that, under some circumstances, interference in the affairs of a sovereign state in the guise of protecting or enforcing universal human rights amounts to "cultural imperialism"-the unjustified or inappropriate imposition of one set of contingent norms on a culture that does not share them. The first, labeled "narrative relativism," does not necessarily reject universal human rights wholesale or suggest that imposing foreign cultural values is morally wrong. Instead, narrative relativism calls attention to the failure of universal human rights to acknowledge the critical reliance of cultures on implicit narratives that inform their normative framework. As Robert Cover succinctly puts it, "No set of legal institutions or prescriptions exists apart from the narratives that locate it and give it meaning."

Universal human rights law-from this perspective-might be dangerous; well-intentioned legal norms may upset key features of a community's sociopolitical order, causing local dissonance that outweighs the alleged benefits of an overarching regime structured by respect for international human rights. Alternatively, international human rights law, in the narrative relativist's view, may prove misguided; alleged universal norms may fail to comprehend adequately the positive roles served by cultural narratives that fail to conform to its, perhaps myopic, prescriptions.

Narrative relativism, under some circumstances, states a legitimate concern for universal human rights. It invites a consideration of the relative desirability of certain kinds of human rights activism that threaten to upset indigenous cultural mores. But narrative relativism, argues, fails to provide reason to abandon the project of universal human rights. First, as some scholars argue, many of its claims-that certain traditional societies value the well-being of the community above individual rights, or that the devaluation of civil and political rights facilitates economic and social stability in developing nations-prove empirical, and evidence tending to establish these empirical claims remains, at best, inconclusive.

Second, and more critically, cultural variations in norms, values, and moral perceptions do not necessarily challenge the idea of an overarching international framework structured around universal human rights; rather, narrative relativism forces one to appraise the extent to which different systems of cultural mores that exist at the level of micro law remain compatible with a macro legal system governed by the standards of universal human rights. However, domestic legal compliance with this component of international law does not demand or even suggest cultural homogenization because values of reasonable tolerance and autonomy form the very foundation of universal human rights law. This observation, standing alone, does not diffuse the relativist challenge.

While universal human rights arguably permit diverse cultural communities considerable latitude to subsist within a common international legal order, by no means do all cultural values and practices conform to its prescriptions. The question also remains whether the fact of cultural pluralism implies that international human rights law should tolerate those that do not. Narrative relativism therefore invites inquiry into a more foundational question: Why does universal human right law-as one peculiar mechanism for promoting human dignity-merit acknowledgment as the paramount international standard by which to appraise domestic legal regimes and cultural practices?

Crude cultural relativism insists that to acknowledge cultural pluralism implies that the coercive imposition of one culture's norms onto another that purports to reject them is morally illegitimate. This Article argues that this position frequently proves a disingenuous, or simply unsupported, empirical claim. Moreover, even assuming its empirical respectability and sincerity, crude relativism remains philosophically unsatisfactory in two principal respects.

First, it suffers from a foundational error of logic. Crude relativism asserts, at once, that all values are relative-culturally and historically contingent-but that, nonetheless, to impose one set of values on an agent or group that rejects them is objectively wrong. It claims, in other words, that one value-the norm against coercive imposition-demands universal respect notwithstanding the descriptive truth of relativism. To embrace crude relativism descriptively, then, requires abandoning the very normative critique of human rights universalism that, ironically, relativists often assume follows from it.

Second, crude cultural relativism presumes that a nation-state's government and its objectives may be identified justifiably with the cultural values and desires of its populace. But several considerations militate against this simple identification, particularly in states that lack genuine democratic institutions, a characteristic feature of most chronic human rights violators. Cultural relativist rhetoric thus often proves more a tool of state elites to vindicate control over their citizenry than a genuine reflection of deeply held cultural values of the populace.

None of these arguments refutes cultural relativism as a descriptive proposition. They establish, at best, that we lack non-contingent criteria-which refer to standards independent of specific historical, cultural, and linguistic contexts-to evaluate competing value hierarchies. But the absence of neutral, non-contingent criteria does not repudiate the normative universality of human rights; it demonstrates, more modestly, that "universal" must not be understood in a transcendental or ontological sense-as a scientific claim about the "true" nature of the world and its inhabitants. Indeed, the emphasis throughout this Article is that a non-transcendental conception of universality is not only empirically accurate, but intrinsically desirable.

To claim that universal connotes "objectively true" is to deny that reasonable individuals can hold disparate, but equally valid, opinions about ultimate questions of value. But the possibility, indeed, even desirability, of these differing opinions-about politics, ethics, the nature of the "good life," and so forth-is inextricably intertwined with the very protections that universal human rights law strives to extend to all individuals, such as freedoms of association, speech, and political and religious belief. Thus, somewhat paradoxically, universal human rights law derives its greatest virtue-and perhaps its most compelling claim to normative universality-precisely from its emphasis on the traditional liberal tolerance of reasonable value pluralism.

But these values cannot be selectively adopted. A state's elite cannot, for example, appeal to the liberal values of reasonable tolerance and autonomy to challenge universal human rights law as "imperialistic"-for failing to extend adequate' tolerance to cultural diversity-but then conveniently reject these very same values when individuals within their polity invoke them in the form of human rights claims. Arguably, this inconsistency can be reconciled. In the former case, it seems, the reference is to the reasonable tolerance owed to groups and to cultural autonomy; in the latter, to individuals and to personal autonomy. Perhaps, then, the former claim need not imply the latter.

But this apparent distinction rests on a mistake: The justification for valuing tolerance and autonomy, as Will Kymlicka has convincingly shown, is inextricably tied to the distinctive liberal conception of the individual or the "self" as agent. Consequently, absent some alternative-non-liberal-justification, any assertion that cultural groups or political entities also merit tolerance and respect for their autonomy is necessarily derivative of-not independent of-the rationale for respecting individual autonomy.

Of course, cultural or state elite remains free to repudiate this value and its concomitant rationale. But it cannot then demand tolerance or respect for "cultural autonomy" as a rhetorical device to deflect criticism of its human rights practices. By contrast, to embrace the values of autonomy and reasonable tolerance is to acknowledge the normative force of universal human rights. Moreover, because the liberal values that find expression in international human rights law do respect the paramount importance of reasonable tolerance and autonomy, "universal" human rights law proves highly inclusive, accommodating, and tolerant of the diversity of cultural traditions and values that comprise the contemporary international community. This is because international human rights law evolved from a tradition that, far from denying alternative, "culturally relative" conceptions of value, emphasizes the liberal presumption of value pluralism.

Finally, the Article concludes by integrating the above arguments with an idea that Jack Donnelly, Rhoda Howard, and other scholars have advanced. Specifically, the normative universality of human rights must be conceived in the context of a historically contingent, but no less valid empirical truth: The Western nation-state-and its attendant cultural narratives-has become the principal actor in international law. Human rights, which developed precisely to counterbalance, as Cover writes, "the rise of the national state with its almost unique mastery of violence over extensive territories," is, consequently, the peculiarly appropriate set of norms to govern contemporary international law.

Universal human rights, then, constitute the appropriate concept for responding to abuses by states and state-like actors, such as paramilitary groups, tribal, or other informal authorities. This may imply that other deeply troubling concerns should not be conceived, strictly speaking, as universal human rights violations. This does not detract from the value or validity of universal human rights law. It simply clarifies, not surprisingly, that human rights ought not to be understood as a panacea for all human suffering or as the exclusive mechanism for promoting a world community conducive to human dignity.

THE CHALLENGE OF CULTURAL RELATIVISM

"Human rights" lends it to multiple rhetorical uses. Like "justice," "liberty," and "equality," the term "human rights" is used to support broad claims and diverse demands. To analyze cultural relativism, however, two basic meanings must be distinguished. First, human rights may be understood philosophically, as the rights that human beings, qua human, possess. In this respect Holmes' dictum that where there is no remedy there is no right must be rejected. It would remain perfectly coherent to suggest that one's human rights had been violated, even if no institution existed to provide legal redress.

As Donnelly clarifies, "Possession of a right, the respect it receives, and the ease or frequencies of enforcement" are quite separate issues.

Needless to say, the mere fact that some human rights are not respected or are inadequately enforced does not, ipso facto, refute their universal possession by human beings. To the contrary, were human rights universally enjoyed, we would have no need for them. Second, we might understand human rights in a strictly legal sense: Human rights would then comprise a particular subset of the domain of legal claims that individuals-and arguably, at times, communities-can advance. In this regard, if no institution exists that, at least in theory, could provide a remedy, no legal human right exists.

Some leading proponents of cultural relativism advocate revisions to the UDHR and post-World War II human rights treaties. Yet the critical issue raised by relativist critiques implicates human rights in the philosophical sense: human rights as weighty, often preemptive, cultural values. Cultural relativists do not typically claim that international treaties lack legal validity because they interfere with sacrosanct cultural traditions. They assert, instead, that the values codified in these treaties and the functional concepts used to enforce them (rights) either (1) impose a value hegemony anathema to their cultural traditions (crude relativism); or (2) often receive interpretations informed by cultural biases that fail to acknowledge alternative, but equally valid, cultural constructions of these legally codified principles (narrative relativism).

Before evaluating these critiques, then the conceptual framework under attack-roughly, Western liberalism and its concomitant concern with rights-warrants preliminary appraisal. Liberalism does not denote a single, clearly identifiable tradition; to the contrary, "right-wing" libertarians, "left-wing" proponents of a vigorous welfare state, and every permutation along the political spectrum in between at times self-identifies as, or is saddled by others with the description "liberal." Liberalism must not, therefore, be understood as a monolithic approach to political philosophy.

Yet several prominent features ascribed to the Western liberal tradition can be identified that different variants of the cultural relativist critique challenge: the primacy of the individual as the fundamental unit of concern and measure of value; a conception of rights as political "trumps" against the demands of the state or community; a commitment to some measure of democratic participation in government; a concern with preserving autonomy; and finally, some notion of equality. But even conceding, for the moment, that most forms of Western liberalism embrace these ideas in one way or another, we must take care not to make any simple equation between the human rights movement and Western liberalism.

First, international human rights did not develop as an identifiable movement until after World War II; whereas liberalism, in its diverse manifestations, claims a much longer history. Second, although human rights evolved from values and philosophical presumptions closely associated with the Western liberal tradition, the modern international human rights movement can embrace certain other substantive cultural values to the extent that they promote human dignity. Finally, no necessary connection exists between being a political liberal and respecting all international human rights.

Some liberals-including self-identified human rights advocates-reject economic, social, and cultural rights, half of the so-called "Universal Bill of Human Rights," as genuine rights. Other liberals-those in the Benthamite utilitarian tradition for example-might regard international human rights as "nonsense on stilts"-though they might be inclined to concede the usefulness of this nonsense. Still others might express support for international human rights while maintaining a deep commitment to Marxist political theory. Yet we need not engage these debates directly to evaluate cultural relativism.

What is at stake is not which liberal values deserve to be included on the substantive "list" of human rights. The crux of the question presented by relativism resides at a distinct level: Does acknowledging the descriptive truth of cultural pluralism require abandoning the idea that human rights-however politicians, international lawyers, philosophers, and others delimit their scope-can, in any meaningful sense, be universal?

Does cultural pluralism show that the very objective of international human rights law-to establish rights that operate *erga omnes partes* despite the disparate cultural and political contingencies that characterize different nation-states-is incoherent? Thus, the next section identifies some of the more prominent features of the Western human rights movement as it has developed, philosophically and historically, in the liberal tradition, and subsequently considers whether the descriptive fact of cultural pluralism renders the normative concept of universal human rights misguided.

PHILOSOPHICAL ANTECEDENTS

These qualifications aside, the human rights tradition remains quintessentially a legacy of Western liberalism. It owes its conceptual origins to a unique Enlightenment-era synthesis of two prominent schools of Western philosophy: natural law and natural rights. The former, which dates to ancient Greek and Hebraic traditions, locates universal moral principles in the order of nature. Aristotle wrote, for instance, that "of political justice part is natural, part legal-natural, that which everywhere has the same force and does not exist by people's thinking this or that."

The idea that certain moral laws exist independently of the human mind because they inhere in the natural order of the universe persisted into the middle ages, at which time Aquinas, among others, linked this notion of natural law to conceptions of a divine will. "It was the fusion of the mythopoeia view that moral values are built into the natural order of things with the doctrine of the immanent operation of divinely revealed moral laws that led to the theory of natural law." Natural law theory thus postulates that certain norms of conduct possess a non-contingent ontological status in virtue of which they transcend the ephemeral features of particular cultures and historical epochs.

Although frequently conflated with natural rights, natural law theory, by itself, provides an insufficient basis for individual claims-whether moral or legal; it includes no necessary connection to the human subject. "The natural law idiom," Thomas Pogge clarifies, "need not involve constraints on one's conduct toward other subjects at all, and even if it does, need not involve the idea that by violating such constraints, one has wronged these subjects-one may rather have wronged God, for example, or disturbed the harmonious order of the cosmos."

Natural rights, by contrast, introduce the human subject as rights-holder, effecting a crucial shift in the locus of universality: from "nature" or "divinity" to "human." Natural rights theorists, including Enlightenment-era luminaries like Rousseau and Locke, commonly posit, whether as an alleged historical fact or a mere theoretical postulate, a state of nature in which humans enjoy certain rights. These natural rights, the familiar story runs, are then collectively traded by individuals to a state in exchange for some form of security.

A strong nexus exists between natural law and natural rights theories, but the pedigree of human rights resides largely in the shift from the former to the latter.

First and foremost, this shift created a class of rights-holders-human beings-empowered to press claims. "To have a right to x," as Donnelly puts it, "is to be specially entitled to have and enjoy x." Second, the shift from natural law to natural rights reoriented the locus of universality-from an external focus on the nature of the universe to an internal focus on the nature of humans:

The adjective "human"-unlike "natural"-does not suggest an ontological status independent of any and all human efforts, decisions and recognition. It does not rule out such a status either. Rather, it avoids these metaphysical and metaethical issues by implying nothing about them one way or the other.

Critically, then, while rights theories frequently evolved from ontological claims-about God or nature-they need not, unlike natural law theory, remain committed to these transcendentalist ideas. Finally, by postulating a contractual relationship between the individual-as-rights-holder and the state, natural rights theory laid the foundation for understanding human rights violations as implying official abuse.

Human rights, in sum, imply three interrelated postulates: (1) They are "held" by a certain class of rights-holders who may "exercise" them or press them as claims upon other agents or institutions; (2) this class includes all and only human beings, qua human-only humans hold these rights because only humans possess the requisite qualities that make human rights conceptually meaningful; and (3) unlike natural rights generally, susceptible to both public and private violation, only official abuses-those committed, at a minimum, under color of state or communal authority-count as human rights violations. From the standpoint of the history of philosophy, then, the universality of human rights resides in either transcendental features of the natural world, or alternatively, in some essential, peculiar features of human beings, qua human.

HISTORICAL ANTECEDENTS

From a political-historical perspective, universal human rights emerged in the wake of World War II. The unique atmosphere prevailing in the post-World War II era, shaped, in particular, by reactions to the atrocities of Nazi Germany, facilitated the extraordinarily rapid success and expansion of the international human rights movement. Indeed, as Louis Henkin observed, only these circumstances made the "creation and adoption [of the Universal Declaration of Human Rights] without dissent" possible; it embodied one of the "marvels of postwar international life."

Yet the post-WWII instantiation of human rights in multilateral treaties and declarations represented the merger, expansion, and modification of several trends in international law that predate the birth of the human rights movement. Steiner and Alston cite four core precedents: first, the laws of war-international humanitarian law; second, the protection afforded aliens by international law, which at times motivated state "humanitarian intervention" to protect nationals residing in foreign states; third, the attribution of individual criminal liability to Nazi war criminals; and fourth, the development of minority rights treaty regimes to protect national minorities during the League of Nations era.

To appreciate the significance of minority rights regimes in the context of the relativist-universalist debate, two ideologies must be distinguished. Value pluralism, the proposition that, within a political community, individual citizens will inevitably disagree about the fundamental goals of life, must be distinguished from cultural pluralism, the coexistence within a polity of two or more distinct peoples, where a people signifies "an intergenerational community, more or less institutionally complete, occupying a given territory or homeland, sharing a distinct language and history." The former concept, though not so-called, informed the political thought of classical liberals such as John Stuart Mill.

It also motivated the concern with factions that preoccupied some of the drafters of the U.S. Constitution. Madison, for instance, remarked that "the latent causes of faction are thus sown in the nature of man.... A zeal for different opinions concerning religion, concerning Government and many other points...." In general, liberals do not deny the fact of value pluralism; to the contrary, a great deal of Western political thought invokes value pluralism as the basic problem that motivates some emphasis on individual rights. But the historical relationship between liberalism and cultural pluralism is ambiguous. Kymlicka argues forcefully that the contemporary notion that states should treat cultures within their territorial boundaries with "benign neglect" is comparatively recent.

Historically, far from endorsing the idea that "the state should treat cultural membership as a purely private matter," Western liberals were attentive to the problems posed by cultural pluralism-not least of which was that its existence threatened the political stability of nation-states. This concern, which first emerged in the seventeenth century when certain religious minorities were afforded interstate protection, grew more prominent in the nineteenth-century due to the predominance of multination-the Hapsburg, Ottoman and Russian tsarist-and colonial empires-Great Britain and France:

It was commonplace in nineteenth-century thought to distinguish the 'great nations', such as France, Italy, Poland, Germany, Hungary, Spain, England, and Russia, from smaller 'nationalities', such as the Czechs, Slovaks, Croats, Basques, Welsh, Scots, Serbians, Bulgarians, Romanians, and Slovenes.

The great nations were seen as civilized... the carriers of historical development.

Needless to say, a similar relationship obtained between the European colonial powers and the diverse peoples of Asia, Africa, and the Middle East that suffered colonization during and prior to the mid-twentieth century. According to Kymlicka, liberals responded to the related difficulties raised by multination empires and colonization in one of two ways: Either they advocated coercive assimilation of the subjugated nationality or colonized people, or they endorsed the idea of certain protections for minority cultures subsumed by these empires.

Pre-twentieth-century liberals did not, however, advance the view that states should ignore cultural membership as an irrelevant, "incidental" feature; rather, "liberals either endorsed the legal recognition of minority cultures, or rejected minority rights not because they rejected the idea of an official culture, but precisely because they believed there should be one official culture."

It was only after World War II that the idea that states should treat cultural disparities with "benign neglect"-that the state's exclusive concern ought to be with treatment of the individual human subject, qua human-became the predominant approach in liberal political thought. Thus, in the aftermath of World War I-with the collapse of the multination Austro-Hungarian and Ottoman Empires and the upheaval wrought by the Bolshevik revolution-the League of Nations sought to create regimes for the protection of cultural minorities by imposing "Minorities Treaties... on the new or reconfigured states of Central-East Europe and the Balkans."

Far from ignoring cultural membership, these treaties-influenced in no small part by Woodrow Wilson's emphasis on the "self-determination of peoples"-demanded precisely the opposite: The newly constituted governments were compelled to guarantee certain group-differentiated rights-language, religion, and education-to minority cultures subsisting within nation-states dominated by other, majority nationalities. In its advisory opinion on Minority Schools in Albania, for example, the Permanent Court of International Justice rejected the

Albanian Government's position that the Albanian Declaration required only that it "grant to its nationals belonging to racial, religious or linguistic minorities a right equal to that possessed by other Albanian nationals."

To the contrary, the Permanent Court of International Justice (P.C.I.J.) held:

The idea underlying the treaties for the protection of minorities is to secure for certain elements incorporated in a State, the population of which differs from them in race, language or religion, the possibility of living peaceably alongside that population and co-operating amicably with it, while at the same time preserving the characteristics which distinguish them from the majority, and satisfying the ensuing special needs.

Here again, consistent with Kymlicka's argument, cultural pluralism receives acknowledgment and appears to require some forms of differential treatment of cultural groups to ensure their protection against the politically predominant culture. Liberalism's purported fixation on the decontextualized individual to the exclusion of certain potential cultural rights and values thus proves less an essential feature of liberalism than of post-War developments in liberal thought-developments that in substantial part motivated the rhetoric of universality that permeates subsequent human rights instruments.

3

Buddhism and the Universal International Human Rights

It is not immediately apparent, then, why "universality," though by no means novel to the Western rights tradition, assumed such prominence in the post-War international public order. Nor is it apparent why concern with ethno-cultural differences and the insulation of minority rights more or less dropped out of the picture after World War II. Several factors, however, help to explain this theoretical shift. First, as Rita Hauser notes:

The universal approach, which looks beyond the boundaries of the sovereign state, was the result both of the horror of the Western world at the scope of Hitler's atrocities and the determined lobbying of interested organizations which made their views known long before San Francisco was selected as the Charter drafting site. Numerous Jewish groups, in particular, promoted the idea of an International Bill of Rights, believing, as they did, that Jews would be protected in the enjoyment of their rights to the extent the rights of others everywhere were similarly respected.

But universality owed its theoretical appeal to more than the desire to affirm certain inalienable rights of man after the horrors of Nazi Germany. It also reflected an acknowledgment that the culturally-based minority rights regimes had failed catastrophically. While these treaty-based rights for the protection of ethno-cultural minorities enjoyed some early successes, Hitler later exploited their existence to vindicate German aggression in the late 1930s. "[T]he issue of German minorities in Poland and Czechoslovakia became a significant, albeit pretextual, precipitating factor for German aggression and World War II."

Consequently, in the aftermath of World War II, the idea of human rights, as inalienable and undifferentiated rights that attach to the individual without regard to cultural identity, found widespread support. Cultural rights were "subsumed... under the broader problem of ensuring basic individual rights to all human beings, without reference to membership in ethnic groups." Universality, then, developed as both a positive affirmation of the naturalistic idea of the inherent "rights of man" after the atrocities of Nazi Germany, as well as a negative reaction against the apparent failure of minority-rights regimes created during the League of Nations era.

Yet the drafters of the UDHR were not blind to the highly precarious empirical status of universal human rights. First, philosophical skepticism about universal rights and natural law enjoys a history as rich as the traditions out of which the contrary ideals developed. Against the Aristotelian natural law tradition of ancient Greece, for instance, stood the moral and cognitive skepticism of the pre-Socratic sophists, famously expressed in the Protagorean maxim that "man is the measure of all things."

Liberalism itself embraces not only natural law and natural rights traditions, but also utilitarianism, whose founder, Jeremy Bentham, famously mocked natural rights as mere "nonsense upon stilts." Contemporary rights skeptics, such as Alasdair MacIntyre, echo this complaint, equating human rights with "belief in witches and in unicorns;" he proceeds to quip that:

In the United Nations declaration on human rights in 1949 what has since become the normal UN practice of not giving good reasons for any assertions whatsoever is followed with great rigor. And the latest defender of such rights, Ronald Dworkin (Taking Rights Seriously, 1976), concedes that the existence of such rights cannot be demonstrated, but remarks on this point simply that it does not follow from the fact that a statement cannot be demonstrated that it is not true. Which is true, but could equally be used to defend claims about unicorns and witches? Natural or human rights then are fictions....

But the problem of forging a list of "universal" rights that confronted the drafters of the UDHR was not only-nor primarily-theoretical. It was magnified and exacerbated both by the number of cultures represented at the United Nations and by the ideological split between the Western allies and the Soviet bloc. Thus, at the time of the UDHR's drafting, as Mary Ann Glendon wrote recently in her commemorative analysis, "the problem of universality loomed large...."

In 1947, in an effort to lay the groundwork for the drafting of a universal declaration of human rights, the UN Economic and Social Council (UNESCO) circulated a questionnaire to prominent scholars and cultural figures worldwide, requesting their views on the extent, nature, and theoretical grounds of human rights. Responses to the questionnaire, as expected, reflected divergent cultural and ideological perspectives; nonetheless, "[t]o the Committee's surprise, the lists of basic rights and values they received from their far-flung sources were essentially similar. McKeon's final report recorded their conclusion that it was indeed possible to achieve agreement across cultures concerning certain rights that `may be viewed as implicit in man's nature as an individual and as a member of society.'"

Yet this consensus, as the Committee readily acknowledged, was tenuous at best, a superficial agreement upon nominal "rights" that masked deep, intractable disagreements regarding their rationale, meaning, and application. Jacques Maritain, French philosopher and member of the UNESCO Committee, noted that no consensus proved possible on what he termed a common "speculative ideology," but that, nonetheless, "we find principles that... constitute *grosso modo* a sort of common denominator, a sort of unwritten common law, at the point where in practice the most widely separated theoretical ideologies and mental traditions converge."

Yet even Maritain's carefully qualified language overstates the degree of this consensus. What the Committee managed to procure for the Human Rights Commission that drafted the UDHR amounted to little more than a short list articulated at a level of generality that rendered the terms susceptible to, not merely different, but at times wholly antithetical interpretations. The Committee concluded, for instance, that "[e]very man has an equal right to justice," without, however, providing any definitional content to this notoriously controversial ideal. Indeed, the vacuity of this "universal right" becomes amusingly apparent in a sentence that shortly follows, which stipulates tautologically that every man has a "right to be protected by law from illegal arrest."

Likewise, the Committee included, under the heading of a "Right to Political Action," the freedom to express ideas and to form associations "provided that such expressions and such associations are not incompatible with the principles of democracy or with the rights of man." Here again, the qualifier eviscerates any content that such a right might prima facie appear to bestow.

John L. Lewis, for example, one of the respondents to the Committee's survey, affirmed the right to democratic association but noted that it requires eradication of "those sections of the community whose interests unquestionably conflict with those of the community [and] are inconsistent with democratic purposes and therefore implacably hostile to real democracy... The crisis can only be solved with full democracy; that is, with the final release of popular power to control economic resources and to accomplish human ends." Whatever the merits of Lewis' remarks, this definition of democracy would hardly resonate with most Western liberal understandings of the word.

Given the constitutional makeup of the United Nations in the immediate post-War era, it is unsurprising that the deepest ideological rift that emerged reflected the antithetical ideologies of, broadly speaking, liberal democracies and communist states-joined by their respective spheres of influence. Respondents thus repeatedly affirmed the importance of liberty as a basic human right but expressed radically different views about the circumstances under which liberty truly exists.

Members of the Soviet bloc emphasized that genuine liberty requires man to be in full control of his economic and social circumstances, free from capitalist exploitation, while Western liberals tended to emphasize the extent to which liberty demands limits on state action. The UNESCO Committee was not, of course, unaware neither of these tensions nor of the precarious nature of the alleged consensus had it achieved. The Committee's chairman, Professor Richard McKeon, concluded that:

The fundamental problem is not found in compiling a list of human rights. The declarations that have been submitted to the Commission on Human Rights are surprisingly similar.... The differences are found rather in what is meant by these rights, and these differences of meaning depend on divergent basic assumptions, which, in turn, lend plausibility to and are justified by contradictory interpretations of the economic and social situation, and, finally, lead to opposed recommendations concerning the implementation required for a world declaration of human rights.

The Committee's final report to the Human Rights Commission conceded as much. Yet it suggested, somewhat paradoxically, that the problem faced in drafting a universal declaration of human rights resides not in "doctrinal consensus" but merely in consensus "concerning rights, and also concerning action in the realisation and defence of those rights, which may be justified on highly divergent grounds."

If we interpret this statement charitably, as merely expressing the conditions under which the drafting of the UDHR's language is a feasible project, then it retains some plausibility. Yet the suggestion that "action in the realisation and defence of those rights" might also proceed from such a consensus remains dubious. This difficulty achieving consensus, moreover, increases exponentially when we recognize that, since the adoption of the UDHR in 1948, the membership of the United Nations has increased from 56 to 185 states.

The United Nations today embraces societies that manifest cultural divergences potentially far more varied and severe than the already intractable Cold War ideological rift that preoccupied the drafters. Indeed, despite the rhetoric of universality, inter-divisibility, and interdependency, which forty-five years later found its way into the Vienna Declaration, the actual 1993 Conference revealed similarly profound disagreements regarding the nature, interpretation, and priority of human rights. In short, genuine consensus sufficient to be termed "universal"-now, as in 1948-exists, if at all, only at a level of rhetorical and linguistic abstraction that provides little guidance as to the practical implementation of human rights.

ALTERNATIVE CONCEPTIONS OF THE LOCUS OF UNIVERSALITY

In 1947 the American Anthropological Association, which was likewise consulted by the Human Rights Commission prior to the UDHR's drafting, affirmed, almost unequivocally, the descriptive fact of cultural relativism: "Standards and values are relative to the culture from which they derive so that any attempt to formulate postulates that grow out of the beliefs or moral codes of one culture must to that extent detract from the applicability of any Declaration of Human Rights to mankind as a whole." Since then, of course, the international community has undergone and continues to experience what has been termed "globalization."

The exponential increase in technology, particularly methods of communication, has facilitated a remarkable growth in economic and cultural exchanges between states, and it seems logical to assume that this increase in cultural exchange promotes an attendant increase in shared values. To some extent, and in certain spheres more than others-economics, for example-there is undoubtedly a degree of truth to this presumption. Yet, perhaps paradoxically, we have witnessed more, not fewer, assertions of cultural and ethnic identification in the post-World War II era, particularly since the end of the Cold War. Francis Fukuyama's "end of history"-brought about by a "universalization of Western liberal democracy"-has decisively failed to materialize.

To the contrary, "modern societies are increasingly confronted with minority groups demanding recognition of their identity, and accommodation of their cultural differences." Even more troubling from the perspective of "universal human rights," these cherished assertions of cultural distinction appear to have at least contributed to, or even played a significant causal role in, some of the most egregious human rights catastrophes since World War II. The hope that global interdependence itself would impel a new era of universal adherence to international human rights norms now seems quixotic.

Empirically, then, the universality of human rights-where "universal" denotes a high degree of consensus among the cultures and nation-states that comprise the international community-emerges as, at best, a useful fiction. "Cultural relativity," as even proponent of universality Jack Donnelly acknowledges, "is an undeniable fact; moral rules and social institutions evidence an astonishing cultural and historical variability."

Yet the normative universality of human rights need not be based on empirical claims about an actual cultural consensus, although it seems apparent that the existence of such a consensus would provide some of the strongest prima facie support for a claim to universality. Universal human rights could be vindicated on several alternative grounds that bear appraisal before examining what consequences flow from acknowledging the descriptive truth of cultural pluralism.

THE HUMAN NEEDS APPROACH

Intuitively, as Donnelly notes, "Human rights are... the rights one has simply because one is a human being." An initially attractive approach, then, would be to locate the source of universality in that which remains definitionally human about us-in natural facts about human beings that do not vary from culture to culture. Thus, one might assert that our need for nutritional sustenance gives rise to a "right to food" and that our need for security gives rise to a "right to physical integrity," which may, in turn, generate certain negative rights, such as the prohibition against torture.

Depending upon how much elasticity we permit the term "need" to assume, one might also suggest that all human beings evince a need for what Rawls refers to as the social bases of self-respect, those traits that permit us to sustain a level of psychological as well as physical health within the context of a cultural community. Rights against enslavement, due process rights, anti-discrimination rights, and others might thereby be drawn within the domain of human rights. Postulating a need for the "social bases of self-respect" disturbs the relatively concrete notion of biological need from which this conception of universal human rights initially appears to derive its attractiveness.

Rawls' concept, however, does retain the virtue of being, at least superficially, neutral as between cultures: The specific social bases needed for self-respect could vary among cultures; yet each could, in its own peculiar manner, satisfy this need. The human needs approach thus appears to promise some conception of universality that does not contravene the descriptive fact of cultural pluralism. Yet a needs-based approach suffers from several, probably fatal, flaws. First, the range of scientifically verifiable human needs remains quite narrow: "If we turn to science, we find an extraordinarily limited set of needs. Even Christian Bay, probably the best-known advocate of a needs theory of human rights, admits that `it is premature to speak of any empirically established needs beyond sustenance and safety.'"

If we introduce needs beyond the physiological, we beg the question of universality, for cultures construct these social needs. While they perhaps remain matters of necessity given the specific mores of a cultural community, these needs also, by definition, emerge as culturally contingent. The "social bases of self-respect," then, proves far too malleable a concept, under which, for instance, maltreatment of *dalits* (untouchables) in the Hindu caste system might well appear justifiable.

Even more fundamentally, however, the needs-based approach to universal human rights suffers from the Humean naturalistic fallacy. It infers certain moral "oughts" from empirical facts that, in themselves, can create no obligations, still less "rights." Finally, while the specific list of human rights that warrant universal status constitutes a distinct inquiry, if we understand the UDHR's language to suggest at least the general contours of these rights, then many prominent human rights remain unaccounted for by a needs-based approach. One might attempt to circumvent this difficulty by expanding the idea of "need" to entail social necessities. But as noted, this simply begs the question, because by definition, it reintroduces cultural relativity-in the form of socially-constructed needs-into human rights.

THE MORAL NATURALISTIC APPROACH

The failure of needs-based approaches to confer universality upon human rights does not, however, exhaust the potential for locating universality in that which is "fundamentally human" about our species. Humans also seem to possess a capacity for moral judgment that distinguishes us from animals. Whether or not we in fact are autonomous agents, to which nebulous concepts like free will-and its corollaries, agency, guilt, responsibility-may properly be attributed, we behave in ways that implicitly assume the validity of these concepts. It therefore may be a *conditio sine qua non* of human civilization that we hold and entertain moral concepts and evaluate each other in terms of these concepts.

Perhaps, then, one can locate the source of universal human rights in man's peculiar capacity for moral judgment and behavior. In part, this is Jack Donnelly's position. "The source of human rights," he writes, "is man's moral nature, which is only loosely linked to the `human nature' defined by scientifically ascertainable needs.... We have human rights not to the requisites for health but to those things `needed' for a life of dignity, for a life worthy of a human being, a life that cannot be enjoyed without these rights." Donnelly's conception, as he readily acknowledges, amounts to no more than a' moral posit.

Yet he believes that universality inheres in man's moral nature, insofar as one accepts the idea that such rights inform our understanding of what it means to lead a "truly human" life. Human rights enjoy universality on this account because "without the enjoyment of (the objects of) human rights, one is almost

certain to be alienated or estranged from one's moral nature...
Losing these rights is morally `impossible': one cannot lose these
rights and live a life worthy of a human being."

Donnelly's account retains a greater plausibility than the
crude human-needs approach To begin, it resonates with the
language of the UDHR and other human rights instruments,
which often invoke, at least rhetorically, the "inherent dignity"
of the human person as the basis of human rights. Unlike the
needs-based approach that purports to ground human rights
without reference to their social context, Donnelly's moral-
naturalistic approach concedes that human rights reflect moral
and social posits. The problem is with his assertion that, absent
these posits, we could not lead "truly human" lives. What
could "truly human" mean in this context?

Throughout most of mankind's history, the very concept
of human rights was unknown-a fact that Donnelly
consistently emphasizes, and yet it would strain credulity to
insist that peoples of the vast majority of civilizations that have
existed to date have not lived "truly human" lives. In fairness,
it bears emphasis that Donnelly intends his statement about
the conditions under which one may lead a "truly human"
life to be understood in context-as applicable to the modern
social and historical epoch in which the nation-state arguably
constitutes the principal threat to human dignity.

He concedes, consequently, that "where there is a thriving
indigenous cultural tradition and community, arguments of
cultural relativism offer a strong defense against outside
interference-including disruptions that might be caused by
introducing `universal' human rights. Such communities, however,
are increasingly the exception rather than the rule," and Donnelly's
argument for the conceptual appropriateness of human rights to
modern international law remains compelling. The problem is
that, by itself, this strategic move proves under inclusive.

The Taliban, for instance, might aptly be described as a
"thriving cultural tradition." But far from providing a "strong
defense against outside interference," the Taliban, at least
facially, appears to exemplify precisely the kind of situation

in the modern world-one in which egregious violations are being perpetrated in the service of an extremist ideology-in which interference under the banner of universal human rights would appear justifiable. One might finesse these circumstances by pointing out that individuals harmed by the Taliban do not consent to this "thriving cultural tradition," thus justifying humanitarian intervention to vindicate their human rights.

Indeed, as argued below, this would be an appropriate suggestion. But this step involves a tacit regression to the modern notion that individuals, not cultural groups, are the basic bearers of rights, as well as the fundamental unit of concern and value-or, put differently, it takes for granted one of the liberal presumptions that cultural relativists challenge in the first place. An additional, though related, difficulty with Donnelly's account of the source of human rights resides in his distinction between something's "being right," which implies a preordained value hierarchy and therefore, cultural relativity, and someone's "having a right."

The latter, it seems, involves a social state of affairs that obtains "universality" when within different cultural frameworks, each of which internally ranks values in divergent ways, individuals retain the right to choose among different values. Here again, however, this seems to amount, at bottom, to a restatement of the very liberal ideals that cultural relativism calls into question; for this distinction resurrects the classical libertarian claim that individuals must be permitted broad liberty to choose among competing conceptions of the good. A characteristic formulation in Donnelly's exposition clarifies this problem. Distinguishing something's "being right" from someone's "having a right," he writes,

Simply because x is right it does not necessarily follow that anyone has a right to x. For example, even if it is right to perform acts of benevolence, such as assisting the needy and hungry, a hungry person does not, ipso facto, have a right to receive food from me, or from anyone else. He is not thereby entitled to my food or my money to buy food: it is my food and my money; I have a right to it.

Donnelly concedes that, under certain extenuating circumstances-where the scarcity of food is connected in certain ways to state abuse-an individual might "have a right" to another person's food. Yet the problem here runs deeper: the exposition of what it means to "have a right" already presupposes a highly distinct set of cultural values. Why, indeed, is it Donnelly, in the proffered example, and not the hungry person, who "has a right" to his food or to his money? Without recourse to, for instance, the Lockean notion that "whatsoever then he removes out of the state that nature hath provided, and left it in, he hath mixed his labour with, and joined to it something that is his own, and thereby makes it his property," it remains difficult to provide a satisfactory categorical answer.

Only our culturally specific intellectual heritage-the values and modes of thought it induces-causes this example to seem so intuitively plausible. Donnelly's philosophical reliance upon a strict distinction between some idea "being right" and someone "having a right" thus remains susceptible to cultural relativist critiques. It proves impossible to say why someone "has a right" without articulating some culturally specific sense of what "is right." Even in a non-legal sense, then, "having a right" and "being right" turn out not, as Donnelly argues, to be conceptually separable-in practice, this distinction collapses.

THE TRANSCENDENTALIST APPROACH

A final possibility would locate the normative universality of human rights in essential or transcendental conceptions of a natural law that operate independently of human society; a view, as noted earlier, that finds classical expression in Aristotle and later in Aquinas' distinction between positive-man-made-and divine or natural law. Yet it bears emphasis that this manner of thought is not unique to Western traditions. All major religious traditions-Christianity, Islam, Judaism, Hinduism and Buddhism-manifest concepts analogous to Aquinas' conception of divine law. They all, that is, assert certain moral precepts as a universal code written into the "true" nature of reality. From the perspective of their proponents, these beliefs, as Diana Eck emphasizes, do not apply merely to a single culture; they lay claim to universal acknowledgment:

When Jewish thinkers speak of the covenant with Noah and the Noachide laws, they are not making a claim that is true only if you are Jewish, but a universal claim about the nature of human responsibility. When Christians speak of human nature as having been dignified by the human incarnation of God in Christ, they are not making a tribal claim that is true only for those who happen to be Christians.... This is also true of Islam in which Muslims speak of submitting to God, or aligning one's life with the god ward human nature with which we are born. It is true for Buddhists when they speak of human life as characterized by suffering... a noble truth that they claim for all, not just Buddhists.

Transcendentalist approaches render claims of universal human rights coherent because they make strong claims about the ultimate ontological status of the world and its inhabitants. But absent genuine consensus on these issues-needless to say, this is lacking-the fact of cultural pluralism compels the conclusion that these schemes will necessarily conflict. Empirical evidence establishing the descriptive truth of cultural pluralism remains too strong to validate scientifically any one of these esoteric metaphysical claims, and "the dangers of the moral imperialism implied by radical universalism hardly need to be emphasized."

Western colonial imperialism, for example, while undoubtedly motivated more by economic than genuine ideological considerations, was in part justified in terms of bringing spiritual salvation-via "universal" Christian law-to the unenlightened peoples of other civilizations. By asserting a transcendental universality for human rights, then, natural law and other ontologically-based theories undermine a central value of human rights itself-the tolerance of reasonable pluralism.

In sum, efforts to locate an actual empirical consensus concerning values "implicit in man's nature as an individual and as a member of society" fail to produce-both substantively and as a matter of hermeneutics-agreement on human rights sufficient to be termed "universal." Furthermore, alternative philosophical approaches that might vindicate the normative universality of human rights, notwithstanding the empirical fact of cultural pluralism, prove philosophically unsatisfactory, potentially dangerous, or both.

CULTURAL PLURALISM RECONSIDERED

The foregoing discussion betrays a troubling silence in the international human rights movement. Talk of universalism pervades human rights discourse. But it finds little support-empirical, historical, philosophical, or otherwise-in the diverse "human rights" practices that characterize the contemporary global community.

Recognition of this descriptive fact invites the following question: When human rights lawyers, philosophers, foreign diplomats, advocates, and others speak of human rights as "universal," are they doing anything more than asserting, for a fifty-year old international political movement, the same dubious transcendentalism that led us to reject religious absolutism? Does the religious extremist's ideological universalism differ meaningfully from that of the human rights activist? Both advance strong normative claims. Both assert these norms universally; they apply to all human beings, not just to one culture. Not least, both believe, albeit to varying degrees, that, at times, violence should be used to deter, terminate, or punish violations of these norms. Holy wars and "humanitarian intervention" rest on common ground in their justification of the use of violence to vindicate norms of human behavior. Can they be meaningfully distinguished?

Conceding the descriptive fact of cultural pluralism permits us to examine more closely what normative implications it indeed supports, and, perhaps as critically, those it does not. To assess the arguments of cultural relativism, then, demands analysis of the normative assertions advanced on behalf of the descriptive fact of cultural pluralism, hereafter presumed unassailable on empirical grounds.

The first form of cultural relativism-narrative relativism,-asserts that because every culture has its own distinctive topos, or cultural vocabulary, human rights may be an inappropriate or myopic functional concept to promote human dignity in certain cultural communities. According to narrative relativism, alternative conceptions of and mechanisms for promoting human dignity-those rooted in the endogenous features of their cultural group-provide a more legitimate measure for evaluating the propriety of their societal practices. The second form of cultural relativism-crude relativism-insists that because conceptions of ultimate value vary from culture to culture, imposing alleged universal norms of behavior on a group that purports to reject them amounts to illegitimate cultural imperialism.

Analysis of these broad normative challenges proves difficult in the abstract. This Part, consequently, uses concrete examples as a vehicle for examining the respective assertions of each. The first section focuses on one aspect of the "Asian values" debate in an effort to expound narrative relativism. In particular, it briefly assesses the claim that certain cultural features alleged to characterize Asian societies render Western conceptions of human rights incompatible with their endogenous cultural values. The second section focuses on crude cultural relativism through analysis of human rights violations perpetrated by the Taliban's regime, which achieved effective control of over two-thirds of Afghanistan's territory in 1996.

NARRATIVE RELATIVISM

Imagine two men holding a captured puma on a rope. If they want to approach each other, the puma will attack, because the rope will slacken; only if they both pull simultaneously on the rope is the puma equidistant from the two of them. That is why it is so hard for him who reads and him who writes to reach each other: between them lies a mutual thought captured on ropes that they pull in opposite directions. If we were now to ask that puma-in other words, that thought-how it perceived these two men, it might answer that at the ends of the rope those to be eaten are holding someone they cannot eat. -Milorad Pavic

Narrative relativism poses a number of conceptually distinct challenges to universal human rights. In the present context, two of these demand appraisal. First, does profound cultural pluralism and diversity preclude the possibility of cognitive consensus on what human rights mean? This Article endorses Donnelly's view that, even if, as appears to be the case, most cultures lack an indigenous conception of "rights," the internationalization of the Western nation-state model has made rights pertinent to nearly all contemporary societies, and cross-cultural cognitive understandings and appreciation of the value of these rights will continue to develop.

This is because human rights involve, at bottom, relations between the individual and the nation-state-or other quasi-state authorities. Second, assuming that certain cultures, though amenable to the idea of human rights, wish to retain their endogenous conceptions of and institutions for promoting human dignity-can the macro legal framework imposed by international human rights law accommodate these alternative values and practices?

This question, the Author suggests, admits of no simple answer. Some cultural practices and values are fully consistent with international human rights law; the two normative frameworks can subsist-indeed, perhaps even complement one another. But others undoubtedly violate universal human rights. This invites the foundational inquiry, to which turns, into why, in instances of conflict, international human rights merit precedence.

COGNITIVE DISSONANCE

To return to the first inquiry, suppose that two people, though members of cultures wholly foreign to one another, agree that Article 3 of the UDHR articulates a genuinely universal human right: "Everyone has the right to life, liberty and the security of person." This nominal agreement may nonetheless veil deep reciprocal misunderstandings. For two individuals rooted in different cultural vocabularies, the right to "life, liberty and security of person" could well be, in the language of Milorad Pavic, "a mutual thought captured on ropes that they pull in opposite directions."

The world's major cultural traditions manifest a superficial "overlapping consensus:" the human rights tradition-a legacy of Western liberal thought-can to some extent be reconciled with its "homeomorphic equivalents" in other cultures. But this consensus must be articulated at an extremely high level of abstraction-most cultural traditions share some belief in human dignity and an aversion to needless suffering and cruelty. How, if at all, does this help advance the universality of human rights? Not, the Author would argue, very much. It decisively fails to justify the use of human rights as the appropriate functional concept for promoting human dignity, as opposed to, for instance, conceptions of social duty and obligation that arguably prevail in some non-Western traditions.

It perhaps draws within the domain of universality some of the most uncontroversial human rights, certain *jus cogens* norms of modern international law-the prohibitions against genocide, torture, slavery and arguably a few others. Beyond these "easy cases," the interpretive challenge posed by narrative relativism stands. Recall, for instance, the sub textual disagreement about liberty that occupied the drafters of the UDHR: Does genuine liberty only obtain when individuals enjoy full control over their economic and social circumstances? Or does it denote, as Western liberals would emphasize, limits on the domain of legitimate state action?

Clearly, different answers to these questions will yield radically different, and probably conflicting, understandings of what the "right to liberty" in fact guarantees. Thus, while crude cultural relativism invokes ethical relativism to challenge universality, narrative relativism makes an argument that, albeit replete with ethical implications, finds its logical foundation in a form of cognitive relativism. Any appraisal of narrative relativist claims will therefore pose acute methodological difficulties. Evaluation demands disengagement from deeply rooted cognitive and linguistic principles that circumscribe our ability to appraise phenomena in the first place.

"Observation of others is so difficult," Michael Reisman notes, "not because other groups... are more complex than ours, but because our own so profoundly shape us, at levels of consciousness so deep that we are often unaware of it." Where the cognitive processes of different cultures do not converge at all, one's evaluation of the other remains, by definition, impossible; no common reference provides the "Archimedes point" from which to derive criterion for evaluating cultural practices and values.

At the same time, it would be foolish to abandon the project of cross-cultural evaluation merely because we lack a perfect set of shared evaluative criteria. First of all, the appraisal of phenomena in the absence of objective criteria is hardly unique to the social sciences; even physics, the quintessential natural science, emphasizes the critical and, at times, determinative impact that the evaluator's perspective exerts upon the object of evaluation. Second, biological similarity means that humans from different cultures will still share at least some rudimentary cognitive processes.

Whatever their culture, different individuals share, for example, similar modes of processing information, capacities for pain and pleasure, and an ability to differentiate rational from irrational chains of thought. Finally, as Bernard Williams emphasizes, core cultural values cannot "merely evaporate because one is confronted with human beings in another society." Cross-cultural human interaction would be impossible if people refrained wholly from appraising foreign cultural practices and values, and from modifying our behavior toward them accordingly. Particularly in an interdependent "globalized" world, international law must strive to develop principles to mediate among the diverse cognitive frameworks that different actors bring to cross-cultural exchanges.

Cross-cultural cognitive relativism, like cultural pluralism, is an empirical fact. This, by itself, is nothing new. Within societies, too, "perception of the same phenomena may vary depending on the culture, class, gender, age, or crisis-experience of the observer." We do not, however, resign ourselves to the nihilistic view that shared perceptions of legal and social norms are impossible. Nor do we abandon attempts at mutual understanding as futile. We acknowledge the difficulties that cognitive disparity generates but strive to ameliorate these problems through the definitional human capacity for communication. Of course, in circumstances of conflict, one or another alternative perception of norms necessarily prevails.

We must, consequently, maintain social and legal mechanisms for deciding which perception, in a given instance, should win out. But this is simply to restate a classic question of political theory: How is a society of diverse individuals possible? To challenge the universality of human rights on these grounds is to transpose a timeless political inquiry to the international plane, and it is not clear what, exactly, this is intended to prove, save for the relatively uncontroversial proposition that no strong cross-cultural consensus about human rights presently exists.

Cognitive relativism may indeed mean that citizens of states with disparate cultural traditions will at times interpret identical provisions of human rights treaties in incompatible ways-pulling a mutual thought captured on ropes in opposite directions. Perhaps an individual whose values have been shaped by Confucian traditions will be more likely to understand the ICCPR's guarantee of "liberty and security of person" to refer to the state's duty to preserve law and order, while a Western liberal will presumably understand this provision to refer principally to her right to protection from arbitrary state interference.

This, however, simply begs the question of which conception, in circumstances of international conflict, should prevail, and this question is normative, not descriptive. Cross-cultural cognitive-narrative-relativism no more repudiates the universal applicability of human rights than intra-societal cognitive relativism repudiates the uniform application of domestic law to a state's diverse citizenry.

THE "TYRANNY" OF HUMAN RIGHTS

With this background in mind, this section considers briefly one aspect of the so-called "Asian values" debate. This blanket label embraces a number of diverse claims, including: (1) that there is claims including: distinct "Asian" approach to human rights; (2) that this approach, rooted in Confucianism, focuses first and foremost on communal welfare rather than individual rights; (3) that Asians prioritize law, social order, and security above individual civil and political rights; and finally (4) that this heavy-handed focus on social order at the expense of civil and political liberties not only resonates with Asian values, but is necessary and appropriate to the process of economic development and modernization.

These claims are in large part empirical, and the debate over their validity forms a subject of continuing academic inquiry and critique. But whatever our view of "Asian values," one premise of these theories is indisputable-the descriptive fact of cultural pluralism. Cultural mores, social rules, and legal institutions vary widely, and homogenization of these norms is not likely to obtain in the near future. Nor, most commentators would agree, would this be desirable. While modern rhetoric at times seems excessive in its praise of diversity "for its own sake," legitimate instrumental, aesthetic, and ethical rationales favor cultural, like individual, diversity. The paradox, however, resides in the fact that a significant subset of these diverse cultural traditions do not themselves value or tolerate diversity.

Human rights do not mandate a monolithic set of values. Nor do they ordain a singular "conception of the good." The protections that universal human rights extend to all human beings permit individuals of widely disparate religious, political, and moral beliefs to coexist within a common international order. At the same time, however, universal human rights, ex-hypothesi, apply with equal force and authority to all human beings. Consequently, cultural practices and values that conflict irreconcilably with international human rights law must yield. In this regard human rights indeed represent a kind of moral and legal "tyranny"-where endogenous cultural practices and international human rights conflict, the former must defer to the latter.

Too often, however, this conflict is portrayed in misleading terms, as a "clash" between diametrically opposed sets of cultural values. Bilahari Kausikan, for example, presents the debate as one between "the individualistic ethos of the

West or the communitarian traditions of Asia? The consensus-seeking approach of East and Southeast Asia or the adversarial institutions of the West?" This misconstrues the problem that "universal" human rights poses-to what extent all the world's disparate systems of cultural values and practices can be reconciled with the overarching framework of law established by international human rights.

Donnelly thus notes correctly, in the context of the "Asian values" debate, that "where traditional practices conflict irreconcilably with internationally recognized human rights, traditional practices usually must give way-just as traditional Western practices such as racial and gender discrimination and the persecution of religious deviants have been required to give way." At the same time, he observes that "internationally recognized human rights leave considerable space for distinctively Asian implementations of these rights."

The crucial point here is that within each state, and within each of its constituent cultural groups and peoples, multiple systems of value subsist. To set up a simple dichotomy between "universal human rights," on the one hand, and "endogenous cultural values," on the other, misconstrues the real problem-to determine, in each case, what degree of cultural or domestic variation remains consistent with international human rights norms. This notion finds expression in the European human rights system's doctrine of a "margin of appreciation." In the Handyside Case, the European Court of Human Rights observed that: it is not possible to find in the domestic law of the various Contracting States a uniform European conception of morals.... By reason of their direct and continuous contact with the vital forces of their countries, State authorities are in principle in a better position than the international judge to give an opinion on the exact content of these requirements... and to make the initial assessment of the reality of the pressing social need implied by the notion of `necessity' in this context of Article 10 sections 2 of the European Convention.

The implementation of human rights need not, that is, be wholly indifferent to salient differences in the prevailing moral and social norms within a state. Some variation is permissible-indeed, perhaps even desirable, because the efficacy of international human rights law ultimately depends on a "process of interaction, interpretation, and internalization of international norms." Progression towards cognitive consensus on the meaning of different human rights may benefit from the flexibility enabled by a "domestic margin of appreciation."

It is clear, for example, that "due process" under international human rights law does not demand the Anglo-Saxon "adversarial" as opposed to the Continental "inquisitorial" model, or vice versa. Functionally equivalent safeguards in each system can independently satisfy its requirements. But it is equally clear that a politically-controlled judiciary-under either model, and whether "Western" or "Asian"-would not conform to international human rights law.

To return to the "Asian values" debate, it is clear that nothing about, say, Confucian values of familial obligation, social duty, virtue, and so forth, necessarily conflicts with human rights law. Like all moral systems, Confucianism can promote human dignity and social stability. Yet, again like all moral systems, its norms can suffer manipulation and political abuse, particularly as the cultural context in which Confucianism developed and thrived deteriorates. De Bary notes that:

The very real social problems attributed to the "individualistic West"-violence, crime, drug and sex abuse, and breakdown of family life, to name only the most obvious-attend the modernization process wherever it goes on, in East or West. Thus it is less a question of Asian versus Western values than a problem of how the forces of a runaway economic and technological modernization are eroding traditional values in both Asia and the West.

Perhaps most critically, then, we should appreciate that that there is nothing uniquely "Asian" about the underlying substantive inquiry that the "Asian values" debate presents-to what extent subordinate systems of morality and social values can subsist within an overarching legal framework structured by international human rights. Contemporary societies throughout the globe must confront this question,   .

and scholars rightly devote attention to articulating principled solutions to the diverse problems it generates. The question, then, that "Asian values" like "Christian values" or any other broadly defined categorization of a group moral code presents is not monolithic.

Depending on how we delimit their scope, some Asian values will prove consonant with human rights law, while others will violate or at least be in tension with it. Similarly, were we to denominate a broad class of microlegal norms "Western values," we would likewise discover that some norms embraced by this crude label conform to human rights standards, while others do not. But note that these case-by-case inquiries presume that the foundational question-which international code provides the appropriate criteria against which to appraise disparate cultural values and practices-has been answered. Once we agree that international human rights law in fact provides the right common standard, we can appraise value systems in terms of their relative conformity to it. Thus, cultural relativists, including "Asian values" proponents, must deny the former premise-that international human rights law provides the right criteria.

Narrative relativism admittedly presents difficulties for implementing human rights, but, as indicated above, these are neither new nor insurmountable. The crux of any critique based on cultural relativism must therefore reside at a more foundational level. It must challenge the notion that the criteria identified by international human rights should not, normatively, be applicable to all the diverse subordinate value systems that subsist throughout the globe-as much within "Western" as within "Asian" states. To defend the normative universality of human rights, consequently, requires us to articulate why, in circumstances where microlegal values and practices conflict with international human rights, the latter merit our respect as paramount standards.

CRUDE CULTURAL RELATIVISM

Culture' is never an essentialist and homogenous body of traditions and customs, but a rich resource, usually full of internal contradictions, and a resource which is always used selectively in various ethnic, cultural and religious projects within specific power relations and political discourse. -Nira Yuval-Davis

On September 27, 1996, Kabul, the capital of Afghanistan, fell to a militant Muslim group known as the Taliban, a name derived from "the Persianized plural form of the Arabic word 'Talib,' which means religious student." The Taliban initially comprised a "small spontaneous group" of religious students who "felt outrage at the behavior of the Mujahidin leaders fighting for power in the city and... decided to take action to end what they saw as corrupt practices, drawing on Islam as a justification for their intervention."

For reasons that remain somewhat nebulous, the Taliban quickly grew into a formidable armed force, receiving military training, ammunition, and weaponry from a number of sources. In October 1994, the Taliban launched a campaign to overthrow the ruling Mujahidin government. Within two years, the group controlled two-thirds of Afghan territory. The astonishing speed and success of the Taliban's military campaign reflected in part the weakness of the "so-called Mujahidin Government," which amounted to a mere "coalition government made up of an amalgam of the seven political parties that had previously formed the Afghan Interim Government."

Yet the Taliban's success also was attributable to its reputation for religious purity and good behavior. By contrast to the diverse governmental forces, paramilitary groups, bandits, and others that had abused sectors of the population following the Soviet withdrawal in 1989, the Taliban quickly formed a reputation, which preceded their incremental military advances, "for behaving relatively well when taking new areas-they did not engage in looting, rape or mindless destruction...."

Yet as they consolidated control over each region, the Taliban imposed rigid behavioral strictures on the population-rules derived from their own stringent interpretation of Shari'a, or Islamic law. It was for the imposition of these rules that the Taliban drew condemnation from the human rights community. Decrees required men to "wear turbans, beards, short hair and *shalwar kameez* and women to wear the *burqa*, a garment the covering the entire body, including the face."

The Taliban prohibited women from working and barred them from education-at least until an "appropriate" Islamic curriculum could be drawn up by religious scholars. This project could not begin, according to Taliban leaders, until they had consolidated control over all Afghan territory. Additional decrees proscribed music, games, and representations of the human or animal form, such as televised images.

What horrified the international community, however, was not so much the rules as it was the shocking punitive methods by which they were enforced. Adulterers were stoned to death. Women who neglected to wear the *burqa* or who accidentally exposed their ankles suffered whippings or public beatings. Shari'a courts, reportedly composed of judges "untrained in the law and basing their judgment on a mixture of personal understandings of Islamic law and a tribal code of honour prevalent in Pashtun areas," issued sentences condemning the convicted to public hangings, strangulation and punitive amputations.

Arbitrary detention, mass executions, indiscriminate killing of civilians-particularly during the battle of Mazar-I-Sharif in which an estimated 2,000 to 5,000 persons were killed-suppression of journalistic freedoms, and other abuses continue to characterize the Taliban's regime. Many of these latter violations reflect the ongoing civil war and the Taliban's somewhat tenuous hold on sovereignty.

The former, by contrast, reflect beliefs and practices that, thoughfully in conformity with cultural norms deemed legitimate-indeed, appropriate-by the Taliban's leaders, strike foreign observers as perhaps the most egregious violations. To what extent, if any, can criticism of these abuses be dismissed as the imperialistic application of foreign norms to a culture that expressly rejects them? The Taliban provide a particularly poignant example of crude cultural relativism.

By contrast to certain "Asian values" proponents-who purport to accept international human rights, rejecting only their "Western" interpretation or imposition-the Taliban pull no punches; they repudiate international human rights law lock, stock, and barrel. Prior to the Taliban's rise to power,

Afghanistan had ratified many of the seminal treaties constitutive of the modern international human rights regime. But the Taliban have stated unequivocally that, should treaty obligations conflict with their understanding of the Shari'a, they will be ignored:

During his visit to Kabul, the Special Rapporteur asked the Attorney-General of the Taliban how they intended to deal with obligations stemming from international human rights treaties. He indicated that if a promise, convention, treaty or other instrument, even if it was in the Charter of the United Nations, was contrary to Shariah, they would not fulfill it or act on it. If the Charter were to proscribe executing a murderer, which the Shariah allowed, "We accept Shariah, our God's convention." The Attorney General added that, "If someone is drinking in public, even if the Covenant or United Nations Charter says they should not be punished, we will. The core of our action and our policy is the law of God, as contained in the Koran. We do not follow individuals, or people or other countries. We follow the law of God."

On November 10, 1995, UNICEF issued a communique stating that, as a consequence of the Taliban's breach of the Convention on the Rights of the Child, to which Afghanistan is party, it would suspend aid to educational programs from which girls had been excluded. Predictably, "this argument made no impression, for the Taliban recognise only the validity of Shar'ia; they do not feel bound by UN human rights instruments, which they regard in good part as vehicles of Western cultural imperialism."

Sher Muhammad Stanakzai, the Taliban's acting foreign minister, responded in kind to international criticism of the Taliban's use of *hudud*, certain punishments prescribed by Shari'a criminal law, including stoning adulterers and amputating the limbs of thieves. "We have not introduced this law," Sher Stanakzai proclaimed on Voice of Shari'a Radio, "This is the law that was revealed by God to Muhammad. Those who consider the imposition of this law to be against human rights are insulting all Muslims and their beliefs."

These statements, needless to say, constitute an unambiguous repudiation of the alleged universality of human rights. The Taliban do not purport to respect human rights in their own, culturally contingent, sense, or to acknowledge rights but accord them a more subordinate role in their overall hierarchy of cultural values. Nor do they claim that human rights mean something different in Afghan society.

Quite the contrary, they view international human rights as part and parcel of the corrupt influences and imperialistic Western practices that they aim to eradicate. Thus, in response to a torrent of international human rights-based criticism of their treatment of women, one Taliban official said the purpose of these laws is "'to protect our sisters from corrupt people.'" On December 6, 1996, the Department for the Promotion of Virtue and Prevention of Vice, a Taliban agency established to implement the moral strictures of Shari'a, stated that its policies ensure the "dignity and honour of a Muslim woman...."

The paradox here bears emphasis: while international human rights presumptively protect the "dignity and worth of the human person," it is precisely this dignity that the Taliban invoke in defense of practices alleged to constitute human rights violations. Imposing punitive measures on the drunkard, the adulterer, or the "indecently exposed" woman does not violate dignity-far from it; such measures, in the Taliban's view, promote it. As Jack Donnelly therefore rightly points out, "alternative conceptions of human dignity amount to challenges to the idea of human rights."

How can advocates of universal human rights respond effectively to the challenge presented by crude relativism? To begin, it will help to restate this challenge in its most general form: because, as a matter of social fact, cultures maintain divergent mores and conceptualize human rights differently, or not at all, the coercive imposition of international human rights norms on cultures that claim to reject them amounts to unjustified cultural imperialism.

"Coercive imposition" is a tautology. But it bears the emphasis, for what is ultimately at stake is the legitimacy of some form of coercion. In short, either (1) the descriptive fact of cultural pluralism means the Taliban should be permitted to order Afghan society in accordance with their culturally contingent-but no less legitimate-interpretation of Shari'a, in which case we tolerate their behavioral strictures and the coercive methods by which they are enforced against members of their cultural community (stoning adulterers to death, amputating the limbs of thieves); or (2) we deny that cultural pluralism means that cultural groups enjoy absolute latitude to structure their social, legal, and political order as they see fit, in which case we also embrace the idea that international actors can and should intervene-through violence at times-to coerce an end to these practices.

We might, therefore, restate the challenge as follows: Does cultural relativism render certain kinds of coercion under the banner of "universal" human rights illegitimate? Before suggesting several answers, this Section canvasses two plausible approaches that, while not without a significant strategic role in the promotion and enforcement of international human rights, do not ultimately confront this challenge directly.

The first shall be called "legal positivist," after the influential and predominant jurisprudential school. The legal positivist acknowledges the descriptive fact of cultural pluralism but suggests that, from the standpoint of international law, cultural relativism remains simply inapposite. Nothing about this relative moral value claim, for the legal positivist, affects the empirical status of the legal proposition that universal human rights-as codified in international treaties to which states remain party-retain binding force.

The second approach, articulated in the compelling work of Abdullahi Ahmed An-Na'im, may be labeled the "cross-cultural consensus" approach. This argument seeks to invoke the cultural resources available in each culture to forge a cross-cultural consensus that invests human rights with universal legitimacy. This consensus-based on the interpretation, reappropriation, and redeployment of alternative schemes of human dignity found in cultures lacking an indigenous "rights" tradition-allegedly bestows upon universal human rights a more genuine legitimacy than external impositions of value.

THE LEGAL POSITIVIST APPROACH

The positivist confronts the descriptive fact of cultural pluralism with a form of legal realism. He does not deny the validity of cultural relativism. Nor does he suggest that human rights inherently possess a greater legitimacy than alternative conceptions of human dignity. The positivist instead repudiates cultural relativism on the basis of empirically verifiable legal facts.

After the UDHR's adoption in 1948 and the astonishingly rapid subscription of nations to the treaties constitutive of the modern international human rights regime, human rights obtained "universality" in virtue of their codification as legal norms binding on nearly all states. Arguably, even states that have not ratified these treaties are bound by human rights law because these norms-or, at least, some widely subscribed subset of them-have crystallized into customary international law. Returning to the Taliban, the legal positivist might point out, as numerous international actors did, that Afghanistan is party to the ICCPR, the Torture Convention, and the Convention on the Political Rights of Women. All of these treaties arguably proscribe the dubious judicial procedures and punishments instituted by the Taliban.

Additionally, international law does not excuse a state party of its treaty obligations simply by virtue of a change in its domestic law or a governmental transition. Thus, for nations that acknowledge international law-or, at least, have a stake in being perceived as a state that abides by its international obligations-legal positivist universality can exert significant pressures to comply with human rights standards. It therefore serves a crucial value: when manipulated with diplomatic and strategic acuity, it can effect positive changes in the human rights practices of certain state actors.

At the theoretical level, however, as the example of the Taliban clarifies, legal positivism fails to answer satisfactorily the crude relativist challenge. Legal positivism is compelling only to the extent that state actors accept one of its axiomatic claims-that legal obligations can exist quite independent of comprehensive moral, philosophical, or religious doctrines.

But the Taliban, far from embracing this dichotomy, expressly repudiates it. Marsden observes that the Taliban's creed derives in part from that of the Muslim Brotherhood of the late-1920s, which proclaimed that Islam is a "comprehensive self-evolving system... applicable to all times and places."

No distinction exists between the secular public world and an alleged private sphere of "comprehensive moral, philosophical or political doctrines." The positivist argument that legal obligations-here, international human rights-survive whatever comprehensive religious or moral doctrines (as well as their instantiation in domestic law and practice) govern society presupposes a real dichotomy between religious and secular law. States that reject this dichotomy will not find positivist universality compelling.

This means that in certain "rogue" states international human rights will not enjoy universal respect; it does not, however, necessarily refute their normative universality. Again, we have conceded that no descriptive consensus supports empirically the existence of universally acknowledged human rights. Recall, however, that the challenge of crude relativism is normative, not descriptive. It claims, not simply that cultural pluralism exists, but that the external imposition of human rights norms on cultures that purport to reject them is somehow illegitimate or unjustified.

THE CROSS-CULTURAL CONSENSUS APPROACH

Alternatively, then, one might seek to repudiate crude relativism by resort to a culture's internal resources. Norms that promote human dignity exist in nearly all societies. Properly interpreted, recast, and reoriented, these norms arguably can be redeployed in the service of human rights; they provide the "raw material" from which to forge genuine "cross-cultural" universality. Like the legal positivists, exponents of this view, such as Abdullahi A. An-Na'im and Charles Taylor, acknowledge the descriptive fact of cultural pluralism but still embrace the universality of human rights.

They argue, however, that any successful rejoinder to the crude cultural relativist must come from within the relativist's own cultural tradition. True legitimacy, An-Na'im writes, requires that "shared moral values be authentic and not imposed from outside.... Values must be legitimate with reference to the norms and mechanisms of change within a particular culture." Taylor likewise concludes that "contrary to what many people think, world convergence will not come through a loss or denial of traditions all around, but rather by creative reimmersions of different groups, each in their own spiritual heritage, traveling different routes to the same goal."

In short, the cross-cultural approach seeks to repudiate the crude cultural relativist challenge by re-appropriating the very cultural traditions relied upon by the relativist to justify behavior that violates universal human rights. Relative to the relativist's own cultural traditions and viewed in the right interpretive light, such behavior appears illegitimate. Understood as a strategic measure, the cross-cultural approach warrants considerable praise.

Rote attempts to compel adherence to human rights norms by citing their codification in international instruments will, as the above-quoted exchange between the Special Rapporteur and the Taliban's attorney general indicates, frequently prove innocuous, particularly where a state's political elite refuses to acknowledge international law. To employ concepts of value and human dignity already internalized by a given cultural tradition may be far more effective. Michael Ignatieff, for example, recounts that, to encourage the Taliban to comply with the 1949 Geneva Conventions, the International Committee of the Red Cross disseminated pamphlets invoking Islamic iconography and maxims, re-appropriating these cultural resources in the service of international humanitarian law.

An-Na'im similarly contends that arguments based upon Shari'a-citing the Prophet's maxim that "if there is any doubt... the Qur'anic punishment should not be imposed"-will more effectively limit the controversial criminal punishments (hudud) imposed by some Islamic states. But note that these examples address the means of realizing an international public order that maximizes respect for the ends promoted by human · rights. They do not address the logically prior question of what ends ought to be advanced by this, or any other, strategy, and as Isaiah Berlin famously observed, "where ends are agreed, the only questions left are those of means, and these are not political but technical, that is to say, capable of being settled by experts or machines like arguments between engineers or doctors."

Yet "ends" are precisely what crude relativism challenges. Undoubtedly, re-appropriating existing cultural resources to promote world convergence on fundamental ends is perhaps the most promising technical method of forging a cross-cultural consensus about human rights-one that might eventually suffice to be deemed true descriptive universality. But this presupposes actors, like An-Na'im and Taylor, who are in fact already committed to the very human rights norms that crude relativism challenges.

The cross-cultural approach begins by presuming that universal human rights represent the desirable end-state. It then inquires how, in a global order characterized descriptively by cultural pluralism, one may effectively establish conditions under which, more often than not, international human rights receive respect. The cross-cultural approach's answer is to manipulate and redeploy each culture's internal resources in the service of human rights. This is not to criticize the "cross-cultural consensus" methodology. It is merely to note that, while laudable as a strategic tool, the cross-cultural, like the legal positivist approach, does not directly address the normative challenge of crude cultural relativism.

Nor do its proponents intend it to do so. In fact, implicit in An-Na'im and Taylor's arguments is the notion that the external imposition of human rights-as conceived in the Western liberal tradition-is not justified in some privileged sense that alternative conceptions of human dignity lack. Rather, the objective seems to reside in amalgamating the most broadly-shareable mores of each society in an effort to achieve an overlapping consensus of basic values that most cultures will respect most of the time. While there may be no reason to object to this goal, it cannot be equated with an international order guided by universal respect for human rights.

OUTRELATIVIZING RELATIVISM

Crude cultural relativism, however, does more than acknowledge cultural pluralism. It infers a questionable conclusion from this empirical fact-"that no transcendent or trans-cultural ideas of right can be found or agreed on, and hence that no culture (whether or not in the guise of enforcing international human rights) is justified in attempting to impose on others what must be understood as its own ideas." This proposition states a fundamental challenge that any successful defense of the universality of human rights must address. To begin, then, we should ask why it strikes us as problematic in the first place.

The answer is that we are disturbed by the idea of imposing on others; it seems to legitimize coercion. Again, we find that arguments about the universality of human rights distill to arguments about the propriety of coercion. Under what circumstances is it justified, in relation to individuals, to cultures, and to states? Needless to say, this question is perhaps the core inquiry of political philosophy, and its comprehensive treatment is beyond the scope of this chapter. But its assessment cannot be wholly avoided, for it speaks to the central question under consideration, i.e., the propriety of imposing human rights on cultures that purport to reject them. Before turning to coercion, however, this Chapter suggests a number of preliminary, though admittedly non-dispositive, rejoinders to crude relativism.

First, independent of the substantive legitimacy of coercion, crude relativism undermines itself. It suffers from the Humean naturalistic fallacy. Simply put, no value claim-a normative "ought"-finds logical support in any purely factual claim-a descriptive "is". Bernard Williams concisely captures this difficulty in his essay An Inconsistent Form of Relativism. The "vulgar relativist" proposition, he notes, reduces to the following syllogism:

That 'right' means (can only be coherently understood as meaning) 'right for a given society'; that 'right for a given society' is to be understood in a functionalist sense; and that (therefore) it is wrong for people in one society to condemn, interfere with, etc. the values of another society.

But this logic is self-evidently pathological. It proposes, at once, that: (1) all claims of right must be understood as relative to the culture making them; but that (2) one such claim-that imposing foreign values on a society that does not share them is morally wrong-merits universal respect notwithstanding the truth of relativism. Crude cultural relativism presumes that the descriptive fact of cultural pluralism compels the normative value conclusion that every culture should tolerate the practices of every other culture. But this latter claim simply does not follow from the former.

As anthropologist Elvin Hatch notes, "To say that values vary from culture to culture is to describe (accurately or not) an empirical state of affairs in the real world, whereas the call for tolerance is a value judgment of what ought to be, and it is logically impossible to derive the one from the other."

The crude relativist's challenge to the "moral imperialism" of international human rights thus suffers from an internal pathology of logic. This rejoinder, however, remains somewhat trivial. It shows only that cultural pluralism does not lead inexorably to the conclusion that no culture may interfere justifiably in the affairs of another. It might still be true that cultural groups should generally refrain from imposing their values onto others that do not share them. A complex system of internalized values in large measure defines a culture. "To be acculturated means to have adopted at a very deep level of consciousness-so deep that one is often unaware of its effect on contemporary behavior-the fundamental postulates of a particular system."

It may therefore be desirable to forbear, where possible, from disturbing these fundamental postulates. Insofar as it upsets the stability of a cultural community, to interpose foreign values may cause more harm than good. Even from a liberal perspective, as Kymlicka argues, "freedom is intimately linked with and dependent on culture" because it "involves making choices amongst various options, and our societal culture not only provides these options, but also makes them meaningful to us."

Yet disparities in cultural values and practices cannot simply be ignored. Indeed, it is precisely because cultural survival depends upon the internalization of certain values that they cannot "merely evaporate because one is confronted with human beings in another society." Few today, for example, would resort to cultural relativism to defend cultural practices that sanction slavery, human sacrifice, or genocide.

These "easy cases" do not show a universal consensus. But they indicate that what Donnelly calls "radical cultural relativism"-the notion that "culture is the [sole] source of the validity of a moral right or rule"-is not the view that most relativists defend when they question the universality of human rights. The issue is rather whether and to what extent cultural pluralism counsels against imposing foreign norms onto a cultural group that does not share them, either because in theory, this imposition is somehow morally illegitimate; or, in practice, the introduction of foreign norms threatens to disrupt the integrity of a cultural community.

In the latter case, however, while recognizing the force of Kymlicka's argument that "access to a societal culture" is a necessary condition for "meaningful individual choice[,]" one must also bear in mind that the very same "societal culture" can at times constitute the principal barrier to individual choice.

For instance, certain Christian sects-the Amish-shield children in their culture from ordinary public education, fearing that this exposure could enable and animate decisions to exit their discrete cultural community. Thus, if one agrees that ensuring "meaningful individual choice"-autonomy-is critical, we must ask whether the extent and nature of cultural "disruption" that might be caused by "imposing" human rights universally will be offset by the value of vesting formerly disenfranchised individuals or social classes with the protections that international human rights law extends to all persons.

Several further difficulties weaken the crude relativist normative challenge. For example, it often presumes a high level of cultural homogeneity within a nation-state. This proves fictitious in two senses. First, the cultural values alleged to characterize a given community are rarely as univocal or ubiquitous as the relativist claims; and second, the interpretation that these cultural values receive often reflects more the self-interest of the elites than it does traditions and practices cherished by the cultural community as a whole.

When the Taliban's acting foreign minister, Sher Muhammad Stanakzai, proclaims, "[t]hose who consider the imposition of [our] law to be against human rights are insulting all Muslims and their beliefs," it is surely not the case that "all Muslims" would agree. As An-Na'im notes, within a single culture, multiple perceptions and interpretations of its constitutive shared values subsist. Cultural pluralism does not, that is, simply stand for disputes between "Islam and the West" but also for internal disagreements among Islamic cultural groups and nation-states.

Likewise, in the context of the "Asian values" debate, Yash Ghai points out that "neither Asian culture nor Asian realities are homogenous throughout the continent." Thus, for example, some "Asian values" theorists claim that Confucian cultural traditions in East and Southeast Asia create greater popular desire for the social order and efficient governance allegedly enabled by authoritarian regimes than for democracy. But the Dalai Lama, as one prominent exemplar of the diverse Buddhist traditions of Asia, expresses the view that "not only are Buddhism and democracy compatible, they are rooted in a common understanding of the equality and potential of every individual."

The point here is not that one view or the other is correct, but rather that we have no reason to assume that the State-to whom universal human rights law principally applies-speaks with a monolithic cultural voice. In the era of the nation-state, rarely, if ever, do territorial boundaries embrace a single cultural tradition? A "cultural" rejection of universal human rights law may therefore reflect not universal cultural norms, but particular perceptions, understandings, and interpretations of these norms.

Which interpretations tend to be at war with the prerogatives of universal human rights? This question invites a more cynical rejoinder to crude cultural relativism. Scholars and human rights activists alike observe that frequently it is not cultural values that inhibit societies from realizing a legal order that respects universal human rights; it is the self-serving manipulation of these values by elites. Authoritarian leaders often invoke cultural relativism to cloak the characteristic abuses of totalitarian rule:

Arguments of cultural relativism regularly involve urban elites eloquently praising the glories of village life-a life that they or their parents... struggled hard to escape.... Government officials denounce the corrosive individualism of Western values-while they line their pockets with the proceeds of massive corruption.... Leaders sing the praises of traditional communities-while they wield arbitrary power antithetical to traditional values, pursue development policies that systematically undermine traditional communities, and replace traditional leaders with corrupt cronies and party hacks.

U.N. Secretary-General Kofi Annan echoed this same conclusion in a recent statement at the Aspen Institute: "It is never the people who complain of human rights as a Western or Northern imposition. It is too often their leaders who do so.... You do not need to explain the meaning of human rights to an Asian mother or an African father whose son or daughter has been tortured or killed. They understand it-tragically-far better than we ever will."

Yet the use of culture to justify human rights violations need not be self-consciously cynical. At times, societal elites-such as the Brahmin caste in traditional Hindu society-rely subconsciously upon deeply ingrained cultural beliefs to legitimize their self-assessment of practices that offend human rights norms. Finally, to the extent that states advance crude relativist objections to universal human rights, we should bear in mind that these arguments assume unjustifiably an identity between government objectives and cultural values. Human rights abuses, as noted above, imply official complicity.

When they are not perpetrated directly by governmental, quasi-governmental, or paramilitary groups, human rights abuses nonetheless enjoy either official sanction or, at the very least, tolerance. Absent some form of official complicity, the abuse perhaps constitutes a crime but not, strictly speaking, a human rights violation. Thus, if crude relativism provides a respectable reason to abrogate international human rights, it must be true that a state's objectives may be identified legitimately with the cultural values invoked to defend the practice at issue. But "the community and State are different institutions and to some extent in a contrary juxtaposition."

Not surprisingly, where many egregious patterns of human rights violations occur, it strains credulity to make this simple identification. In fact, when human rights abuses occur on a massive and systematic scale, it is frequently because the state, or, more commonly, one cultural or national elite that seizes control of the state seeks to suppress or destroy certain other cultural, ethnic, or political groups within its territory.

The war in the former Yugoslavia is a case in point. Likewise, in the Rwandan genocide of 1994, it was not culture per se, but a political elite's manipulation and exacerbation of preexisting socio-cultural divisions within Rwandan society that caused the systematic slaughter of Tutsi.

Again, in the People's Republic of China of the 1960s and 1970s, nothing about Chinese-still less "Asian"-values sanctioned the massive destruction and terror of the Cultural Revolution. Indeed, ironically, this human rights catastrophe involved an attempt to eradicate traditional Chinese cultural values in the service of a state ideology that, far from being shared by its citizenry, grew out of the radical ideas of a long-dead social critic of nineteenth-century industrial Europe. In short, particularly in states that lack democratic institutions, the crude cultural relativist's identification of the state-and its objectives-with the cultural values of its people remains dubious.

APPLYING THE REASONABLE TOLERANCE

The above arguments cast doubt upon the empirical accuracy and sincerity of cultural relativist challenges to universal human rights. But assume that a state's practices conform to the values of many of its citizens. Assume further that its population is relatively homogeneous and that the state's elite pursues policies that genuinely reflect many of its people's cultural values. Finally, assume that these values manifest an alternative conception of human dignity, but one that is largely incompatible with international human rights law. Under these circumstances, do human rights enjoy some privileged status that merits their application to a culture that appears to reject them? This Part concludes that, even in such an implausible scenario, they do.

In this context, the following discussion revisits the example of the Taliban. For its leaders, structuring Afghan society according to their interpretation of Shar'ia promotes human dignity, insulates men and women from corruption, and shields citizens from the corrosive influence of decadent Western practices. The Taliban are not unique in this respect. Many groups impose strictures on their members to preserve existing social arrangements and to prevent the deterioration of, or to reestablish, "traditional" cultural mores. These strictures force individuals to obey societal norms, often in violation of international human rights law. At the same time, the crude relativist argues, these alternative cultural arrangements merit tolerance; it would be wrong for foreigners to coerce societal compliance with international human rights.

The debate thus returns full circle to the question of coercion. In practice, the objections sketched above often betray the disingenuousness of crude relativism. But a compelling defense of universal human rights must interpret the position charitably for the argument's sake. We need to appraise whether cultural pluralism, by itself, indicates that certain kinds of coercion intended to enforce international human rights are illegitimate. But what aspect of coercion would render it "illegitimate" or "unjustified" in any context? Obviously, we do not disapprove of all forms of coercion. Without violating human rights, states compel citizens to pay taxes, to serve on juries, at times to enlist in the army, and so forth. Therefore, we have no difficulty with forcing children to attend school and receive an education. But we balk at the Taliban's strictures that force women to behave in certain ways and that forbid them certain forms of education and employment.

In the liberal tradition, the salient difference resides in the understanding of the nature of the coercion in each case. Isaiah Berlin defined coercion as "the deliberate interference of other human beings within the area in which I could otherwise act." Where this interference serves, broadly speaking, the institutions that preserve human freedom and choice-as education, taxes, and jury duty all arguably do-it does not strike us as illegitimate. By contrast, where coercion interferes substantially with human freedom and choice, it becomes untenable.

It is one thing to require people to do jury duty or to vote, and quite another to compel people to attend a particular church or to follow traditional gender roles. The former are intended to uphold liberal rights and democratic institutions, the latter restrict these rights in the name of cultural tradition or religious orthodoxy.

The quintessential idea that motivates this distinction is the peculiar liberal conception of the self. For this reason, the following discussion, which expounds the source of respect for autonomy within the liberal tradition, applies, first and foremost, to individuals. It applies to communities only insofar as they can genuinely be understood to enable the kind of meaningful individual choice that the liberal tradition venerates. It would remain perfectly coherent for a community-based or patriarchal society to reject this idiosyncratic conception of the self and its concomitant concern with individual autonomy. But then to purport to reject the universality of human rights on cultural relativist grounds requires that the proponent of relativism explain why coercion-in the form of imposing international human rights law-is illegitimate.

Absent some presently unarticulated alternative, the contention is that cultural relativism necessarily appeals, albeit tacitly, to the liberal principle of autonomy. An appeal to autonomy, however, is only available to the extent that the rationale for valuing autonomy holds true. This rationale, in turn, is inextricably linked to a belief that the individual is the fundamental unit of concern and source of value. Cultural relativism therefore cannot embrace autonomy to reject the universal applicability of human rights, but then dispense with autonomy in relation to the very source of its value and rationale-the liberal conception of the individual. Liberals understand the self as an agent, a being capable of formulating personal projects according to widely diverse values.

Robert Nozick-one exemplar of this tradition sets forth this vision of the self-and its many philosophical assumptions in *Anarchy, State & Utopia*. We conceive of the sell he writes, as "sentient and self-conscious; rational (capable of using abstract concepts, not tied to responses to immediate stimuli); possessing free will; [and] being a moral agent," as a being that is able "to regulate and guide its life in accordance with some overall conception it chooses to accept." Liberals therefore try to establish social and legal institutions that do not interfere with each person's autonomous pursuit of his or her values.

The rationale for this principle of tolerance is neither obvious nor obviously correct. It stems from the controversial assumption that no one set of values-no single "conception of the good"-is right for everyone. This claim could be metaethical, empirical, or both. It could mean that, as a matter of metaethics, personal, cultural, and societal differences render certain values worthier of pursuit for some people than for others; or it could mean that, empirically, even if one set of values is in fact right for everyone we cannot know this. But critically, note that in either case the rationale for valuing autonomy reduces to the same basic claim-that choice is the prerequisite for individuals to give meaning to their lives.

So stated the argument against coercion appears highly quixotic and by no means shared by the world's diverse cultural traditions. Many religious, moral, and cultural doctrines, far from disclaiming knowledge of the good life, advance strong conceptions of it that demand universal assent. The Taliban-though they are hardly unique in this regard-do not recognize a Rawlsian distinction between, on the one hand, mere "political" conceptions of right that can be switched on and off as one moves in and out of the public political arena and, on the other hand, comprehensive private moral and religious doctrines.

Quite the contrary, the latter encompass and ordain the former. Moreover, even assuming we do acknowledge this distinction, as Kymlicka rhetorically asks, "We know that some people will make imprudent decisions, wasting their time on hopeless or trivial pursuits. Why then should the government not intervene to protect us from making mistakes, and to compel us to lead the truly good life?"

The answer, he emphasizes, resides in human fallibility. We recognize that, "[s]ince we can be wrong about the worth or value of what we are currently doing, and since no one wants to lead a life based on false beliefs about its worth, it is of fundamental importance that we be able rationally to assess our conceptions of the good in the light of new information or experiences, and to revise them if they are not worthy of our continued allegiance."

A liberal conception of "rights as trumps" against the demands of the community or the state finds its justification in two interrelated ideas: First, that everyone must "have the resources and liberties needed to lead their lives in accordance with their beliefs about value...;" and second, that individuals also need the information and liberty to "question those beliefs, to examine them in light of... an awareness of different views about the good life" and, if warranted, to revise them.

Human rights, as one peculiar subset of rights generally, seek to protect human dignity by preserving each person's ability to choose among the diverse conceptions of ultimate value that different cultures embrace. We live in a world, not of competing relativisms-"these values embody the good for a circumscribed set of persons leading lives in this particular cultural context"-but of competing universalisms-"these values embody the good."

Paradoxically, then, the feature of comprehensive "conceptions of the good" that proves most adverse to an international order structured by respect for universal human rights is dogmatic universalism-the claim that one system of value prescribes what "is right" for everyone and can therefore be justifiably imposed, through violence if necessary, on others. At first glance, this appears to beg the question. Does not the phrase "universal human rights" imply precisely such a system of values? Is it not precisely this "imperialistic" feature of international human rights that cultural relativists reject?

These questions indicate that liberalism's preoccupation with "rights" does not render it, as some argue, wholly neutral towards different conceptions of the good. It cannot tolerate any conception of the good life that requires suppression of the conditions under which free and informed choice by individuals remains possible. Simply stated, liberalism rejects institutional arrangements that do not preserve autonomy.

Yet clearly, some cultural value systems, which in the view of their adherents promote human dignity, actually demand the repression of autonomy. By restricting women's educational opportunities, the Taliban destroy the conditions under which women can make free and informed choices about what values-and, consequently, what life and vision of human dignity-they wish to embrace. Human rights, then, do not permit cultures absolute latitude to structure their socio-political and legal arrangements as they choose; in this respect, they may fairly be deemed "imperious."

But at the same time, human rights do not compel any one particular set of values. Within constraints delineated by the autonomy principle, international human rights provide an overarching political and legal framework that permits individuals and cultural units relatively broad latitude to structure their social circumstances and to pursue their values as they see fit. International human rights therefore prove far more inclusive of diverse conceptions of cultural value than alternative functional concepts for promoting human dignity.

Most non-rights-based conceptions of human dignity insist upon a singular substantive conception of the good; they therefore demand adherence to specific values, ideologies, and attendant behaviors. The human rights tradition is unique in that it does not demand adherence precisely because the universal human rights tradition, far from denying pluralism and far from denying diverse conceptions of cultural value, is animated by the distinctively liberal presumption of reasonable value pluralism. With this background in mind, recall that crude cultural relativism challenges the alleged "intolerance" of universal human rights as illegitimate-an unjustified imposition of foreign values on a cultural community that does not share them.

But what could "illegitimate" mean in this context? Crude cultural relativism, after all, vehemently defends the proposition that conceptions of legitimacy are culturally determined. Yet, as has been seen, it fails to support its own argument in this regard because it unjustifiably infers a normative conception of legitimacy from a mere descriptive fact. To substantiate its challenge, then, cultural relativism must appeal to some other principle-other than merely "the truth of relativism"-that can differentiate legitimate from illegitimate coercion. The liberal tradition-and the distinctive conception of "human rights" to which it gave rise-suggests one: roughly, respect for individual autonomy.

"What distinguishes liberal tolerance is precisely its commitment to autonomy-that is, the idea that individuals should be free to assess and potentially revise their existing ends." But crude cultural relativism cannot rely on the autonomy principle to repudiate the universality of human rights while at the same time violating this principle in relation to members of its own society. As Arthur Schlesinger observed in the context of the debate over multiculturalism, "One of the oddities of the situation is that the assault on the Western tradition is conducted very largely with analytical weapons forged in the West."(240) the same can be said, in short, of the vast majority of cultural relativist objections to universal human rights.

Other principles for differentiating legitimate from illegitimate coercion in the context of diverse cultural communities do exist. The most well-known, the Ottoman "millet" system, permitted Greek Orthodox, Armenian Orthodox, and Jewish communities subsisting within the Ottoman Empire to structure their internal affairs as they saw fit, though "their relations with the ruling Muslims were tightly regulated." Historically, this system provided a relatively humane and stable system of tolerance among religious groups.

Yet it permitted these groups to impose restrictions internally on the autonomy of their respective members, and theoretically, it is not clear on what basis-other than the pragmatics of ruling an empire-this distinction could be justified. A millet - like system remains plausible today. In a rough sense, international law traditionally proceeded from an analogous principle, regulating relations among states but permitting each sole authority over matters "essentially within its domestic jurisdiction." But after abandoning transcendental concepts of right, the appropriate inquiry becomes whether, regardless of its presently unarticulated theoretical justification, this system would be desirable today, in an interdependent global community of highly diverse peoples and states.

Crude cultural relativism emphasizes correctly that conceptions of human dignity respond to the prevailing social and cultural features of the society in which they develop. But to accept this premise invites the following question: Which mechanism for promoting human dignity responds most appropriately to the threats to human dignity posed by contemporary social and historical contingencies? Jack Donnelly, Rhoda Howard, and other scholars have observed that international human rights are peculiarly well-suited to protect persons from the threats to human dignity posed by the modern nation-state, market economies, and industrialization.

These conditions do not exist to the same degree in all regions of the world. But today, they penetrate virtually every state, culture, and society, Western and non-Western alike.

This may explain why "when Chinese students cried and died for democracy in Tiananmen Square, they brought with them not representations of Confucius or Buddha but a model of the Statue of Liberty." The liberal value of individual autonomy that finds expression in universal human rights law resonates with the particular needs of human beings faced with threats to human dignity posed by the modern nation-state and its instrumentalities.

Absent a transcendental justification, which is both undesirable and dangerous, resort to the liberal principle of autonomy to vindicate the universality of human rights does not provide a philosophically-hermetic rebuttal to the relativist's charge that human rights "impose" foreign norms. But one must appraise this challenge, not in isolation, but in context and by reference to its logical alternative-an international laissez-faire system that permits elites (often those who control the military) to impose their conception of the good upon subordinate groups and individuals, armed with the machinery of the state.

In practice, cultural relativism rarely states a sincere call for cultural tolerance; in theory, cultural relativism lacks any coherent theoretical ground to demand tolerance. At the outset, then, one has reason to view cultural relativist claims with skepticism. But universal human rights law also claims two affirmative policy justifications. First, it is maximally inclusive.

Within limits dictated by the autonomy principle, international human rights law accommodates the greatest diversity of alternative cultural conceptions of human dignity; in other words, it is the most tolerant of cultural pluralism. Second, international human rights law is the uniquely appropriate mechanism to counterbalance the threats to human dignity posed by the nation-state, its offshoots, and its instrumentalities. To acknowledge the universality of human rights, then, is not to deny cultural pluralism or the relativity of value. It is to recognize the normative force of the system of international human rights in the face of cultural relativist challenges-which, in the end, appear to state little more than demands for international legal tolerance of intolerance.

4

Human Rights Drama Featuring Burma

The World Trade Organization ("WTO"), an organization described as "arguably the most boring international group in the world," recently held a ministerial conference that drew a huge group of demonstrators, showing the growing resentment that large numbers of people feel toward the WTO. The establishment of the WTO in 1994 and its corollary system of dispute resolution in 1994 provided a strengthened means of resolving trade disputes, in comparison to the earlier General Agreement on Trade and Tariffs ("GATT"). The only way that a panel report containing recommended remedial provisions can not be adopted is for a Member country to appeal the report, the parties to agree to non-adoption, or for a consensus of the Dispute Settlement Body ("DSB") to agree upon non-adoption.

In addition, the Dispute Settlement Understanding contains heightened enforcement provisions that establish a procedure for the DSB to monitor compliance with the report and approve sanctions by the complaining country if non-compliance is found. While the DSB has succeeded in strengthening enforcement of GATT and its related agreements, it may also be seen as a major source of the growing resentment of many people toward the WTO. By authorizing a non-judicial body the ability to resolve questions of violations of an international agreement, and by agreeing to be governed by resultant sanctions, the WTO Members have sacrificed a major aspect of their sovereignty.

Certain issues, even ones justifiably removed from the sphere of "free-trade," are now, according to the WTO and the DSB, beyond national legislation. Therefore, in many circles, the WTO is seen not only as the embodiment of capitalist corporate ideals, but also as a supranational enforcer able to impose those ideals on unwilling nations. With nations ceding the power to legislate in certain areas and subjecting themselves to an international enforcement mechanism, questions naturally arise. Does the agreement relate rationally to the areas in which it is empowered to act? Does the international organization charged with this power, and the agreement under which it operates, take into sufficient consideration the ancillary goals and ideals of the member nations of the agreement? If not, do other methods of achieving these ancillary goals exist in the international arena?

This Article, by analyzing the dispute that has arisen out of the Massachusetts-Burma selective purchasing law, posits that in the recent fervor to attain the goal of free trade, the idea that "trade serves at best as an instrument for achieving goals societies seek" has been lost. As a consequence, the ability of nations to legislate in certain areas-those either marginally related to the concept of free trade or vital enough to warrant exceptions to the strict application of free trade agreements-has been severely compromised. Unfortunately, this may hamper the ability of sovereigns to deal with the issue of human rights in countries that are seen as consistently violating the most basic rights of its citizens.

Applying the GPA in this manner may further alienate the WTO and the notion of free trade generally, in the minds of a public already dissatisfied with WTO policies and procedures. As a result, this type of application of the GPA may be detrimental to the cause of other free trade agreements in the future. In making these arguments, this Article argues that international trade agreements should recognize that "trade is a means to an end, not an end in itself."

THE CURRENT BURMESE REGIME'S VIOLATIONS OF HUMAN RIGHTS

The least contentious issue in the entire dispute about the Massachusetts Burma Law is the existence of gross violations of human rights in the present Burmese regime. The Court of Appeals for the First Circuit expressed this notion succinctly with the following statement: "There is one matter on which the parties are agreed: human rights conditions in Burma are deplorable." Consequently, the court did not inquire further into the matter.

While perhaps not completely germane to the legal controversy put before the District Court of Massachusetts and the Court of Appeals, the issue of the existence and the extent of human rights violations in Burma should have been given more than cursory attention in the subsequent legal dispute. Therefore, in an effort to provide a more complete picture of the situation than has generally been exposed by legal proceedings and constitutional analysis, a short history of the current Burmese regime and its treatment of its citizens is necessary.

THE BURMESE REGIME

Burma, officially named the Union of Myanmar, lies in Southeast Asia, bordered by Bangladesh, China, India, Laos, Thailand, the Andaman Sea, and the Bay of Bengal. Slightly smaller in size than Texas, Burma is plentiful in natural resources but has remained in poverty for much of the time since its independence from the United Kingdom in 1948. From 1886 until its independence, Burma was treated as part of British India, and one writer has commented that the legacy of colonial rule greatly influenced the isolationism that remained the trademark of the nation until the late 1980s.

This isolationism found its greatest expression in the rule of General U Ne Win, who became dictator after a 1962 military coup ended fourteen years of fledgling democracy. Aided by tumultuous internal strife among the many ethnic minorities in Burma; national fears of incursion by neighboring countries;

a single party political structure; complete power over the national press; and strict controls on ingress of foreign journalists and egress of Burmese citizens, the General propelled his country along the "Burmese way to socialism."

This ultra-nationalist policy based upon communist principles sequestered Burma from both the Communist Bloc and the Western community. Under General U Ne Win's control, the country virtually shut itself off from the rest of the world, enforcing a "non-aligned policy" that, until only recently, prohibited the nation from forging any strong strategic or economic alliances and kept public attention from focusing on Burma.

Due to continual clashes between ethnic minorities; the harsh political and social controls over the populous; the lack of attention paid to the regime by the world community; a culture of accepting adversity as an element of strong Buddhist beliefs; and a Burmese trait of selfless respect for authority, General U Ne Win faced little opposition from his countrymen until March 1988, when student protests began in earnest.

THE DECLINE IN THE BURMESE ECONOMY

In the fall of 1987, the Burmese government withdrew a large amount of currency from circulation in Burma. The move was possibly aimed at stifling the drug trafficking industry, which appeared to be run largely by ethnic rebel armies. The effect, however, was to significantly deplete the savings of many ordinary Burmese people. Students protested this decision, but the protests remained small. Apparently, the students were unable to garner any great support for their protests, possibly due to the deference to authority mentioned above; the long history of living under authoritarian rule; and an economy that may have been healthier than most observers could see from the official statistics.

The withdrawal of currency, though, occurred at a time when the Burmese economy was weakening even further. Public sentiment in the fall of 1987 was not strong enough to propel a backlash against the government, but after a few months of living under harsher economic conditions, things began to change. Western influences possibly added to the growing rancor. Reports in early 1988 suggested that, despite extreme isolationism, the government reluctantly tolerated Western tourist excursions.

Tourists brought in U.S. dollars, which became a staple of the Burmese economy, fostering a black market that paid approximately seven times the government exchange rate. Also, western movies, music, and television shows entered Burmese culture, adding a breath of diversity long denied by the xenophobic military regime. Following a sharp decline in the official economy, firsthand experience with the power of a strong currency, and imported visions of Western freedom, the Burmese people replaced their docility with public protest.

Early in 1988, the death of a student provided the impetus for the people of Burma to express their long-restrained dissatisfaction with the government. In March, an argument between students and villagers in a Rangoon tea shop led to the death of one student, apparently due to police action. Students, angered by the death, began a series of protests that lasted approximately one week. Many believe that the student protests arose out of the earlier fall protests, which had stagnated due to lack of support. Although largely unreported in the Western press, protests continued in the following months as support increased.

In July, the protesters achieved one of their goals; twenty-six years after seizing control of Burma, General U Ne Win officially resigned as head of the government, citing the pro-democracy student protests, which ended in the deaths of numerous citizens. Although officially out of office, many believed that U Ne Win remained in control of the country throughout the several subsequent changes of official leadership of Burma; even today, he likely continues his influence.

General Sein Lwin, appointed by the government, took control from General U Ne Win on July 26, 1988. The General had been in charge of the riot police that attempted to contain the earlier protests. Due to this notoriety and the belief that the resignation of General U Ne Win was merely a ruse, the protests ending the twenty-six year reign of the dictator continued in Rangoon. Across the country, minor disputes between ethnic minorities continued to erupt into full scale anti-government protests, and the military and riot police continued to brutally suppress the rioters.

It was reported that the military, at times, fired into groups of unarmed women and monks. A letter endorsed by 170 lawyers of the Rangoon Bar Council, a Burmese governmental organization, asserted that during the rioting, "the army shot and killed nurses on duty, people in their homes or coffee shops, and pedestrians in the streets." After holding power for just seventeen days, and under extreme pressure from fierce rioting, General Sein Lwin resigned the presidency of Burma. In the final five days leading up to his resignation, the government acknowledged that ninety-five people died in the violence, but other reports listed at least 3000 deaths in Rangoon alone.

One week after the resignation of General Sein Lwin, the first civilian leader of Burma in twenty-six years entered office. Attorney General Maung Maung, one of only two civilian members of the presidential cabinet, was selected the next president of Burma by the ruling government. Many in Burma believed that he had been chosen to appease the people, and to give the impression that military rule was at an end, while control remained with the military establishment.

However, even if Mr. Maung Maung was able to wield power himself and not merely as a puppet of General U Ne Win, he still would have been a very objectionable leader in the eyes of the Burmese people. Mr. Maung Maung had close political and ideological ties to U Ne Win and had personally inscribed the principles of the "Burmese Way to Socialism" into the Burmese constitution of 1974. The Burmese people believed that, even if Maung Maung could exert independent control, the principles and ideologies that resulted in the economic devastation and the disregard for basic human rights in Burma would still be enforced.

The protests for democracy against the government continued, drawing millions into the streets. Outraged at the brutality of the suppression of protests in Burma and convinced that the unrest and danger would not be quelled by the most recent change in government, the U.S. Senate and the House of Representatives each penned resolutions condemning the violence in Burma, and the U.S. Department of State prepared for the evacuation of U.S. citizens from Burma. In another attempt to appease pro-democracy activists who protested in the streets to express displeasure with the recent change in government, Maung Maung promised democratic elections later in the year.

The promise did not change the attitude of the Burmese people and did little to quiet the public protests, because many believed that General U Ne Win continued to hold power. After twenty-six years of dictatorial control, few believed that U Ne Win would acquiesce to a call for real democratic reform. For approximately one month, the protests against the rule of Maung Maung continued, during which time various groups contemplated the idea of forming an interim government.

The former Prime Minister of Burma, U Nu, who had lost his position in the coup of 1962, actually formed an interim government but did not receive support from the public or other opposition parties. The most prominent opposition leaders concluded that the current regime would have to resign before an interim government could be formed. Any interim government would be doomed to failure without the support of the military because of the military's vital role in Burmese society and politics.

Unless the current government resigned, the formation of an interim government would force the military-historically very loyal to U Ne Win and the ruling establishment-to decide whom to support. The opposition forces were not willing to wager that the military would disavow historic allegiances in favor of a newly formed, idealistic government. Therefore, the opposition parties waited, hoping that Maung Maung would commit to democratic reform.

MILITARY COUP LEADS TO LITTLE CHANGE IN POWER

In September, Maung Maung ordered the resignation of all military personnel and civil servants from the Burma Socialist Program Party ("BSPP"), the ruling political party. On September 18, perhaps in response to the forced resignation of the military from the BSPP, another change of government occurred in Burma. The Defense Minister, General Saw Maung, appointed by former ruler Sein Lwin over the summer, initiated a military coup to take complete control of the Burmese government and set up the "Organization for Building Law and Order in the State."

This military council enumerated its position when it stated: "in order to halt the deteriorating conditions on all sides all over the country, and for the sake of the interests of the people, the defense forces have assumed all power in the state." Once again, the Burmese people believed that the change in the government was not an actual shift in power. One reporter described the apparent military takeover as a "false coup" designed to maintain the power of the BSPP-still be headed by U Ne Win-with a weak puppet as the officially recognized head of the government.

This interpretation comports with the analysis that the forced resignation of the military from the BSPP-intended to signify to the Burmese people that the upcoming elections would be truly free and not influenced by the military-was a political tactic rather than an accommodation of future democratic elections. By effectively abolishing the BSPP, the government wanted to be perceived as acceding to the public's desire to end the one party system of rule in Burma. However, combined with the military coup that followed shortly thereafter, almost certainly led by U Ne Win, the only effect was to rename the persons in control of the government.

From the speculation that the coup was a reaction by the military to its forced resignation from the BSPP, one may draw the conclusion that the forced resignation was designed to anger the members of the military. Military anger with the BSPP would shift its loyalty from the official party to the leaders of the ensuing coup. Therefore, in the eyes of the public, the official government would change hands, and the military would change allegiances, but no real change of power would occur.

Whether the change in government was in name only or was a real shift in power, the effects remained the same. Shortly after the coup, the military dispersed demonstrators in Rangoon, and the council, headed by General Saw Maung, ordered a curfew and banned groups of more than five people. Less than a month after the takeover, the new government killed 1000 civilians and fired thousands of government workers. One reporter claims that videotapes of the violence after the coup show soldiers killing wounded students after the demonstrators were dispersed.

Rangoon was described as being under "virtual military occupation," and thousands of students were reported to be fleeing to areas controlled by ethnic rebels in hopes of obtaining military training and arms. Also, although Saw Maung again promised free elections, the elections originally scheduled for late in the year were rescheduled to "sometime in 1989," or only after "three conditions were met: peace would have to prevail; the battered rail and road network would have to be made secure; the basic food and shelter situation would have to be improved."

With the effects of twenty-six years of social, political, and economic stagnation to frustrate the achievement of these criteria, the military government showed that it planned to retain its hold on Burma for the indefinite future, with elections coming only when the government so desired. In an apparent attempt to temper the repression and to bolster the promise of free elections, the Saw Maung regime permitted political parties to form. 233 parties formed by April 1989, including the National League for Democracy ("NLD").

Named as General Secretary of the NLD was Daw Aung San Suu Kyi, the daughter of General Aung San, who had been the major force in the independence movement in Burma in the 1940s, but who was assassinated shortly before Burma gained its independence from Britain in 1948. Over the next few months, Suu Kyi gradually assumed the role of popular leader of the NLD and spokesperson for the democracy movement in Burma. In early 1989, the military government of General Saw Maung, which came to be known as the State Law and Order Restoration Council ("SLORC"), set a general time frame for the democratic elections but continued its attempts to repress dissent.

In March, after protest rallies, the SLORC renewed arrests of dissenters, hauling in approximately 1000 people, including 300 members of the NLD. In July, the SLORC put Aung San Suu Kyi and another leader of the NLD under house arrest, not allowing them contact with other NLD members or leaders. Reports indicated that the government continued to arrest anyone that advocated human rights or democracy, attempting to eradicate dissent in Burma. According to a senior Western diplomat, "The government seems to be clearing the field of anyone in opposition. People who were active last year continue to be picked up."

Due to the continued detention of large numbers of political dissenters, the government removed regular criminals from many of the jails to make room for political prisoners. The main jail in Rangoon reportedly released 17,000 criminals to free space for opponents of the government. Reports also claimed that the government often detained individuals with no political ties or involvement for up to five days in harsh conditions and released them with an admonition not to become involved in politics. In the weeks leading up to the one-year anniversary of the massive protests in which thousands of people had been killed, the military detained at least 1,000 members of the NLD to stifle any commemoration of the previous year's events.

REGIME REFUSES TO ACCEPT RESULTS OF DEMOCRATIC VOTE

Despite the efforts of the government to stifle public dissent and detain political protesters, elections set for May of 1990 occurred on schedule and appeared uninfluenced by corruption, though they could hardly be called fair. The ban on gatherings of more than four people continued to be enforced, squelching public debate, and each party running for election was allowed only one campaign address, which was censored. In spite of daunting challenges it faced: election restrictions; the detention of thousands of its members; and the continued house arrest of its two main leaders, the NLD captured more than eighty percent of the parliamentary seats for which it was vying. Not surprisingly, the ruling military regime, embodied by the National Unity Party, the successor to the BSPP, won only 10 seats out of 485.

Despite the landslide victory of the NLD, the prospects for a change in the actual government of Burma were dim. Prior to the election, the ruling regime stated that before any exchange of power would occur, a new constitution would have to be drafted by the new parliament. After the election, the military stalled attempts by the NLD to take power. Although the NLD appeared ready to submit a constitution based on the democratic constitution of 1947, under which Burma had been governed until 1962, the military refused to meet with the NLD and refused to call a national assembly to begin work on the new constitution.

Throughout the following years, the military regime continued its repression of the members of the NLD and to stall the process of writing a new constitution. Aung San Suu Kyi was kept under house arrest until July 1995, when the military felt that the democracy movement had lost enough momentum so as to threaten no longer the military regime. At various times, the military proposed measures to begin forming a constitution, but these efforts often included the requirement that the military be given a large role in any future government.

Needless to say, these measures were seen as unacceptable to the proponents of true democratic reform. Aung San Suu Kyi, after her release from house arrest, began to work on the drafting · of a new constitution with the NLD, but the military government indicated that such a document would not be accepted.

By enacting a law that made the writing of a rival constitution a crime, the military clearly expressed its intent to maintain a firm hold on any constitutional process in Burma. This intent has not dwindled in the ensuing years. In 1999, nine years after the democratic elections, a Burmese governmental official stated: "You can't cry over spilled milk now. And if you're going to stick to demanding that the government should hand over power, I don't think that is very realistic."

HUMAN RIGHTS ABUSES OF THE REGIME

The 1988 protests and the ensuing actions of the Burmese government provide a chilling account of the reprehensible abuses that the Burmese regime imposed upon its people to retain and strengthen control of the country. The killing of thousands of protesters; the arrest, detention, and torture of many thousands of other protesters; the detention of hundreds of members of opposition political parties, including the leaders of the main opposition unit; the severe restriction of social freedoms; and the extreme repression of virtually all democratic ideals serve to introduce the human rights abuses present in Burma today.

The list of other abuses of which the Burmese regime is accused includes: extrajudicial killing; torture; forced labor; forced child labor; forced relocation of entire villages; rape committed by military personnel; invasion of personal privacy; confiscation of personal property; restrictions on access to information; repression of religious activities; and discrimination against ethnic minorities. Since journalists have been either banned completely or severely restricted in the areas that they could visit alone, and since no foreign or national human rights organization has been allowed to operate in Burma, the scope of human rights abuses in Burma has been severely underreported.

The primary source of information has been refugees who have escaped to bordering countries, such as Thailand. From these reports, which detail scores of brutal acts, one indication of human rights abuses of the Burmese military has been the apparent ease and nonchalance with which it has indiscriminately killed fellow citizens. The program of extrajudicial killings in Burma was extensively detailed in a report issued by Amnesty International.

Although issued in 1988, reliable sources indicate that the program of extrajudicial killings, especially of ethnic minorities, continues presently. In its efforts to control the ethnic rebellions that have plagued the country since its independence in 1948, the military regime of Burma has subjected the inhabitants of various ethnic regions to extreme abuse and death in a number of ways.

Reports indicate that to ensure that militant rebel factions receive as little support as possible, the government has often placed entire villages under strict control: (1) restraining free movement; (2) relocating villagers; (3) allocating the amount of food or money that the villagers may possess; and (4) maintaining strict curfews. Persons that are caught in violation of these controls are sometimes killed on sight. Amnesty International stated in its report: "Porters and guides caught trying to escape are often killed, as are villagers who run away when they hear the army is coming."

Although the SLORC has often denied these abuses and cited its attempts to "make peace," evidence shows: the military has continued in the 1990s to kill villagers for having real or alleged sympathies for anti-government forces. In addition to killing villagers and those allegedly supporting local insurgents the military common tortures its detainees. One rice farmer interviewed by Amnesty International described a frequent torture method used against villagers: shin rolling.

"The interrogator tried to force information out of me by rolling a large bamboo pole over my shins, up and down, increasing the pressure until the skin began to strip off... After a few minutes of this treatment, the skin came off, but the guy kept rolling the bamboo over the exposed bone, causing terrible pain."

Other favourite methods of torture include: (1) detention in underground pits; (2) wrapping victims' heads in plastic sheets until the victim nearly suffocates; (3) near-drowning;

and (4) near-strangulation. Many Burmese people are also killed when the military forces villagers to work as porters. These porters are most often used in the areas of Burma in which the government is fighting ethnic insurgencies. The military, often facing mountainous terrain with no roads and having no mechanized transport, uses human labor to carry food, ammunition, and other supplies, and uses locals familiar with the geography of the region as guides for their military expeditions.

Not only are the villagers forced to labor for the military; they are rarely, if ever, paid for their work, and they are also maltreated and forced to engage in dangerous activities for the benefit of the military. Reports suggest that porters are frequently mistreated for not carrying a large enough load or for not walking quickly enough. Porters are also frequently worked to death or killed for not working hard enough. In addition to using conscripted porters to perform grueling manual labor, the military also forced them to act as human danger detectors its forces. Reports show that porters are frequently forced to walk ahead of the military through areas that are suspected of being mined.

As human mine sweepers, these civilians-pulled from their homes or from the streets of their villages-are forced to risk their lives. Also, accounts relate that porters have been forced to dress in the uniforms of the army to patrol insurgent areas unarmed. In these patrols, the civilian porters serve as defenseless decoys for the army, drawing the fire of rebels and alerting the military to their location. Until the late 1980s, the porters were mainly used to support military operations in ethnically controlled insurgent areas, but with the gradual opening of the Burmese economy after 1988, the government began using forced labor for infrastructure projects as well. These projects included the building of railroads, an airport, roads, and an oil pipeline.

During the period 1992-97, Human Rights Watch/Asia estimated that approximately two million Burmese people were used for forced labor to make the Burmese infrastructure more attractive for foreign investment and tourists. Current reports indicate that the institution of porterage is still widely used in Burma. "The forced use of citizens as porters by the army-with attendant mistreatment, illness, and sometimes deaths-remained a common practice" in 1998, according to the United States Department of State. The State Department report of human rights conditions in Burma in 1999 stated:

The Government did not honor its repeated pledge to prevent its officials from using their authority under the country's Towns Act and Villages Act to mobilize forced labor. In June the Government responded to sanctions that the International Labor Organization (ILO) imposed on it for its use of forced labor by unilaterally withdrawing from the convention on forced labor administered by the ILO.

Along with the indiscriminate killing of citizens and the imposition of forced labor upon civilians, the military government also commonly practices forced relocation of citizens. As part of the "four cuts" strategy to disable ethnic rebels-cutting off food, funds, information, and recruits to the insurgents-entire villages are often relocated away from areas of rebel activity. The new locations often lack even the most basic features of adequate living areas, such as sanitation facilities, access to water, electricity, and health care facilities.

From 1988 to 1990, the government relocated an estimated 500.000 people from their homes. Further, as Burma attempts to attract foreign investment, the government began to relocate citizens not only to counter ethnic conflicts, but also to hide "shanty towns" from the view of investors, and to renovate possible tourist areas. In addition to various forms of military brutality, Burma also engages in overt ethnic and religious discrimination. Burma recognizes three different levels of citizenship, each with different levels of rights: full citizenship, associate citizenship, and naturalized citizenship, each with different levels of rights. A full citizen must prove Burmese ancestry back to pre-1823 British occupation.

An associate citizen is one who had one or more ancestors who were citizens of another country. Finally, a naturalized citizen is the offspring of a full citizen and an associate citizen. The discriminatory efforts focus on associate citizens, who are not allowed to own land, hold elected office, or become doctors or engineers. Associate citizens are also severely restricted in their movements within the country. Indirect discrimination also occurs, in that many ethnic minorities who could prove the requisite ancestry back to pre-colonial times are effectively barred from obtaining their citizenship documents. The government has often failed to register these people by making the registration process unavailable in local areas, and associate citizens are frequently not allowed or unable to travel to central locations to register.

Religious intolerance hostility toward non-Buddhist religions occurs frequently in Burma. The military regime has long enforced a policy of promoting Buddhism as the "true" religion of the Burmese people, attempting to instill in the populous the belief that to be a "true Burmese," one must follow Buddhism. The government has forced the conversions of children to Buddhism, destroyed Christian churches, and conscripted Christians and Muslims to build Buddhist religious facilities.

In order to maintain a dictatorial hold on Burmese society, the military has repressed freedom of expression for the past thirty-eight years. Foreign sources of information were largely unavailable for much of this period, with access to foreign newspapers and magazines subject to government censorship. Domestic media services are controlled completely by the state. Domestically produced books, magazines, and films are scrutinized by a "Press Scrutiny Board."

Since most materials are submitted to the board only after substantial expense has been incurred by the publisher, publishers use self-censorship to ensure that their investment will not be wasted by subsequent government revisions. In addition, censorship violations potentially result in seven years in prison for publishers, providing a healthy incentive to stay on the censor's good side.

The effects of censorship and the lack of access to foreign printed material cannot generally be circumvented by electronic means. Realizing that electronic communication could deal a damaging blow to the repression of speech and the isolationism favored by the ruling elite, Burma enacted laws requiring a license for any facsimile machine or computer modem. In addition, for most of the 1990s, the government closed the universities to prevent further student protests.

THE BURMESE LEGAL SYSTEM

The Burmese legal system provides few rights to prisoners and detainees. Many prisoners are detained for up to three years without a trial, and trials do not provide prisoners with most basic judicial norms. Defendants are often denied access to counsel before and during trial. When defendants are allowed counsel, the attorney often simply bargains with the judge for the least harsh sentence for his client. Members of the NLD are usually denied counsel, and when counsel is available for political prisoners, one report suggests that the counsel's role is mainly to serve as mere moral support for the defendant.

Even if counsel played a normal role in court proceedings, the judiciary in Burma is subjected to influences that make it unlikely to act independently in its decisions. First, the judiciary is tied to the military rulers of Burma. The SPDC appoints the members of the Supreme Court of Burma. With the approval of the SPDC, the justices select the lower court judges. This naturally presents conflicts, most notably in trials of political prisoners, where it is believed that the government exerts its influence to determine the outcome of the trial in advance of any proceeding.

Also, bribery appears rampant in the judiciary. The judges typically earn an equivalent of $300 per year, providing ample incentive for parties to attempt to buy their way to a favorable decision. By many accounts, the people of Burma have become increasingly dejected by the continuing history of brutal repression in their homeland.

Few would argue that the present situation in Burma is not a saddening example of a people being subjugated to the whims of a powerful military elite. What does provoke heated arguments, though, is the method by which to express the world's desire for the situation in Burma to improve, the manner in which influence should be used to encourage or compel Burma's regime to respect the most basic human rights of its citizens, and the tools to be used to promote peaceful transition from repressive regime to just governance.

INEFFECTIVENESS OF TRADITIONAL METHODS

INTERNATIONAL SANCTIONS ON BURMA

Beginning in 1988, in response to the brutal repression of the student protests in Burma, the international community enacted measures intended to ease the tensions in Burma and compel the military regime to appreciate and respect human rights. Due to the internal political, economic, and social situation in Burma, however, these measures have largely failed to effect any substantial change in the Burmese regime.

Because of the "Burmese Way to Socialism" instilled by General U Ne Win, Burma remained economically isolated from the rest of the world for twenty-six years. Although the country possessed vast reserves of natural resources such as oil, natural gas, timber, and precious gems, a failure to economically exploit these resources caused Burma to fall from a "rich" country to one of the poorest countries in the world, garnering a vast amount foreign aid. Knowing that a large part of Burma's capital flows came in the form of aid, the first response by countries wishing to influence Burma was to cut off this aid. Believing that without the foreign aid, the Burmese regime would be more willing to change, the major suppliers of aid to Burma cut off most non-humanitarian aid in late 1988.

In October 1988, three large aid donors, the United States, West Germany, and Japan, halted aid to Burma. The combined yearly aid to Burma of these three countries equaled approximately $152 million, and Burma also lost an additional $200 million in Japanese loans. Burma's foreign reserves dwindled, and the country was described as "virtually bankrupt."

These decisions to halt aid showed the contempt the world community felt for the brutality of the military regime during the summer of 1988, and were designed to influence the government to change its tactics. Rather than weakening authoritarian control of the country in order to regain foreign aid, the government-for the first time in approximately twenty-six years-opened its borders to foreign investment. Not surprisingly, many investors initially remained wary of entry into such a volatile market, but a few, mainly in Thailand, were tempted by the abundant natural resources Burma had to offer and immediately capitalized on the new market.

Through a gradual increase in the amount of foreign investment, Burma was able to compensate at least partially for the loss of direct aid formerly supplied by foreign governments. According to data reporting the levels of Foreign Direct Investment (FDI) in Burma, $56 million of FDI was attained in 1989-90, with the United States and the Netherlands representing the largest contributors. By 1990-91, the level of investment had increased to $225.1 million, with the United States and the Republic of Korea being the largest investors.

The cutoff of aid from Western countries was also ameliorated by increased Chinese interest in Burma. After the 1988 student protests, the military became increasingly aware that future social disturbances posed a great threat. The military was also concerned about the likelihood that past and future political uprisings would provide an impetus for the many ethnic insurgent factions to increase rebellious activities to take advantage of the disarray caused by the massive protests. In light of these realizations, the military leaders of Burma began purchasing large amounts of arms from China in 1989. With a more intimate relationship between China and Burma forming due to the arms sales, China saw an opportunity to increase its influence on Burma.

From this strengthened relationship, Burma received greatly increased trade ties with China and opportunities for Chinese development loans. Desiring to wield as much political influence in the region as possible, China established a relationship with Burma that it strove to maintain. Even though Burma may have wished to retain a more independent relationship with China, it now had a "Big Brother," with all the added implications, to provide needed economic and military support. Increased trade with China reduced the coercive effect of the cutoff in foreign aid. Therefore, one traditional method of influencing rogue states proved completely ineffective in Burma.

Diplomatic and humanitarian attempts to deal with the oppression of the Burmese people have proven to be equally ineffective. In addition to ending aid to Burma, the United States imposed an arms embargo, which was easily circumvented through Burma's relationship with China. A 1995 visit to Burma by Madeline Albright, then-U.S. Permanent Representative to the United Nations, engendered excuses and justifications by the Burmese government for its past actions, rather than a dialogue geared toward the resolution of the tensions between Burma and the rest of the world.

As the Association of South-East Asian Nations (ASEAN) prepared to accept Burma into the economic group, the United States and the European Union retracted their opposition to the joinder of Burma to the group, calling for ASEAN to take the lead in encouraging talks between the opposition and the military government. The UN has repeatedly issued resolutions condemning Burma for its abuses and calling for an end to the violation of human rights in the country, but to no avail.

The UN High Commission on Human Rights established the position of a Special Rapporteur ("Rapporteur") for Burma in 1990 to make trips to Burma and report on human rights situations. For a few years, the Burmese regime allowed the Rapporteur entry to Burma; then, in 1996, the government denied the Rapporteur access and has since not allowed the UN official into the country. The International Society of the Red Cross negotiated with the SLORC to gain access to political prisoners.

Finally, in 1995, the Red Cross, completely discouraged by the military regime's failure to grant access to the prisons, withdrew from the country. Subsequently, the Red Cross has been able to return to Burma and obtain limited access to prisoners, although it has claimed that many political prisoners were removed from a prison in Rangoon so that the Red Cross would be unable to see or speak with them. In addition, the Burmese government has continually rebuffed the efforts of the International Labor Organization ("ILO") to secure Burmese adherence to its international obligations. In retaliation, the ILO effectively ejected Burma from the organization and will not allow re-admittance until Burma stops using forced labor.

WEAKNESSES OF CONSTRUCTIVE ENGAGEMENT

While it is obvious that various diplomatic measures and the withholding of aid have failed to promote respect for human rights in Burma, the next step remains unclear. Some groups argue that sanctions should be continued against Burma and should be tightened, while others tout "constructive engagement" as the proper tool for promoting human rights and democracy. Proponents of constructive engagement argue that, all too often, sanctions fail to have a substantial effect on the practices of that country.

In addition, it is argued that economic sanctions have negative repercussions that inure to the innocent citizens of a rogue state, outweighing any benefit from the sanctions. Therefore, instead of relying on an ineffective tool that harms the people it intends to help, proponents of sanctions insist that economic incentives and the benefits from profitable economic activity will more effectively promote the same aims as sanctions. In sum, proponents assert that capitalism will triumph.

The principle behind constructive engagement is that with free trade, instead of sanctions, rogue states are allowed and encouraged to enter into economic transactions with whomever they please. These economic transactions will cause capital flows into the country, very often in the form of foreign direct investment.

Proponents of constructive engagement argue that these increased capital flows and the resulting increased wealth for citizens in the country, from either new jobs created by foreign investors or increased demand for existent production capacity, will gradually lead to political and social changes.

It is often claimed that in developing countries with poor wages and poor labor conditions, the introduction of foreign-owned businesses will heighten labor standards and the level of pay. Proponents argue that the higher labor standards to which foreign businesses have become accustomed outside of the target country will eventually affect the target country's labor system, almost as if by social osmosis.

It appears that adherents to the policy of constructive engagement believe that, by entering foreign markets, businesses, rather than maintaining the status quo of the host country and taking advantage of the opportunity for cheap labor and the ability to circumvent costly standards of treatment, will infuse the labor climate of the target country with greater pay and worker protection in the long run.

Proponents argue that the increased economic and social wealth for the citizens of the target country and its increased presence in the world community, will generally lead to faster improvement in the political and social situation than with sanctions. This improvement appears to be possible in two general ways. First, the country and its political and social climate, through the influence of wealth, security and foreign values, may "evolve" from a restrictive or oppressive state into a more open, protective state cognizant of, and responsive to, its citizens' appeals for change.

This evolution would be aided by private and public appeals to the government for change. Governments supportive of economic ties with the target country could use the increased interactions between the two governments to state privately their concerns and desires for reform and could offer future incentives (the classic carrot and stick situation). The same appeals could be made publicly, and foreign governments could threaten to sever economic ties, appealing to the economic self-interest of the country and its people.

The second possibility is that the increased wealth, security, and power of the citizenry will manifest itself in increased political dissent. As the fruits of engagement are distributed throughout the economy, a "middle class"-

motivated by the taste of what economic and social freedoms have to offer-will develop with the intense desire to change the government and the increased power to do so. The theory suggests that change would occur through rebellion against the country's current government.

What the proponents of constructive engagement for Burma fail to realize, though, is that the conditions necessary for the policy to be effective are not present in Burma. As Madeline Albright noted after her trip to Burma in 1995, "`Constructive engagement' must be, in fact, `constructive.'"

To be constructive, the policy must be able to work its influence upon either or both of two factors. First, if a base level of respect for the rights of the citizenry exists, increased economic and social integration with the rest of the world may subtly influence the target country and its leaders to gradually allow change in the country. Eventually, the theory says, greater involvement with more refined and respectful nations will cause the target country to evolve into a country more conscious of the need for, and more willing to allow, greater protection and freedom for the people.

The influence for change would come about not only from an internal evolution of respect for the populace, but also from external pressures. To maintain the increased involvement with the rest of the world, the target country would seek to create an air of respectability in itself. The views of foreign nations would gain in stature as the target country attempts to promote itself as a country worthy of continued and expanded economic engagement. Secondly, increased economic activity with the outside world could work its influence upon the people at large, rather than the government.

As the theory goes, increased demand for the nation's labor force and the creation of new jobs that accompanies the influx of foreign investment will cause an increase in the wealth and stability of the people. Buoyed by small tastes of what economic and social freedom could entail and strengthened physically and morally by newfound wealth, the people will have greater incentive and capability to throw off the control of their intolerant regime. Upon further analysis, it seems that the policies, politics, and economic realities present in Burma are not conducive to the goals of constructive engagement.

For the past thirty-eight years, the military regimes of Burma have shown willingness to murder, torture, enslave, repress, and discriminate against the citizens of the country. In the twelve years since the technical ouster of General U Ne Win, Burma has resisted change, even in the face of political and economic pressure from much of the world community.

Even after the large increase in the levels of foreign direct investment in Burma since 1988, no real strides in the realm of respect for human rights have occurred. The combination of many factors largely unique to Burma may account for the failure of economic cooperation with the outside world to have positive effects. The first, and perhaps most subtle factor to be considered, is the social and political climate that has been predominate in Burmese recent history. Long before the present regime instituted its own social and political repression, British colonialism repressed and abused the Burmese people, creating an air of distrust of foreigners to form in the Burmese consciousness.

After British colonial rule ended, Burma was allowed little time for this distrust of foreigners to wane before General U Ne Win instituted his "Burmese Way to Socialism," officially instituting fear and distrust of anyone or anything non-Burmese. For twenty-four years, Burma was effectively cut off from the rest of the world, not only economically, but also socially and politically.

Simply put, Burma has not had the necessary time to evolve from a nation fearful of the influences of foreigners to a nation that can be subtly and positively influenced by mere economic cooperation with the rest of the world. For such intangible and indirect changes to occur in the national mindset or the social and cultural norms and morays of the Burmese people, there must be a conduit through which capitalism can succeed. Unfortunately, for Burma, such a conduit remains largely lacking. One way in which involvement may positively affect the general social and political climate in a target country is through the increased flow of information.

With greater access to a wider variety cf sources of news and opposing viewpoints, the populace may begin to think more for it, may begin to question the status quo, and may feel more confident in its own expression of dissent. Also, the people may learn that they are not as alone as they once thought. Not only may they feel themselves to be an increasingly greater part of the world community, sharing in the events of the day and the ensuing discussion and dialogue, but they may also see that the world actually cares about their domestic situation. Sympathizers never before known of may be revealed, providing moral support and feeding the people's hope and determination to be free.

In Burma, however, the flow of information is anything but free. Despite increased engagement with the outside world, censorship still rules the day. Foreign newspapers, magazines, films, television, books, and videotapes all face distribution restrictions. Those media sources legally allowed into Burma or produced domestically face heavy state censorship, which that eliminates any material likely to damage the image of the present regime. Technological innovations may also prove incapable of increasing, to any large degree, the flow of information to Burma.

Fax machines, computer modems, and other devices that would enable the free, or at least less restricted, influx of information and that would allow the outside world to have a degree of unrepressed contact with the Burmese people continue to be strictly controlled by the military regime. Although in some areas the enforcement of these strict controls has been lax, the laws requiring licenses for these devices remain in force, awaiting enforcement when the junta deems it necessary. Direct contact with foreigners interested in seeing positive change in Burma could also prove to be a conduit of information, but this would not occur today in Burma.

Foreign journalists continue to be severely restricted in their ability to even enter Burma and once there, in the ability to have contact with the opposition. Humanitarian non-governmental organizations ("NGOs") are permitted only a very small presence in Burma, and human rights NGOs face an outright ban on operations, thereby limiting the contact between aid workers and the Burmese population.

The government usually grants tourists limited duration visas to certain restricted areas, thereby limiting the contact they may have with the people. In any event, the Burmese people may remain wary of having meaningful contact with foreigners, even if and when the opportunities may present themselves. The threat of harassment and possible detention remains over the heads of citizens that discuss anything other than mundane matters with foreigners.

Another factor needed for "constructive engagement" to attain its goals is the ability of foreign investment or other increases in economic activity to economically and socially benefit the people of the target country. In theory, a stimulated economy will produce not only financial benefits for those employed directly as a result of new or increased foreign investment, but will also stimulate the economy of the country in general by widely dispersing the increased wealth and attendant benefits.

In this model, workers employed by or, as a result of, increased foreign investment will receive better pay and treatment than those in the typical domestic employment will. The increased wealth will be spread to the community at large, promoting general economic growth. Employees receiving better labor standards will become accustomed to the more humane treatment and will be more likely to demand similar treatment in the future. The stimulated economic growth will lead to improvements in infrastructure, allowing the growth to be sustained and heightened.

The government, through increased inflows of cash, will be able to provide improved social services for its citizens, leading to a happier, healthier, and better educated populace that will be increasingly desirable to foreign employers, providing ever increasing opportunities for sustained economic growth. Eventually, economic growth will lead to the formation of a middle class with a heretofore unknown power of political persuasion, better able and more willing to express its views to the government and more likely to have its views listened to by those in political power.

Economic integration will tend to provide a gradual shift in the political and social climate in the host country. Through capitalism, respect for and protection of the population and its basic human rights will either evolve naturally in those in political power, or will be superimposed upon the rulers of the country through the will of a populace with increased political and economic power and the influence of foreign industry and governments. The target country will likely be quite intent on maintaining economic ties with these foreign players and will therefore be more susceptible to political and moral persuasion by those whom the target country wishes to keep happy.

As logical and reasonable as the model of constructive engagement may seem, it is difficult to believe that economic activity, without more, may lead to a positive shift in the political and social climate of Burma. Unfortunately for the people of Burma, the social and political situation in the country and the increased economic interaction outside Burma tend to lessen or even negate the potential benefits from "constructive engagement." First of all, Burmese citizens may actually receive an extremely small amount of the financial rewards of economic engagement with foreign firms and investors. Approximately one-third of the foreign investment in Burma flows to the oil and natural gas industry, which remains under state control.

Rather than private businesses or individuals capitalizing on the profits and opportunities from one of Burma's greatest assets, the state receives nearly all of the benefits: offering itself as the sole joint venture partner for foreign firms in this field. Furthermore, approximately one-third of all investment in Burma is accounted for by the tourism and hotel industry, in which the military regime also plays a large role. The government also maintains a monopoly in the export of rice, the prime agricultural product of Burma, and in teak wood, pearls, jade, other gems, metals, and minerals.

The Burmese government also controls the fisheries, communications, public utilities, defense, and banking and finance industries. A 1995 International Monetary Fund report stated that government-run monopolies controlled fifty percent of all Burmese exports and controlled forty percent of all imports. The government's explicit monopolistic control of vast areas of the economy serves only as an introduction to the role of the state in the Burmese economy.

In addition to maintaining economic control by holding monopolistic power over certain industries and resources, the Burmese government also wholly owns a huge number of operations in all areas of the Burmese economy. Despite recent efforts to privatize a small percentage of these holdings, in early 1999, the government still owned 1,609 enterprises in Burma. These holdings are largely in the form of State Economic Enterprises ("SEEs") operated by diversified governmental ministries. However, a number of enterprises are also owned and operated directly by the military, providing foreign currency for the maintenance of economic stability and military political control.

The government, rather than the population as a whole, receives the greatest amount of direct benefits-profits and cash flows-from increased economic ties with the outside world. In theory, this would not absolutely prevent Burmese society from receiving the benefits of economic integration, assuming the government engaged in some beneficial redistribution of the new wealth. However, this does not appear to be the case in Burma. The expenditures of the government have historically been to support the military. Speculation on the percentage of the government's budget spent on the military ranges from approximately thirty-three percent to sixty percent.

From 1988 to 1999, the Burmese military expanded from a force of approximately 180,000 troops to at least 350,000. Given that during this time Burma was not involved in any aggressive or defensive military actions with other countries; had no real outside enemies against which to defend; and junta entered into cease-fire agreements with a large number of ethnic rebel factions, this military buildup was less of a protectionist security measure, and more of an attempt to perpetuate the power and control of the ruling military government.

Some foreign corporations recognized the failure of "constructive engagement" to positively affect the Burmese government. Levi Strauss pulled out of the country in 1992, stating that "Under present conditions, it is not possible to do business in Myanmar without directly supporting the military government and its pervasive violations of human rights." As public sentiment against the military regime in Burma grew stronger over the following two years, Liz Claiborne also decided to cease its Burmese operations, articulating the following reasoning for its withdrawal: "Though the facilities with which we work have complied with our strict human rights standards, we cannot support the activities of this country's current government."

The most telling example of how economic engagement may support or promote continued violations of human rights in Burma may be the Yadana natural gas pipeline, a project that has brought the subject of human rights violations in Burma into the U.S. legal system. In this novel litigation, the plaintiffs are attempting to hold Unocal, a California oil company, responsible for acts of "forced relocation, forced labor, torture, violence against women, arbitrary arrest and detention, cruel, inhuman or degrading treatment, crimes against humanity, the death of family members, battery, false imprisonment, and assault," allegedly committed by the Burmese military in furtherance of the pipeline project.

The theory of the case is that the actions of the Burmese military in relocating villagers; forcing villagers to work on infrastructure projects related to the pipeline; forcing villagers to work on the pipeline itself; and committing various other human rights violations may be attributable to Unocal. This is because the SLORC, the alleged cause of these abuses, acted as an agent for the Myanmar Oil and Gas Enterprise, Unocal's partner in the Yadana joint venture.

Unocal denies that any human rights violations have occurred because of the pipeline project and those actions by the military government are completely separate from Unocal's role in the joint venture. Two documents obtained by human rights groups, however, suggest that Unocal implicitly and explicitly knew of, and may have been complicit in, human rights violations related to the Yadana pipeline project. Whether or not Unocal is deemed legally responsible for these alleged acts, the reports support the contention that serious human rights violations have occurred in Burma because of the pipeline project. This negates, at least in the short term, much of the argument that economic engagement with Burma will promote the social and economic welfare of its citizenry.

One possible benefit of constructive engagement is the distribution of economic benefits from foreign investment throughout society. One method to attain this goal is to use a socialist approach, in which the government reaps the greatest benefit and redistributes it through social welfare programs. In part due to the tremendous assets expended on the military, the government has failed to provide increased social services to the Burmese people. The Burmese education system has been devastated by the disinvestment in social and human re sources.

Formerly a leader in Southeast Asia in terms of education, Burma has slipped greatly in the last few years. In the mid 1980s, the country boasted an official literacy rate of 78.6%. It appears that Burma has not been able to maintain this figure in the 1990s, with only twenty-five percent of the children that enroll in school completing the mandated five-year educational program and thirty-nine percent of school-age children not attending school at all, largely because of the cost. Theoretically, primary education in Burma is free, but parents are required to pay the costs of textbooks and various supplies and also to make contributions for school improvements; as a result, many families in Burma are unable to utilize the educational system.

Those parents that are able to afford these costs often face additional costs. As the salaries of teachers remain quite low, they sometimes extort additional payments from parents to supplement their income, and, at times, parents must pool together their money to pay the teachers' salaries. Although the status of health care in Burma has improved in the last few years, much more emphasis needs to be placed on health and medical services in the country.

The government has been slow to provide increased services. In 1998, only sixty percent of the Burmese population had any access to primary public health services, the second lowest figure in the region. In remote regions, this figure may be much lower. In addition, doctors are paid meager salaries in Burma, necessitating supplements to their incomes. To achieve this, doctors often engage in private practices apart from their government positions. This not only makes access to health care more expensive, but also tends to alleviate health and medical statistics in Burma, since only figures gathered by health care workers in their official capacity are tallied for official statistics.

Therefore, the true incidence rate of such diseases as AIDS, malaria, and tuberculosis may not be known, causing the health situation in Burma to look more favorable than the real situation.

Despite a doubling in 1997 of the budget for health services, supplies of equipment, drugs, and other medical supplies, the number of treatment facilities, and the amount of money for health care worker salaries remain inadequate to provide sufficient services to the people of Burma. Malnourishment remains a prevalent problem in Burma (approximately forty-three percent of children under five-year old are mildly or moderately malnourished, and approximately sixteen percent are severely malnourished). Access to sanitary drinking water also remains a large problem (approximately sixty percent of the population has access to safe and convenient water sources).

Through the aid of various NGOs, opportunities for Burma to deal effectively with these problems exist. Despite the increased wealth provided to Burma by economic engagement, the government has failed to utilize this wealth and opportunity. The lack of attention focused on the improvement of educational and health services for the people of Burma not only shows a disregard for the welfare of the population, but also provides indications that development and economic integration with the outside world may not prove to be sustainable in the country.

The nature of economic ties with Burma supports an argument of constructive engagement in general, or as applied to certain countries with special circumstances. As noted earlier, constructive engagement must actually be constructive to have a positive effect. Many believe, however, that engagement with Burma actually serves a detrimental purpose in that economic ties with the country-both directly and indirectly support-the military regime.

After a visit to Burma in 1995, Madeline Albright noted the direct and indirect support that economic ties with the country engender for the military government. She commented on the how hard relief organizations in Burma have to work to ensure that relief actually went to the citizens in need, rather than to the government itself. She added: "Democracies should be ashamed to encourage their businesspeople to be `first in Burma' for this would provide the SLORC with the booty it needs to resist mounting pressure for a political opening."

This "booty" consists of not only physical assets, but also the possibility that economic assistance and integration show implicit international acceptance of the military regime's practices and policies. With the military regime's virtually omnipresent presence in the Burmese economy, particularly with regard to foreign investment and trade, economic engagement-touted by many as the vehicle of choice for engendering political and social change in Burma-may not prove "constructive." Rather than providing direct monetary benefits to private citizens, engagement with Burma tends to direct foreign capital and profits to the government, enriching the ruling junta and providing it with the assets necessary to continue the repression of the Burmese people that has become typical over the last thirty-eight years.

APPLICATION OF THE MASSACHUSETTS BURMA LAW

In 1996, Massachusetts became the first state in the nation to take its own stand against the government of Burma. Buoyed by the previous success of anti-apartheid divestiture laws, and the increased public attention focused on the repressive regime of Burma, Massachusetts passed "An Act Regulating State Contracts with Companies Doing Business with or in Burma (Myanmar)." Commonly referred to as the "Burma Law," the Act aimed to severely restrict the commercial ties between Massachusetts's state agencies and any entities economically tied to Burma.

To achieve its aims, the statute prohibits any state agency, state authority, or either house of the Massachusetts legislature from procuring goods or services from entities listed on a "restricted purchase list." The restricted purchase list, established by the secretary of administration and finance, includes all the entities that are deemed to be "doing business with Burma (Myanmar)" and is directed to be updated at least once every three months.

Certain exceptions to the prohibition are contained in the Burma Law, such as an exemption for the situation in which procurement is essential and the only offer or bid for the procurement contract comes from an entity on the restricted purchase list. In addition, a general exemption applies to entities operating in Burma for news-reporting purposes or for purposes of providing goods or services for international telecommunications, and an exemption allows the requisition of certain medical supplies from an entity on the restricted purchase list.

The last exception, covering procurement contracts for which bids from both listed and non-listed entities have been received, allows a covered state entity to purchase from an entity on the restricted purchase list only if "there is no comparable low bid or offer by a person who is not on the restricted purchase list." A "comparable low bid or offer" is defined as a bid or offer that is within ten percent of the lowest received bid or offer. In effect, a ten percent surcharge is added to each bid or offer received from a listed entity, and the procuring agency or authority is then allowed to take the lowest bid or offer. In sum, these exceptions, although well enumerated, seem rather sparse in practice.

EFFECTS OF THE MASSACHUSETTS BURMA LAW

In the two years in which it has been in force, the Burma Law proved to be effective in causing a few companies to pull out of Burma and has, arguably, had much greater indirect effects by focusing public attention on Burma and its repressive regime. Just seven months after enactment of the law, four large companies: Apple Computer, Eastman Kodak, Philips Electronics, and Hewlett-Packard ended their ties with Burma to avoid the Burma Law. Although perhaps not directly attributable to the Burma Law, J. Crew, Levi-Strauss, Motorola, and Walt Disney also pulled out of Burma in 1996, apparently in response to the growing boycott against companies involved with Burma.

In January 1997, PepsiCo, Inc., which had been a major target of a consumer boycott, because of its business in Burma, completely ended its relationship with the country, citing "our assessment of the spirit of current US government foreign policy." Implicit in Pepsi's statement was a concern about impending U.S. sanctions against Burma.

However, because there was debate in Congress as to the appropriate level of sanctions, from limited restrictions on certain business activities (which would have allowed Pepsi to retain its then present involvement in Burma) to complete disengagement, a "wait and see" policy could have been followed by Pepsi. By taking action before federal sanctions passed, it is logical to assume that Pepsi was concerned not only with federal sanctions, but also with the possibility of stricter state and local sanctions influenced by the Burma Law, as well as with the pressure of growing consumer discontent.

William Weld, the Governor of Massachusetts at the time of the passing of the Burma Law, expressed a corollary purpose of the law: "it is my hope that other states and the Congress will follow our example and make a stand for the cause of freedom and democracy around the world." [sic] This goal was satisfied to a certain degree. Since the enactment of the Burma Law in Massachusetts, fifteen cities, including Los Angeles, which passed its selective purchasing law after the Massachusetts law was held unconstitutional, and two countries have passed legislation relating to Burma.

Perhaps most importantly for business interests, the Massachusetts law and its consequent constitutional challenge has aided supporters of boycotts against companies doing business in Burma. Massachusetts state representative, Byron Rushing, the drafter of the Burma Law predicted that if states and localities are unable to use selective purchasing laws: "What you'll see is a lot more individual boycotts of companies." Speaking of such consumer boycotts aimed at members of the National Foreign Trade Council ("NFTC"), the lobbying group suing to invalidate the Burma Law, commented: "Potentially, it could be a very serious problem for some companies."

THE CONSTITUTIONAL CHALLENGE TO THE MASSACHUSETTS BURMA LAW

The enactment of the Burma Law in 1996 received attention in a group of law review articles both attacking and defending the Act's constitutionality. The arguments against constitutional validity focused mainly on Massachusetts's invasion of the exclusive realm of foreign relations power of the federal government. The Supreme Court, in two cases in 1937 and 1942, described the foreign affairs power of the federal government as "Complete power over international affairs is in the national government and is not and cannot be subject to any curtailment or interference on the part of the several states. In respect of all international negotiations and compacts, and in respect of our foreign relations generally, state lines disappear."

It later stated that "In our dealings with the outside world the United States speaks with one voice and acts as one, unembarrassed by the complications as to domestic issues which are inherent in the distribution of political power between the national government and the individual states." A review of these cases indicates that they dealt with the Roosevelt-Litvinoff Agreement between the United States and the Soviet Union, and thus can be largely distinguished from the Massachusetts case.

The Litvinoff Agreement cases concerned the applicability of New York law in relation to application of the Agreement. New York argued that application of the Agreement, which would have entailed implicit validation of the Soviet nationalization of Russian businesses, violated New York public policy. One may therefore argue that the opinion of the Court stands for the proposition that state law may not contravene federal laws or agreements already in place, rather than the proposition that States may never engage in activity that relates to foreign countries.

Possibly the only Supreme Court case that has dealt explicitly with state infringement on the foreign affairs power of the U.S. Government is Zschernig v. Miller. In Zschernig, the Court set a general guideline for the determination of whether a state statute impermissibly interferes with the foreign affairs power of the federal government. The court concluded that the statute under scrutiny "has a direct impact upon foreign relations and may well adversely affect the power of the central government" and "seems to make unavoidable judicial criticism of nations established on a more authoritarian basis than our own." The Court contrasted this determination with Clark v. Allen, which held that a similar California statute was constitutionally valid.

In that case, the Court concluded that the California statute would have only "some incidental or indirect effect in foreign countries" and that "the case seemed to involve no more than a routine reading of foreign laws." Therefore, the general test flowing from Zschernig involves a determination of the degree to which a state action affects foreign countries, and of the degree of scrutiny to which the action subjects foreign countries. A state law implicating the foreign affairs power of the federal government, and not contradicting existing federal legislation or executive action, may be constitutional if it does not too greatly affect foreign countries or unduly inquire into the actions of foreign governments.

Consistent application and explication of this general test-determining what is "too far"-has eluded courts dealing with the foreign affairs power. The Supreme Court has not yet explained the practical application of the Zschernig test, so one may still argue that the Burma Law does not meet the test.

In addition to the argument that the Burma Law does not facially violate the principles enunciated in Zschernig, proponents of the Act offer another theory. They argue that the considerations of the "market participant exception" that are commonly applied to the dormant Commerce Clause should also apply to the Foreign Commerce Clause and the foreign affairs power. Under this theory, considerations such as (1) whether a state acts as a market regulator or purchaser/seller; (2) whether the state action is discriminatory in character; (3) whether a legitimate state interest exists; and (4) the degree to which a state action actually affects commerce potentially remove the negative presumption against the validity of state action in the realm of foreign affairs. In making this argument, Massachusetts argued that if it acts as a market participant, the statute is not discriminatory in nature; the statute has only indirect effects; and a "legitimate local purpose" exists to support the Act.

Furthermore, opponents of the Burma Law, have argued that it is unconstitutional under the dormant Commerce and Foreign Commerce Clauses. Like the dormant Commerce Clause, the dormant Foreign Commerce Clause vests ultimate authority over foreign commerce with the federal government, notwithstanding a lack of affirmative action by the federal government. In addition, commentators have argued that the Court applies stricter standards to Foreign Commerce Clause issues than to traditional interstate commerce issues. The distinction rests on the premise that foreign commerce deserves heightened standards of analysis due to the interest of the federal government in maintaining a unified policy and approach to foreign commercial relations. Thus, any state action that attempts to regulate foreign commerce, absent a proper exception or congressional endorsement of that action, would seem to face an almost insurmountable challenge to its validity.

Given the real and potential problems that legislation such as the Massachusetts act posed for a number of American economic interests, the NFTC, on behalf of its members on the Massachusetts restricted purchase list, brought an action against the Burma Law asserting that:

The Burma Law is invalid because it (1) intrudes on the federal government's exclusive power to regulate foreign affairs; (2) discriminates against and burdens international trade in violation of the Foreign Commerce Clause; and (3) is preempted by a federal statute and an executive order imposing sanctions on Myanmar.

The District Court-A Violation of Foreign Affairs Power The district court briefly discussed the Foreign Commerce Clause and preemption arguments, but did not base the decision on either of these, instead focusing on the alleged violation of the foreign affairs power of the United States federal government. The district court broke its constitutionality analysis into two parts: whether the Constitution grants exclusive foreign affairs power to the federal government, and whether the Massachusetts Burma Law impermissibly burdens U.S.-foreign relations.

In determining that foreign affairs are an exclusive federal power, the court quoted the Supreme Court's warning in Pink: "power over external affairs is not shared by the States; it is vested in the national government exclusively." The district court also used Zschernig as further support for federal exclusivity over foreign affairs, asserting that the net result of Zschernig is that states and localities must defer to the federal government if their actions will affect foreign affairs. The district court also used Zschernig to determine that the Burma Law is burdensome on U.S. foreign relations, pointing to amicus briefs from both the EU and Japan as evidence that the Burma Law violates Zschernig in that it is a non-federal law affecting foreign policy. Specifically quoting the Zschernig test, the district court stated that the Burma Law is unconstitutional because it has more than an "indirect or incidental effect in foreign countries," and a "great potential for disruption or embarrassment."

THE COURT OF APPEALS-IMPINGING ON FOREIGN POWERS OF THE UNITED STATES

In contrast to the relatively sparse district court opinion, the Court of Appeals for the First Circuit touched on nearly all of the major arguments in its de novo review of the lower court opinion. The court of appeals first determined that while the federal government has dominion over foreign affairs, state activities in this arena are not completely excluded. Quoting the Restatement (Third) of Foreign Relations Law of the United States, the court of appeals noted that states may have a role in foreign affairs, so long as their actions do not "impinge upon the authority or the foreign relations of the United States." Thus, the central question is whether the Burma Law impedes the foreign relations of the United States. The court of appeals responded that it did, citing the district court's focus on the disruption the law has caused within the EU and ASEAN, among others.

Massachusetts argued that Zschernig stood for the proposition that a state may lawfully intrude on the federal government's foreign power dominion if the interest is sufficiently strong. However, the court of appeals struck down that argument by stating that Zschernig does not require a balancing test of state and federal interests, but rather that Zschernig essentially creates a foreign powers bar over which the states cannot venture. Massachusetts again tried to evade Zschernig by using Barclays Bank PLC v. Franchise Tax Board as support to limit Zschernig's scope, asserting that Barclays allows only Congress to determine if a state is violating a federal foreign affairs policy. The court struck down this interpretation of Barclays, which, if accepted, would have essentially overruled Zschernig. The 1st Circuit thus upheld Zschernig as good law.

The court of appeals continued to discuss, and subsequently dismiss, further Massachusetts's arguments for the constitutionality of the law, including the market-participation exception. The market-participation exception, which was omitted from discussion by the district court, was briefly analyzed in the decision of the court. The exception, which has been applied only in situations dealing with the dormant domestic Commerce Clause, was succinctly disposed of by the court of appeals, which determined that it explicitly had been limited to specific dormant domestic Commerce Clause instances and should not be extended. The court of appeals also determined that the law violated the Foreign Commerce Clause, mainly through facial discrimination; hindrance of the federal government's ability to speak with one voice; regulation of conduct beyond its borders; and lack of local justification for the law.

Massachusetts's final argument dealt with implicit approval, arguing that because Congress knew of the Burma Law before it passed the federal act and did not condemn the Act, Congress implicitly approved it. The state cited Barclays, in which the Court found that Congress had implicitly permitted the use of the reporting method at issue because it had studied the method and surrounding issue and considered but did not pass legislation that would have overruled the method.

However, the court of appeals dismissed comparisons to Barclays. First, Barclays concerned the Commerce Clause, not the Supremacy Clause. Second, Barclays involved taxation, traditionally a state activity, rather than foreign affairs, traditionally a federal activity. Third, Congress frequently discussed the taxation issue in Barclays, thereby making a determination of implied consent much easier than in this case, in which Massachusetts argued that virtual silence should equal implied consent. Fourth, in Barclays, Congress ultimately was silent when it came to the specific tax issue, whereas in this case Congress passed legislation specifically relating to Burma. The last conclusion leads into the preemption argument, which although it is a small part of the appellate court opinion, this is the main-essentially sole-focus of the Supreme Court.

THE SUPREME COURT-PREEMPTION

Congressional preemption can come in two forms: express preemption, where Congress specifically states its intent to overrule existing law with a federal action, and implied preemption, which is more difficult to discern. The Supreme Court has established that implied congressional intent to preempt exists where (1) a federal statute is so pervasive that it completely occupies the area of law; (2) the federal and state law cross so often that it essentially would be impossible to follow both; or (3) to enforce the state law "stands as an obstacle to the accomplishment and execution of the full purposes and objectives of Congress."

In addition to one of the three requirements above, if the statute regulates an area traditionally occupied by state law, the congressional intent must be "clear and manifest." However, as the court of appeals points out, usually a case for preemption is the reverse situation: a state is interfering in the federal sphere rather than the federal government interfering in the arena of the states. Thus, after determining that Congress implied preemption, it is necessary to examine the state regulation to determine whether it was preempted by federal law.

In Hines v. Davidowitz and its progeny, the Supreme Court established that a state law will be preempted in at least two instances. One, when Congress, through either express or implied intent, indicates that federal law shall "occupy the field," and two, when the state law interferes with a federal law, regardless of whether Congress has occupied the field. In the latter instance, evidence of state interference includes situations in which it is virtually impossible for a party to comply with both the state and federal laws, and where "under the circumstances of a particular case, the challenged state law stands as an obstacle to the accomplishment and execution of the full purposes and objectives of Congress."

The Supreme Court found that the federal act preempted the Burma Law. The Court's reasoning was trifold. First, it found that Congress's intent was to authorize the President to have complete as well as flexible control over sanctions against Burma. The federal act gives the President much power and discretion in determining appropriate interactions with Burma; therefore, the Court stated that "it is just this plenitude of Executive authority that we think controls the issue of preemption."

Second, the Court determined that Congress specifically intended that economic pressure against Burma be limited, and that the Massachusetts statute, by penalizing all companies engaged in business activities in Burma, went beyond the intended congressional mandate. Thus, if Congress exempted a certain business from its actions in Burma, the Burma Law could still penalize the business, a situation the Court found to be unacceptable. Third, the Court found the state law directly conflicted with the President's authority under the federal act. Through an analysis of the Congressional Record, the Court determined that Congress intended for the President to be able to control U.S. sanctions against Burma without state or local interference.

ITS IMPACT ON HUMAN RIGHTS

The Supreme Court's decision is quite anti-climatic. With all of the protests and controversy surrounding this issue, the Court had an opportunity to take a definitive stand on the manner in which this country deals with human rights violators. In reality, however, the effect of the Supreme Court decision is not what is enunciated, but what is omitted. The Court, in focusing only on preemption, permits two different conclusions. The decision might stand for the proposition that the Court is completely eliminating the issue. The Court's decision might mean that state action against foreign human rights violators is so beyond the scope of state action that it does not warrant further discussion.

On the other hand, the Court might have opened the door to state and local foreign affairs actions when the federal government has not yet spoken. Thus, while the Court has answered the question specifically raised by the Burma Law, it has arguably not affected future state and local legislation. This actually could be quite meaningful. Given the relative ease of passing state and local legislation versus federal legislation, state and local laws could affect foreign governments for some time before a federal law preempts them.

This possibility leads back to issues regarding the WTO. In order for the WTO to effectively impact human rights violators, it must have the complete support of its Members. The Supreme Court decision implies that states and localities can erode the ability of the United States to "speak with one voice." This could lead to dissension in the WTO, as well as massive world pressure on the United States to close the loophole. If the purpose of state and local legislation is to eliminate human rights violations in countries such as Burma, then closing the loophole is not the answer.

As seen by the effects of the Burma Law, sub-national entities have the ability to effect change in foreign economies, which can lead to a change in human rights policies. While the WTO is supposed to be engaging in "constructive engagement," it does not seem to be working. Thus, if sub-national entities are not permitted to participate, one could argue that the top priority of the United States and the WTO is not to eliminate human rights violations through free trade but, as the Seattle protesters illustrated, to make money. On the other hand, perhaps procurement agreements-whether local, state or federal-are not the solution to end human rights violations, especially in Burma. Burma, in its more than thirty-eight years of isolationism, is no stranger to a lack of outside investment.

With the exception of the approximately twelve years that the country opened its doors, Burma has existed on its own. However, giving the country a taste of democracy through outside investment, and then withdrawing that investment after only eight years, just places Burma back on the same, albeit harmful, "Burmese way to socialism." How can the wrongs of Burma be rectified? Perhaps free trade, without restrictions and guidelines as envisioned by constructive engagement, is the answer, despite the shortcomings of using economic incentives to improve human rights.

Free trade-in its purest form-may in time give the country the taste of capitalism that it needs to break free from its oppressive regime. While the federal government and Massachusetts had human rights reform in mind when they passed procurement laws, by essentially forcing industry to retreat from Burma, they may have unwittingly reversed any potential positive steps. In fact, they may have sent Burma back into the depths of isolationism, because "Trade is a means to an end, not an end in itself." While recent events seem to indicate that constructive engagement might not work in Burma, it is also clear that sanctions have failed as well.

However, this should not end attempts to reduce the number of human rights violations in Burma. Perhaps the answer is to insure that the international community clearly communicates its condemnation of the Burmese regime through the process of constructive engagement. By using trade not purely as an economic tool as the WTO favors, but as a means to achieve freer societies, we could satisfy multiple obligations: (1) making money through the uninhibited passage of goods across borders; (2) allowing citizens to freely participate in this exchange; and (3) aiding economic development.

Although judicially settled (for the time being), the issue at hand rings loud and clear in this country and abroad. Needless to say, the protests will continue; the matter will brew; and voices will be raised in the future. Perhaps this is not a matter for the courts, or for any one country, but rather a global issue, begging for a multilateral approach and a well-devised system of sanctions. To leave the problem as it is now invites danger and disregards the slow but constant movement towards giving human rights a greater voice.

Wasn't Burma a British colony invaded by the Japanese during the Burmese campaign? So how do you compare "human rights" with "human rights"? Threats of military intervention are screeched at President Mugabe's Zimbabwe. But for the missing monks of Burma, for the murdered citizens of Burma, there is a pounding silence.

There now follows a highly emotional broadcast rant on behalf of the "So What" party. Please note my branded logo at the top of your screen. "Good Evening. Do not adjust your set. As you'll soon realise, I know nothing at all about Burma or about the Burmese people. So What?! Where is Burma-sorry, 'Myanmar'? It's not a little country-50 millions people-far, far away. Have you heard of it? Yeah, right. Wasn't there a war there during the war? World War Two to you, ignoramus! A lot of jungle fighting. Seen any really old black and white films lately? Hero man in jungle with gun. Best friend behind him, enemy thingy in front, grenade thrown, best friend soon dead. Man with gun angry.

The Burmese jungle. Weren't there Japs and Brits involved? Remind me, wasn't Burma a British colony invaded by the Japanese? The something campaign? The Burmese campaign? Correct. Forgotten history. Never learnt history. Funny how learning dates turns out to be vital not boring. When did wars begin, when did they end? Important facts, important things, dates. You can't mess about with beginnings and ends. You're either right or you're wrong. No lottery choosing of numbers is adequate. 1947: Aung San, independence leader, is assassinated. January 1948: Burma gets its independence from Britain. Later, there follow decades of military rule.

August 1988: the Burmese people's pro-democracy revolt, provoked by economic incompetence, ends with at least 3,000 killed by the military regime. August 2007: the removal of fuel subsidies means a 500%-correct, a five-fold-increase in natural gas prices which leads to a doubling of petrol and diesel prices, and bus fares. Poor people use the buses. Burmese people are very poor people, some 'experts' say as poor as 'sub-Saharan Africa', that global euphemism for extreme poverty. In mid-August 2007, peaceful protests against the fuel price increases start on the streets. By September 2007, these protests have turned into mass pro-democracy demonstrations led by thousands of monks. Hundreds of thousands march on the streets of Burmese cities.

'Mandalay', how terribly romantic the name of that city still sounds! But I'm not so keen on ruby-robed Buddhist monks dying there or in Rangoon. Revulsion is not the word. How to describe a sickness inside when it is the involuntary 'Oh' you breathe out, the physical step you take backwards from the television set, your guts emptied. Your stomach pulls you away from watching such pure evil. Walk backwards. Try to rid yourself of ruby-coloured robes and their hidden, discarded, then displayed blood. Alms for the monks? Dead Japanese photographer-but his photo life album will live on. What a thing when the soldiers, they shoot their own people! What a thing when the monks, they become the real opposition to the military!

Half a million Burmese monks and nearly the same amount of soldiers and assorted generals. But who will arm the monks? They only have their Father: the Lord Buddha. Buddhism: probably the most peaceful, peace-loving, peace rendering religion of this sordid little world. The religion that welcomes all. Chant that! A leaving-present from my friends in Cambodia. It sits on top of my book cabinet, sheltered by layers of books on each side, and adorned with orange bead-bracelets. What say you Richard Gere, friend of the Dalai Llama and actor-Buddhist-in-chief of Hollywood? What say all you other actors, actresses, singers, entertainers, models, stars, celebrities, whatevers of the luvvie fraternity? The ones who have stuffed their chanting, charm beads-loving Buddhist credentials down our eyes and ears for the last two decades.

What! Nothing to say now that Buddhist monks are being shot dead on the streets of Burma? What! No airwaves to grab, as Buddhist monks are searched for in their own monasteries, raids by soldiers and police in the middle of the night, monks hauled out of their sacred religious sanctuaries? What! No comfy sofa to chat your internationally important views from, as Buddhist monks are beaten with truncheons and rifle butts and then driven away in vans to detention camps for more beatings and torture? What! No gala opening to spout peace words from, as you stand on the ruby-red carpet as Buddhist monks are disrobed and sent to 'work'? What! No photo opportunity with a neutrally opining 'world leader', as Buddhist monks go into hiding, thousands of police and soldiers swamp and patrol the cities now under curfew?

No. There are no angry words, no anguished chanting, no action from the Buddhist kingdom of Hollywood. They're hunting monks in Burma but-so what?! 'Americans are outraged by the situation in Burma where a military junta has imposed a 19-year reign of fear.' President Bush at the UN General Assembly in September. 'If the monks go against the rules and regulations in the authority of the Buddhist teachings, we will take action under the existing law.' Brigadier General Thura Myint Maung, Burma's minister for religious affairs.

'China hopes that all parties concerned show restraint, resume stability through peaceful means as soon as possible, promote domestic reconciliation and achieve democracy and development.' Wen Jiabao, Chinese prime minister. The UN's Security Council is held in an arm lock by China, Burma's very friendly neighbour, because of China's vested interests in Burma. It probably has nothing to do with Burma's rich deposits of natural gas, oil, and timber, plus their rubies, sapphires and other precious stones. Did you know that 90% of the world's rubies come from Burma?

What a thing when 'international intervention' is effectively reduced to threatening a country with the unsuccessful staging of 'their' Olympic Games! What sports do you guys play? What 'games' are you holding? Right! We don't like you and we're not going! We're going to play with ourselves. A boycott of the Olympic Games in 2008 will only works if as many as possible include themselves out. The militarisation of a religion is a weirdly beautiful thing to behold. Of course! The generals who 'rule' Burma from their new jungle city of Naypyidaw (pronounce that, mate, spell that!) must be Buddhists, too, surely? What's it like to issue the command to round up, terrify, beat, torture, shoot, kill, the same men of the cloth that you go to for spiritual peace and harmony?

How many soldiers are Buddhists in a country of citizens held hostage by a peace-wielding, strait-jacketing religion? Do soldiers put food in a monk's alms bowl? Do monks continue to accept food given by a soldier? Devoted to a religion or revolt for a revolution: which would you choose? The world is overrun by generals. Who does give them their generally available medals for killing people? What a waste of metal, ribbons and braiding! What do they do, what have they done, to deserve their medallions?

Generals, it appears to me, are fast becoming the most despised people of our age. They are bringing the honourable institution of the army into gross disrepute. And what about Aung San Suu Kyi? What about her? Pronounced: 'Hang Sang Sue Chi', she's Daddy's little independent daughter-heroine, all peace, all non-violence, married to an Ox-FORD man, pin up poster girl (aged 62) for the world's lefties sunning themselves in LA Land. How is the house-sitting going? Nice lakeside vistas. What did you talk to that pleasant UN envoy, Mr Ibrahim Gambari, about? No communicating.

And now the generals have shut down the internet, having crushed the protesters, killed hundreds, homing in on the 'leaders' of the demonstrations and those who dared to applaud them, now they want to shut up the bloggers, black out the photographs, freeze the videos, cut off the mobiles, stop the texts, down the phone lines. End all messaging now or die. How do you compare 'human rights' with 'human rights'? What I mean is that the West says: 'Mugabe' commits 'human rights violations' in Zimbabwe, and that the empty supermarket shelves and the hyperinflation prove that. Zimbabwe holds elections, but, apparently, there is 'no democracy'.

But in the same breath, with only a small pause for a commercial break, the West goes on to say that the murder of hundreds of Burmese people by their own military and the vicious crackdown on little acts of freedom that is now taking place are also 'human rights issues'. Senior General Than Shwe does not hold elections. There is no democracy in Burma. What now constitutes human rights violations in our neo-modern world? Threats of military intervention are screeched at President Mugabe's Zimbabwe.

But for the missing monks of Burma, for the murdered citizens of Burma, there is a pounding silence. Dialogue is wanted by the West when the generals get round to wanting it. Is there a Level of Unacceptability Index for Human Rights Issues? If there isn't, there should be. Although that would imply that some human rights violations are acceptable! Where 'Mugabe' would figure on such an index compared to the obscenities the world witnesses in Burma, I leave you to calculate.

5

Buddhism and Human Rights
The Problem

The United Nations Universal Declaration of Human Rights of 1948 raises the problem of how the concepts of human rights are compatible with the cultures and practices of those civilizations where the concept has not taken a firm root. The concept of human rights, as expressed in the UN Declaration, is regarded as alien, or as an imposition of foreign, namely Western, powers on the lives and minds of non-Western people whose cultural development does not go along the same path trodden by the West. In the case of Thailand (formerly Siam), which was not directly colonized by any Western powers, the concept is also generally regarded as foreign, and the Thai word for human rights - Sitthi Manussayachon - still rings an unfamiliar sound.

For most Thais, the word simply conjures up the image of someone who disregard the traditional pattern of compromise and harmonization of social relations; someone, that is, who is quite out of touch with the traditional Thai mores. However, the mores themselves are changing. As the country is surging toward industrialization, and as the people are ever estranged from the traditional way of living, more Thais are beginning to realize the need for human rights. This is well attested by the Black May incident of 1993, when scores of Thais lost their lives fighting for democracy against the army.

The discourse of Thai people is beginning to presuppose the basic premises of human rights, even though these are not spelled out explicitly. The situation is that of a dynamic where traditional mores are being left behind and the people are groping for a new one. This situation, then, raises, the problem of how to accommodate human rights within the constitutive beliefs of Thai culture. Since the core of Thai beliefs is represented by Buddhism, a problem then ensues concerning how to reconcile the religion and its way of life with the new mores, part of which is the conception and actualization of human rights.

In this chapter I shall investigate the situation, comparing and contrasting two famous thinkers in contemporary Thailand - Sulak Sivaraksa and Phra Dhammapidok (Prayudh Prayutto). The former is a noted scholar of political philosophy and social critic who has often been given a hard time by power holders for his daring outspokenness and truth telling. The latter is a Buddhist monk and scholar. He is an author of a book, Buddhadhamma, which is widely recognized in Thailand as one of the most lucid expositions of the Buddha's teaching. His thoughts on Buddhist views on various aspects of life are very well respected. Being a respected monk, he has never been in trouble with the authorities.

Although both are steeped in the Thai Theravada tradition, however, their views on the role of Buddhism regarding problems of society, including that of human rights, diverge in a significant way. While Sulak favors a kind of socially engaged Buddhism in which the religion is seen as an instrument toward betterment of the society in terms of justice, democracy and respect for human rights, Prayudh Prayutto tends to be more conservative, and for him Buddhism seems to be more concerned with the cessation of suffering at the individual level rather than trying to improve society at large. I shall try to show in this chapter how both thinkers deal with the problem of the relation between Buddhism and human rights, accentuating the key problem of the relationship of Buddhism toward its social environment.

For more than three decades Sulak Sivaraksa has been a leading voice of conscience for the Thai people. His continual and courageous criticisms of successive unjust regimes have given him a lot of trouble with the authorities. During the time when seemingly all sectors of the Thai society were effectively silenced by totalitarian regimes, his was the sole voice raised against them, aiming at raising the awareness in Thai people of the true meaning of democracy and justice. Sulak calls for a return to the real roots of the Thais, and examination of imported Western values and technologies.

He rails against Western educated intellectuals in his society who appear to worship Western techniques and ways of thinking without really understanding the roots and historical contexts of those techniques and thinking. That is, he persistently criticizes the normal attitude among Thai bureaucratic planners who blindly adopt the Western models without critically examining whether they really lead to "good life." He calls for a return to the traditional pattern of Thai life. This call, however, does not mean he is advocating a nostalgic glorification of the past. In fact he has many stinging words directed against aspects of Thai history. But the call is part of his campaign against the rampant consumerism in Thailand today. For him Thais should abandon consumerism and return to their indigenous culture with a strong critical attitude.

Sulak thinks that Buddhism is anything but a religion devoted solely to an individual search for salvation with no regard for the social environment within which such search takes place. He is often vehement against monks who abandon the true teaching of Buddhism and become mere instruments of power wielders to legitimize their rules. In Sassana Kap Sangkhom Thai, one of Sulak's most important works, he writes:

The saying that Buddhism is concerned only with individual salvation is a complete neglect of its basic principle, that is, the denial that individual soul exists. The Buddha's teaching concerns only individuals, but it is also involved with something wider, which cannot be other than the society and politics. And this is what the Buddha often said in the Pali

canon, which is the main scripture of the Theravada tradition.
. The attempt to understand Buddhism without its relations to
the society is an error. Buddhism is an attempt to relate with
the individual's serious disease. It is primarily a way to defeat
limitations of the *atta* in a way that brings in involvement with
the social and the political. Until Buddhists are well aware of
this fact, their adherence of Buddhism cannot help them get
rid of their *attâ*.

That is, the supreme goal of Theravada Buddhism,
attainment of the state of extinguishment of all defilements or
nibbana (Sanskrit, nirvana), is not possible if the Buddhist cuts
himself or herself out of his or her involvement with the social
and the political, according to Sulak. Since Buddhism teaches
that existence of a self is an illusion, to try to proceed to *nibbana*
by getting this individual self of mine to arrive at salvation is
thus a contradiction. Rather one must be aware that one's own
self is indistinguishable from that of all others, and in fact that
there is no underlying self behind the momentary
consciousnesses which are constantly in flux.

This means for Sulak that an individual must relate to
others, and any attempt to cut oneself off from such relation
is a presupposition of an individual self in the first place. This
idea of the impossibility of attaining *nibbana* without
dissolution of the individual self and relation toward others,
then, is the core of Sulak's view on the relation between
Buddhism and human rights.

The ideal form of society is one where its members are all
free from self attachments. However, Sulak realizes that such a
society is only an ideal, and Buddhism has to compromise with
its social environment in order that its teachings be accessible to
the outer circle. That is, the original Buddhist community, which
at first consisted only of arahants, later included more laypeople
so that its teachings could reach them and change them for the
better. Thus the ideal community of the selfless arahants form
an ideal, or a standard on which ethical and moral judgement of
lay societies are based. Thus such violations of human rights
as slavery, torture, etc. could only be a movement in the

opposite direction to the ideal, for these violations all result from strong attachment to the self of the violators of human rights.

Without any attachment to the individual self, without the consciousness of "Me" and "Mine" as Bhikkhu Buddhadasa teaches, there is no motive to violate any of the rights enshrined in the UN Declaration. Instead, respect for human rights follows naturally from such non-attachment. Nevertheless, for Sulak it is not enough for setting the ideal ethical standard which can be used to evaluate social actions. There must be political action by the ruler to actualize and to enforce human rights.

According to Sulak, the action of the political ruler is directly related to the well-being of the people as a whole. Sulak states that the political ruler and the people are two parts of a tripartite relation, whose remaining part is the Sangha community. The three parts all necessarily depend on one another and have duties toward one another. The king, or the political ruler, has the duty to care for the well being of the Sangha and the people, as well as protect them from harm and danger. The Sangha, on the other hand, has the duty to teach the Dhamma to the king and the people, and to remain steadfast as the moral exemplar. The people, then, have the duty to remain righteous and pay allegiance to the king and the Sangha.

If one part, on the other hand, does not follow the path of righteousness, for example, if the king is unjust, or if the Sangha does not follow the teaching of the Buddha, then serious calamities occur. The tripartite relation theory stems from the time of Emperor Asoka, who reigned as a Dhammaraja, the supreme benefactor and upholder of the Buddhist religion. According to Sulak, It is true that the Sangha community has never been as powerful as the Western clergy. It never has as much power. But it has a countervailing power. In what way? In legitimacy and righteousness. If the king does not follow the dhamma, he is the adhammarâja, and is thus vulnerable to destruction. But if he is a dhammaraja, then he will depend on the Sangha community. The Sangha acts as one who looks after the people. It teaches the people to pay respect to the dhammaraja. It is a countervailing force against the king, preventing him from being too harsh on them. It strives for moderation.

Thus in ancient times there were a counterbalance to absolute monarchy. The monarch has to remain on the path of righteousness; otherwise he would not receive legitimacy from the Sangha, and his overthrow would then be legitimate. The idea, however, is hardly applicable in the present time, for the political ruler of contemporary Thailand is hardly a model of the Dhammaraja ruler:

I would like to tell you about the present situation. I would like to say that in the present society, the tripartite dependency does not work any more, especially after the overthrow of absolute monarchy in BE 2475. Those who came to power, including the original perpetrators in BE 2475, all came to power through unscrupulous means. No matter how well intentioned they were, they came to power through betrayal and unjust seizure of power with no trace of legitimacy...They came in and abolished the existing constitution, and set up a committee to draft a new one. Then there would be an election.

All these are merely means to legitimize the power wielders themselves. These people cite their upholding of the monarchical institution, because people still believe that this institution is the source of legitimacy. People still believe that the king is still dhammaraja. The political power holders want the monarchical institution to support them.

In Sulak's eyes, the legitimacy of the monarch as Dhammaraja in Siam stopped with the overthrow of absolute monarchy and founding of representative democracy in 1932. However, the holders of political power since then were almost all unjust and unrighteous, so there has been no real Dhammaraja in the country since the founding of democracy. This point is the motif behind Sulak's repeated criticisms of all those who come to power in Thailand through the unjust means of coup d'etat.

For Sulak, these means of coming to power are gross violations of human rights, for the military who usurp legitimate power based on the will of the people do not respect the principle of democratic will nor do they have any sense of human dignity and rights as, for example, enshrined in the UN Declaration. The Dhammaraja is the ruler who is steadfast in the path of justice and righteousness. He acts in accordance with the Dhamma, which is the way the nature of thing is. To act contrary to the Dhamma, therefore, would be to act in a way that is contrary to nature. Calamities in various forms result. Thus, the contemporary rulers of Thailand, even though they do not claim to be kings, nonetheless have to act in accordance with the Dhamma. Otherwise they would lose all their legitimate claims to power, and are thus subject to criticisms, censure and overthrow.

For Sulak, the concept of human rights is clearly indigenous to traditional Thai culture, of which Theravada Buddhism is an essential part, and it is ironically the imposition of Western ideas that result in loss of such rights in contemporary Thailand. As I have already mentioned, Sulak views the traditional Thai village life as where the quintessentially Thai identity and values lie. This view is the motive behind Sulak's repeated criticisms of consumerism. In the traditional Thai life, there were also some cases of injustice and violations of human rights, to be sure. But these are small scale and tempered by the adherence to the Buddhist teaching by all parts of the society.

On the other hand, the imposition of the ideas of consumerism, greed and exploitation of the natural environment, which Sulak quite rightly regards as originating from the West, is perpetrated by power holders who are unrighteous and who are mere pawns of Western governments and multinational corporations. The imposition of these Western ideas, then, is a symptom of Thailand's loss of identity due to their misconception that whatever is "Western" is better and more desirable than the traditional way.

The way of life of the traditional village is destroyed, resulting in Thais being alienated from them. Gross violations of human rights follow from the acts of these unrighteous governments. Since greed and selfishness underlie the power holders' attitudes, it is natural for Sulak to see that human rights suffer as a result of the imposition of Western ideas rather than that human rights result because of such imposition. According to Sulak Sivaraksa, then, the relation between Buddhism and human rights is such that respect for the latter is already there in the teaching of Buddhism.

Since Buddhism teaches non-existence of the individual self concerns for others and dissolution of selfish attitudes naturally follow. Human rights for Sulak are not only the preserve of the West; on the contrary, Sulak's repeated criticisms of the West show that blindly following the Western model results in loss of human rights. Thus what is needed is not such blind following, but a critical attitude and a deep respect of one's own cultural heritage. For Sulak genuine respect for human rights would not be possible if Thais still look down on their heritage and uncritically accept anything coming from the West without seeing its potential danger.

IN PHRA DHAMMAPIDOK

In one of his lectures given to the lay audience on "Education for Peace," Phra Dhammapidok outlines some of his ideas on the relation between Buddhism and its social environment as follows:

In order to solve this problem (i.e., loss of peace) Buddhism teaches that we need to attend to the root cause. Everything depends on its cause. An effect is a result of a cause. We need to see where the cause is. But here there are so many causes.

Why are people making war? Because they hate each other or sometimes their interests come into conflict. Sometimes it's because their views are different...They are attached to the view that their own particular religion is the best; anyone else's are all bad. These are all the world's problems. In sum, Buddhism teaches that these problems are all caused inside the minds of human beings. Before they are expressed externally as killing, using weapons, throwing grenades, using planes to bomb, etc., these actions must originate in the mind first. Human beings need to intend before they act. Hence the problem first arises in the mind.

The problem arises in the mind. What does the mind contain? It contains the knot of the problem for which the Buddha already gave a principle. We are talking simply and clearly, so we need some Buddhist terms. They are packed with meanings. If we use ordinary people's language we will have to talk for a long time. But if we use the Buddhist terms we need only three of them. They represent almost everything. The Buddhist terms indicating the root causes inside the mind which compel humans to act in ways that are recognized as loss of peace are: (1) Tanha (desire), (2) Mana (self-aggrandizement), and (3) Ditthi (belief, attachment to one's viewpoint).

These ideas represent almost all of Phra Dhammapidok's view on the relation between Buddhism and its social environment. The problem, according to him, springs originally from inside the mind and is ultimately solvable only by uprooting these causes. Thus for him the role of education is of paramount importance, for it alone is capable of going inside the mind to change it for the better. It is not surprising, then, that he is intensely concerned with the problem of education, and has written numerous books and given countless lectures on the role of education.

For him education does not limit itself only to the level of self perfection leading ultimately to *nibbana*; he also points out various shortcomings in the education system of modem Thailand. Here is where his thought is most likely to be in the category of social criticism. However, the most important role of education is none other than the perfection of an individual in such a way that he realizes the Dhamma and gets rid of all defilements, or at least tries to improve him according to the Buddha's teaching the best he or she can.

Nevertheless, his main point regarding the relation between Buddhism and society is clear. Since society is composed of individuals, the only way that social problems can be solved in such a way that no problems could arise any further is that all individuals in that society attain the state of selflessness. Effort by individuals at education and self perfection counts for the most in his view. Phra Dhammapidok's idea on the primary importance of mental motivation figures prominently in his view on human rights. In a lecture given at the 1993 Parliament of the World's Religions in Chicago, he presents his view on the issue, which, due to its importance, I am quoting here in full:

The concept of human rights arose from a historical background of division, segregation and competition. Human rights are a necessary protection from aggression from other parties, an answer to a negative situation: when humanity is plagued by aggression and contention, it is necessary to devise some protection from aggression. Human rights have led to the establishment of laws and regulations devised to try to maintain harmony within human society. Within developed countries these qualities are very effective and as such are very useful to the global situation.

While human rights are useful within the environment of dissension, they are not very far reaching. They are only a compromise. Compromise is not capable of leading human beings to true unity and harmony. Compromise is a situation in which each side agrees to give in a little to the other in order to attain some mutual benefit. A quality of force or mental resignation is involved. As long as human beings do not outgrow their old ways of thinking, it will be impossible to bring about true peace in the world. The concept of human rights is useful in an age of fighting and contention, or when human thinking is divisive and separatist, but is not enough to lead humanity to true peace and harmony.

In essence, the concept of human rights has three major flaws:

Firstly, the concepts themselves are flawed. They have resulted from a background and basic attitude of division and segregation, struggle and contention. This situation led to an attempt to assure self-preservation and protect mutual interests, which became human rights. Human rights must be obtained through demand.

Secondly, human rights are a convention, they are a purely human invention and do not exist as a natural condition. They are not "natural rights." Being a human invention, they do not have any firm and lasting foundation of truth. They must be supported by laws and they must be accepted by all parties in order to work. They are not lasting. If human rights are to be lasting and firm they must be connected to natural reality. In order for human rights to be founded on natural reality, human mentality must be developed to a stage where people are prepared to preserve human rights. Only in this way will human rights be sustainable.

This leads us to the third flaw of the concept of human rights, which is that it is a purely social convention, dealing with social behaviour. It does not consider the quality of mental motivation within the individual. Social behaviour must always be connected to mental motivation, which is both the instigator and the guiding influence of that behaviour. If the mental foundation is faulty, or there is not a good foundation within the mind, then instead of leading to a good result, the result will be more and more contention.

The basic idea is clear. Human rights, according to Phra Dhammapidok, are results of contention among individuals. Thus at best they represent a way of living together which is not optimal. Pure motivation, which is not based on hatred or contentious feelings, is necessary to achieve the ideal, and activists who struggle for human rights would not be moving toward the ideal if their inner motivation is not pure. There is a gap between the ideal community and one where human rights are necessary. Since human rights, for Phra Dhammapidok, are but social invention, they are contingent and not necessary for the ideal community. In such a community, where hatred and divisiveness is not known, there is no need for human rights.

These rights are necessary when individuals are not free from divisiveness and delusion; they form a basis of laws, for example. But it seems that for him human rights are superseded when the community has developed and achieved the state of the ideal. Right social regulations, according to Phra

Dhammapidok, consist of those which promote the spiritual development of the individual. He distinguishes between the Dharma, which is natural law, and Vinaya, which is human law. Since human rights serve to secure peace and order for a society, a safeguard against unbridled aggression, they could be regarded as a form of the Vinaya.

However, the latter derives its value only from its being the means toward realization of the Dharma or natural law, which for him means "man's internal independence and freedom." The role of the others is also necessary, for the monk could attain the supreme end only through material help provided by others. An orderly and peaceful society is a necessary condition for the monk to attain such state. On the other hand, the monk who realizes the true Dharma is of tremendous help to the others in showing them the Path.

The concept of human rights in Phra Dhammapidok's view is also related with that of the social kamma (Sanskrit, karma). This is the kamma committed by the society as a whole. When a society allows itself to be led by an unjust and unrighteous dictator, for example, it incurs the social kamma and has to pay for the consequences. The dictator may even not be a person, but an idea, for example consumerism. Thus a consumerist society, in which its members do not critically reflect on the danger of the idea, incurs a social kamma. Thus, in the same manner as the individual kamma is overcome when the individual follows the path leading to Enlightenment, at the social level the same is the case when the society as a whole follows the same path. Phra Dhammapidok thinks that this is a rationale in Buddhism for an endorsement of social action. In order to cure a society suffering from bad social kamma, a kind of social action aiming at creating a favorable condition necessary for spiritual development of individuals is required.

In sum, Phra Dhammapidok's view on Buddhism and human rights is that he sees the latter as resulting from divisiveness and contentions among individuals, which are not favorable toward realization of individual perfection. This does not mean, however, that for him human rights have no role to play at all. On the contrary, in order that individual perfection be possible at all, the external environment must be favorable, and for that to be so the society, it seems, need to endorse human rights.

He is not clear, however, on the question of whether the concept of human rights are impositions from the West, but presumably this point does not matter much for him. If a community is full of divisiveness, then a conception of human rights is necessary, and this seems to be the case for any community. Though the rights are necessary, they are never sufficient, and he is at pains to point out that if they are applied without the right conditions of the mind, then they will only lead the people astray, and will not be effective toward realizing the perfection at all. The right condition of the mind is then of primary importance.

A COMPARISON AND CONTRAST

While there are obvious agreements on many issues, a basic difference between Sulak and Phra Dhammapidok on the nature of Buddhism and human rights is clear. While Sulak views human rights as an integral part of the end of Buddhism, Phra Dhammapidok views them as merely a means. It can be said that both Sulak and Phra Dhammapidok are examples of how Thais cope with the problem of how best to adapt their belief system in the face of contemporary developments. The two, it appears, go different ways. The difference seems to come from the fact that both perhaps view the nature of human rights differently. Sulak views them as constitutive of the ideal end of Buddhism; Phra Dhammapidok believes they are symptoms of divisiveness.

Perhaps Sulak thinks that the effect of human rights is primary. That is, when the society is just and righteous, there is naturally a respect for human rights already. The legal or political aspect of such rights, as well as their enforcement, would not be necessary and would then be ignored. On the other hand, Phra Dhammapidok seems to think that human rights are inseparable from their legal and political aspect. That is, they are parts and parcels of procedural justice. Since law and politics are only needed when individuals are not enlightened, human rights then are not part of the ideal community.

Who is right, then? I am afraid that that would be out of the scope of this chapter. Perhaps this question should not be raised at all. The question, nonetheless, accentuates the problematic of the relationship between Buddhism and its social environment. Thus an advantage of the question is that we now appreciate its inherent difficulty more fully, and realize that a lot more work and thinking needs to be done before an answer can be glimpsed. As has been often noted, the concept of "human rights" tends to be based on modern Western European assumptions that, to a large extent, can be traced to earlier Judeo-Christian and Greco-Roman concepts; assumptions that are alien to many, if not all, of the innumerable Buddhist traditions.

It is not so often noted that it is difficult, if not impossible, to make sense of the concept of human rights - as opposed to some of the particular items that are lumped together under that rubric - within the common law tradition that prevails in England, in the English speaking nations of North America, in the British Commonwealth, and in other countries whose political and judicial institutions have been inherited from England, a legal tradition that can be traced back without interruption to feudal practices and that is based on centuries of judicial precedents, not on rational deductions drawn from positive legislation or abstract principles.

As Eugene Kamenka has pointed out:

The belief in human rights as a great moral value, a UNESCO symposium characteristically insists, is not a specifically western or Judeo-Christian contribution to the world. It is to be found in all the great moral documents of mankind, and in all its aspirations since primitive times. If the concept of human rights is to have any specific meaning, is to be seen as implying a view of man and society, this is untrue.

The concept of human rights is a historical product which evolves in Europe, out of foundations in Christianity, Stoicism and Roman law with its *jus gentium*, but which gains force and direction only with the contractual and pluralist nature of European feudalism, church struggles, the rise of Protestantism and of cities. It sees society as an association of individuals, as founded - logically or historically - on a contract between them, and it elevates the individual human person and his freedom and happiness to be the goal and end of all human association. In the vast majority of human societies, in time and space, until very recently such a view of human society would have been hotly contested; indeed, most cultures and languages would not have had the words in which to express it plausibly.

Of course, all human societies have had a concept of suffering and most of them have had a concept of human worth, of justice, of fair dealing, of meeting one's obligations. But the society of the great seventeenth- and eighteenth-century social contract theorists, the society of the right-and-duty-bearing individual standing in external "contractual" association with other right-and-duty-bearing individuals, the society which the great German sociologist, Ferdinand Tonnies, called the Gesellschaft, is a modern, European phenomenon. The Greeks, like the Chinese, saw man in a familial, social and cosmic setting; and their concern was not with rights but with duties, and with balance, harmony, moira, dikee and jus, a balance that transcended the individual, that made society part of a great cosmic pattern and that rested on a network of obligations, not just to individuals but to forces and institutions, human and divine, that shaped and transcended such individuals. Men in pre-modern societies lived in a Gemeinschaft that saw man as part of a social organism, a structured community based on a common religious tradition, a hierarchy of power, a network of mutual obligations that made and shaped men, rather than served them. Even in Roman law as the Romans and their immediate successors knew it, there was a concept of right, and certainly of duties - but no concept of rights.

The common law, like the Roman law, has a concept of right, and a concept of duty, but it has no concept of rights in general, of rights in the abstract. And the Buddhist tradition, like those of the classic Greeks and the Chinese, evolved within a Gemeinschaft, within a community of monks and nuns and householders, or, more precisely, it evolved within a community that consists of all the myriad of interdependent beings. As Masao Abe tells us:

The Buddhist view of "human rights" is significantly different from that found in the Western tradition. Strictly speaking, the exact equivalent of the phrase "human rights" in the Western sense cannot be found anywhere in Buddhist literature. In the Western notion of "human rights," "rights" are understood as pertaining only to humans; nonhuman creatures are either excluded or at most regarded as peripheral and secondary. "Human rights" are understood not from the nonhuman or wider-than-human point of view but only from the human point of view - an anthropocentric view of human rights.

By marked contrast, in Buddhism a human being is not grasped only from the human point of view, that is, not simply on an anthropocentric basis, but on a much broader trans-homocentric, cosmological basis. More concretely, in Buddhism human beings are grasped as part of all sentient beings or even as a part of all beings, sentient and non sentient, because both human and nonhuman beings are equally subject to transiency or impermanency. (That nothing is permanent is a basic Buddhist principle.) If this universal impermanency that is common to both human and nonhuman beings is done away with, the problem of life and death peculiar to human existence cannot be properly resolved. Both the Buddhist understanding of human suffering and its way of salvation are rooted in this trans-anthropocentric, cosmological dimension.

As one who aspires to follow the Buddha Dharma and who has studied and practiced and taught the common law for these last forty years, it strikes me that there is at least one reason that explains why neither of my traditions makes use of the concept of human rights: both traditions are of practices that are concerned with arriving at a goal starting from the way things are right here, right now in all of their interdependent complexity, not starting from philosophical speculations as to how things must - or should - be in a radically simpler world without much ambiguity.

The goal in this chapter is to explain why the concept of human rights is not likely to be useful in either following the Buddha Dharma or in practicing of the common law. The follower of the Dharma and the common law practitioner are both concerned with the particular, with this particular case, right here, right now; the concept of human rights, on the other hand, is so abstract and general, and so incoherent, that it is not likely to lead to right understanding, or even to right conduct, in terms of either practice. More importantly, both the follower of the Dharma and the practitioner of the common law are concerned with processes - with practices, with the flow of particular interrelated moments - in a world that is continually in flux and that has no room for unchanging absolutes like "human rights" that are deduced by a rigidly ahistorical rationality.

I should make clear, however, that it is not my intent to denigrate the interest that is sought to be protected by the proclamation of any particular "human right." It would be hard for anyone in our Western society, and especially for one who tries to follow the Buddha Dharma, to oppose the protection of most of those interests. Nor am I raising objections to the use of the term "human rights" as a convenient phrase to refer to complex desiderata or as a rhetorical device or skillful means for advocating right conduct on the part of those who govern others, even though I doubt that talk of human rights is very skillful when addressed to those, like the vast majority of Buddhists, who are not party to the traditions of Western Europe.

The following remark by an international lawyer and diplomat from Thailand who received his legal training in the West, strikes me as a very sensible approach to human rights for one within the Buddhist tradition:

We live in a multicultural world, where the light in which a person sees cultural values depends on the social environments to which he is accustomed. To admit the reality of such a wholesome world is a giant step toward a closer appreciation of a more tolerable concept of human rights. If we are aware that a world of distinct cultures exists and eventually accept it, we will recognize and ultimately tolerate different cultural values and therefore essentially different concepts of human rights. After all, the international instruments proclaiming the Rights of Man or the International Covenants of Human Rights merely incorporate the views and concepts advocated by the authors and draftsmen of those instruments, who have invariably been trained in Western or European legal traditions.

It is, in this spirit that to suggest in this chapter that, though followers of Buddhist traditions do value most, if not all, of the interests underlying the rhetoric of human rights, they may not have much use for the label itself, which is, after all, a product of the traditions of Western Europe and the parochial histories of that region. There is little that is wrong, and much that is right, with the Western European concept of "human rights" when that concept is viewed from within that tradition; but problems arise when efforts are made to impose that concept with all its Western trimmings upon traditions - like those of Buddhism - that have quite different concepts, if only because they have quite different histories.

6

A Coherent Concept

Although the concept of human rights is the product of recent historical processes, such rights are often invoked as if they were timeless absolutes discoverable either by rational thought or by checking to see if they are listed in various declarations of the United Nations, and in particular in that body's "Universal Declaration of Human Rights." Viewed in the latter fashion, the listing of rights seems to have much in common with the list that Borges reports appeared in a Chinese encyclopedia, for the "rights" listed in the Declaration seem to comprise little more than a disparate aggregation of claims, privileges, powers, and immunities that are not connected to one and other in any coherent fashion. A sampling of the various rights proclaimed by the Universal Declaration of Human Rights should suffice to make this point clear.

Article 1:

All human beings are born free and equal in dignity and rights. They are endowed with reason and conscience and should act towards one another in a spirit of brotherhood.

Article 8:

Everyone has the right to an effective remedy by the competent national tribunals for acts violating the fundamental rights granted him by the constitution or by law.

Article 10:

Everyone is entitled in full equality to a fair and public hearing by an independent and impartial tribunal, in the determination of his rights and obligations and of any criminal charge against him.

Article 16:

1. Men and women of full age, without any limitation due to race, nationality or religion, have the right to marry and found a family. They are entitled to equal rights as to marriage, during marriage and at its dissolution.
2. Marriage shall be entered into only with the free and full consent of the intending spouses.
3. The family is the natural and fundamental group unit of society and is entitled to protection by society and the state.

Article 17:

1. Everyone has the right to own property alone as well as in association with others.
2. No one shall be arbitrarily deprived of his property.

Article 18:

Everyone has the right to freedom of thought, conscience and religion; this right includes freedom to change his religion or belief, and freedom, either alone or in community with others and in public or private, to manifest his religion or belief in teaching, practice, worship and observance.

Article 21:

1. Everyone has the right to take part in the government of his country, directly or through freely chosen representatives.
2. Everyone has the right of equal access to the public service in his country.
3. The will of the people shall be the basis of the authority of government; this shall be expressed in periodic and genuine elections which shall be by universal and equal

suffrage and shall be held by secret vote or by equivalent free voting procedures.

Article 23:

1. Everyone has the right to work, to free choice of employment, to just and favorable conditions of work and to protection against unemployment.
2. Everyone, without any discrimination, has the right to equal pay for equal work.
3. Everyone who works has the right to just and favorable remuneration ensuring for himself and his family an existence worthy of human dignity, and supplemented, if necessary, by other means of social protection.
4. Everyone has the right to join trade unions for the protection of his interests.

Article 25:

1. Everyone has a right to a standard of living adequate for the health and well-being of himself and of his family, including food, clothing, housing and medical care and necessary social services, and the right to security in the event of unemployment, sickness, disability, widowhood, old age or other lack of livelihood in circumstances beyond his control.
2. Motherhood and childhood are entitled to special care and assistance. All children, whether born in or out of wedlock, shall enjoy the same social protection.

Article 26:

1. Everyone has the right to education. Education shall be free, at least in the elementary and fundamental stages. Elementary education shall be compulsory. Technical and professional education shall be generally available and higher education shall be equally accessible to all on the basis of merit.
2. Education shall be directed to the full development of the human personality and to the strengthening of respect for human rights and fundamental freedoms. It shall

promote understanding, tolerance and friendship among all nations, racial or religious groups, and shall further the activities of the United Nations for the maintenance of peace.

3. Parents have a prior right to choose the kind of education that shall be given to their children.

Now what is one to make of this congeries of "rights?" Certainly it is apparent when one examines them, even in a cursory fashion, that many of them presuppose the existence of social institutions - such as trade unions and professional education and the United Nations itself - that did not exist at the time of the historical Buddha (or at the time of the founding of the common law, for that matter) and that clearly, however important they may be for particular persons at particular times, are not central, or perhaps even germane, to the Buddha's teachings.

Some of these postulated institutions, such as trade unions or the individual ownership of "property," may not even be consistent with the organization of modern societies in accordance with Buddhist teachings. Thus, for example, the division of a community, the Gemeinschaft, into two antagonistic groups of "labor" and "management" does not seem to be in accord with the Buddha's teachings and the idea of abstracting this cup and this field, and so forth, into an intangible undifferentiated sort of object called "property" that is subject to being "owned" by an individual who can do with it as he wishes, quite without regard to that individual's relations with the greater community, also seems far removed from anything that the Buddha taught.

It is also apparent that the language of the Declaration is a peculiar mix of vagueness and specificity, which can perhaps be explained by the exigencies of negotiating an agreement among parties who were not really in agreement about its terms, or even about the rights that it should protect, though it hardly seems appropriate in the definitive declaration of the fundamental and universal rights that supposedly are possessed by everyone, or at least everyone whom we classify as human.

In particular, from the standpoint of a common lawyer, there is the troublesome vagueness about whoever it is against whom the rights listed in the Declaration are asserted, and about the specific nature of the rights. Thus it is all very well to say that everyone has the right to work, but exactly who is supposed to be the employer? And exactly what is the work that is being claimed? Of course, one can say that the rights are asserted against the state, or against society, but that does not quite make sense to one brought up in the common law tradition when there is no means of enforcing, or even specifying the exact content of, those rights.

One of the major maxims that have influenced the development of the common law is *ubi jus, ibi remedium,* "where there is a right there is a remedy." Although this maxim is often used to justify the creation of new remedies, it also supports the argument that the absence of a remedy proves that there is no right. Furthermore, the common law simply has no way of giving a remedy against something as vague as "society" and it has never really been able to supply remedies against the state (as opposed to individuals who purport to be acting as agents of the state). The common law, moreover, to revert to our earlier example, though it might in theory supply a remedy by which a claimant could obtain a particular job, has never had a way of enforcing a claim to "work" without reference to some particular job.

From the Buddhist perspective on the other hand, considering that the absence of one's self lies at the center of the Buddha's teachings, it is difficult to imagine a Buddhist, qua Buddhist, according much reality to - to say nothing of clinging to - a recent, and rather dubious, mental construct like a state or a society. Nor, to return to our particular example, are traditional Buddhist societies likely to be able to make much sense of the concept of a "right to work," a concept that is only intelligible within a tradition that radically divides labor from capital and the employed from the employer (and both from the unemployed) in a fashion which would be incomprehensible in any traditional Gemeinschaft.

From a Buddhist point of view, the trouble would seem to lie not only in the illusory nature of the purported rights, but also in their implicit denial of the fact of *dukkha*, the fact of the ubiquity of suffering and of the unsatisfactory nature of all conditioned things. It hardly does for one to say to an unemployed steel worker in the United States that he has a right to work even if he does not have a job, or for one to tell a peasant tilling a rice-field in Southeast Asia that she has a right "to a standard of living adequate for the health and well-being of himself and of his family, including food, clothing, housing and medical care and necessary social services, and the right to security in the event of unemployment, sickness, disability, widowhood, old age or other lack of livelihood in circumstances beyond his control."

Such claims seem more like a denial the truth of suffering than a step leading to its cessation. Surely it does not profit a man to tell him that he as a right to security in this world of impermanence, as if he could in some way avoid the consequences of sickness and old age - or even of death, which is, after all, the ultimate case of "lack of livelihood in circumstances beyond one's control." Although it may make us feel that we have accomplished something to declare that everyone has a right to happiness, or to its pursuit, the fact of *dukkha* remains a fact.

The world of dew-A world of dew it is indeed, and yet, and yet... °

Of course it would be nice if everyone had work, and not too much of it, if everyone had enough to eat and a roof over their heads, if everyone's dignity - everyone's Buddha nature - were universally recognized. But that°is not the way things are right now. And although one may - and as a Buddhist perhaps should - aspire to bring about such changes, the Buddha's teaching, as I understand it, is that one should not to cling to such aspirations, or to any other cause of suffering, including rights. From this point of view rights seem more like an incitement to clinging than a cure for suffering.

HUMAN RIGHTS AND COMPASSION

His Holiness the Dalai Lama has been a tireless advocate for human rights in a global context. Some leaders and moral theorists of non-Western cultures - and some contemporary Western moral and political theorists - have argued that the assertion of fundamental human rights is merely an accidental feature of the moral outlook of modern Western moral and political theory. The extension or imposition of this moral framework and its demands on non-Western cultures, they argue, is an instance of cultural imperialism and hegemony, incompatible with and disruptive of those cultures.

Some in the West have even argued that this framework has outlived its usefulness even in Western cultures and that the overcoming of modernism should include the abandonment of a moral and political discourse grounded in rights. His Holiness has consistently rejected this view, and has urged in his public statements and in his writings on morality and politics that the demand for the recognition of human rights is indeed universal in scope, and that to the extent that a culture deprives its citizenry of fundamental human rights, that culture is morally deficient. It follows from such a view that to demand of a society that it respect some fundamental set of such rights is not an instance of illegitimate cultural imperialism but an instance of mandatory moral criticism, even if it is not so experienced by those to whom such an effort is directed at the time.

On the other hand, His Holiness, grounded in, and advancing with considerable eloquence, the tradition of Buddhist moral theory rooted in the teachings of the Buddha, as transmitted through texts such as Aryadeva's Four Hundred and Santideva's Guide to the Bodhisattva's Way of Life has been a consistent exponent of the view that moral life is grounded in the cultivation and exercise of compassion. He has urged in many public religious teachings, addresses, and in numerous writings that the most important moral quality to cultivate is compassion, and that compassion, skill in its exercise, and insight into the nature of reality are jointly necessary and sufficient for human moral perfection.

This view, is of course, not original with His Holiness. It is the essence of Buddhist moral theory. On the other hand, His Holiness is certainly the most eloquent exponent and advocate of this moral position of our time, and his application of this moral vision to public life and to international relations is highly original and of the first importance, justly recognized by the conferring of the Nobel Peace Prize. For instance in one recent discussion His Holiness writes:

To me it is clear that a genuine sense of responsibility can result only if we develop compassion. Only a spontaneous feeling of empathy for others can really motivate us to act on their behalf.

Democracy is [the system] which is closest to humanity's essential nature. Hence those of us who enjoy it must continue to fight for all people's right to do so... We must respect the right of all peoples and nations to maintain their own distinctive characters and values.

Now at first glance, there is nothing surprising about this pair of commitments - that to the universality of human rights and that to the cultivation and exercise of compassion as the foundation of morality. Both seem laudable. Both seem to be prima facie "noble" moral commitments. But a second look may raise deep and difficult questions. A number of influential moral theorists have recently argued persuasively that moral theories grounded in rights and moral theories grounded in compassion are fundamentally incompatible with one another.

Moreover, they have argued that liberal theories are critically deficient - that they fail to account for and to provide guidance in our morally most important circumstances - matters of interpersonal relations where sentiments, attitudes and behaviors are of moral significance, but where questions concerning the rights and duties of those involved are at best beside the point. If these critics of liberal moral theory are correct, focusing on rights and duties impoverishes our moral discourse and distorts our moral vision and is to be abandoned in favor of a morality grounded exclusively in compassion and attention to interpersonal relations. Importantly, responses to this view have typically defended liberal theories against compassion theories, arguing that the former are indeed adequate to the full range of moral questions, and that compassion theories, to the extent that they get matters right, are no more than restatements of liberal theories.

The interesting thing about this response is not whether or not it succeeds, but that it concedes to the compassion-theorist the most important point - that rights and compassion are in tension with one another. And if that point, on which the parties to this debate concur, is correct, then His Holiness' advocacy for both of these approaches to morality would turn out to be incoherent. On the other hand, if his moral vision is - as I will argue that it in fact is - both coherent and compelling, seeing just how that is so international relations is highly original and of the first importance, justly recognized by the conferring of the Nobel Peace Prize. For instance in one recent discussion His Holiness writes:

To me it is clear that a genuine sense of responsibility can result only if we develop compassion. Only a spontaneous feeling of empathy for others can really motivate us to act on their behalf.

Democracy is the system which is closest to humanity's essential nature. Hence those of us who enjoy it must continue to fight for all people's right to do so...We must respect the right of all peoples and nations to maintain their own distinctive characters and values.

Now at first glance, there is nothing surprising about this pair of commitments - that to the universality of human rights and that to the cultivation and exercise of compassion as the foundation of morality. Both seem laudable. Both seem to be prima facie "noble" moral commitments. But a second look may raise deep and difficult questions. A number of influential moral theorists have recently argued persuasively that moral theories grounded in rights (to which I will henceforth refer as "liberal" theories) and moral theories grounded in compassion are fundamentally incompatible with one another.

Moreover, they have argued that liberal theories are critically deficient - that they fail to account for and to provide guidance in our morally most important circumstances -

matters of interpersonal relations where sentiments, attitudes and behaviors are of moral significance, but where questions concerning the rights and duties of those involved are at best beside the point. If these critics of liberal moral theory are correct, focusing on rights and duties impoverishes our moral discourse and distorts our moral vision and is to be abandoned in favor of a morality grounded exclusively in compassion and attention to interpersonal relations. Importantly, responses to this view have typically defended liberal theories against compassion theories, arguing that the former are indeed adequate to the full range of moral questions, and that compassion theories, to the extent that they get matters right, are no more than restatements of liberal theories.

The interesting thing about this response is not whether or not it succeeds, but that it concedes to the compassion-theorist the most important point - that rights and compassion are in tension with one another. And if that point, on which the parties to this debate concur, is correct, then His Holiness' advocacy for both of these approaches to morality would turn out to be incoherent. On the other hand, if his moral vision is - as I will argue that it in fact is - both coherent and compelling, seeing just how that is so critique of institutions, as opposed to the mere bland comparison of democracy with tyranny as two interesting alternatives for ordering society.

Second, positive rights such as these are always quite specific rights to particular actions by particular individuals or institutions. Fundamental negative rights are rights against everybody. My child's right to an education is a right that the local school system admit him to school. The shopkeeper on the corner is irrelevant to this right: he can neither satisfy nor violate it. But my right to life is satisfied by all who do not kill me, and can be violated by any assailant. We can identify three more specific functions rights serve, and which are central to defining the liberal moral outlook: they create a domain of free expression; they establish clarity regarding life expectations; they enable moral criticism. Each of these functions is complex, and deserves examination.

Human flourishing - both at the individual and at the social level - requires the freedom of expression to be realized in a number of ways. For an individual to experience him/herself as creative, as responsible, as a being whose views matter; who is taken seriously; who can interact spontaneously and genuinely with those with whom s/he lives it is essential that s/he be able to express his/her views without fear of persecution. Moreover, for a society to flourish it is essential that as many voices be heard as possible, and that no views be suppressed.

The suppression of speech harms not only the individual whose voice is silenced but also the community deprived of what might have been the correct view of a crucial matter, or the beauty of a work of art never created. And of course a society of individuals each of whom fears to express his/her views is a miserable one. Social and individual flourishing hence require respect for the right to free speech. But of course not all speech is protected absolutely. Speech may be slanderous. Speech may be used to menace, or to deceive. So it becomes important to demarcate the domain of speech to be protected.

This is notoriously difficult, and almost certainly cannot be done explicitly by any clear set of general principles. But we can at least note, given the general motivations just sketched for the protection of speech, central cases of speech that merits protection: speech critical for individual self-development, such as that related to scholarship, art, or the development of bonds of friendship of family is clearly to be so protected. Moreover, speech related to the political process, to debates regarding social policy, and to the pursuit of religious practice is also to be protected. In short, those domains central to individual and collective flourishing, in order to contribute to those goals, must be domains in which one can advance views free from the fear of censorship. This is what the freedom of speech is.

But rights protect not only discourse and discursive practices such as the creation of art and the practice of religion. They also allow us to organize our lives rationally, and to plan our lives with the confidence that our plans have some chance of success. That is, rights ensure a relative clarity of expectations. That others will respect our rights to property, for instance, allows us to plan to put that property to use. That others will respect our right to move freely allows us to plan travel, and to plan a career or course of action that will involve travel. And it is of course the recognition of these rights and their instantiation in a set of institutions enforcing them that allows this confidence necessary for rationally lived lives, free from the terror of the unexpected crushing of legitimate expectations.

Rights have yet another central role in our moral lives. They make moral criticism possible. It is important to remember that among our most ethically significant activities is our criticism of ourselves, our fellows, and of alien practices. The role of rights is most central in the latter case. For, sadly, we often find ourselves encountering in the world practices that we find morally abhorrent and wish to condemn and even to extirpate. And we often find that those engaged in those practices not only show reluctance to abandon them, but defend them as morally acceptable.

And to make matters more disturbing, the participants in these practices may urge that our condemnation represents an illicit - even culturally imperialist - universalization of the parochial moral prejudices of our own culture to their very different context. They argue that just as they don't interfere with our moral practices, we should leave their very different culture intact and mind our own business. A case in point is the rejoinder of the government of The People's Republic of China to pressure from Western governments and from non-government human rights advocacy groups, as well as the statements made by representatives of this government at the 1994 conference on human rights in Asia.

In these statements this government asserted that such putative fundamental rights as that to free speech, freedom of emigration, freedom to practice religion, etc...and indeed the entire framework of individual human rights are artifacts of Western liberalism, and that any attempt to impose respect for such a set of rights on Asian cultures is simply a new version of imperialism. Now, leaving aside how the debate between the Chinese leadership and its critics ought to turn out, let us notice what the liberal discourse of rights does for its exponents in this debate: to put the matter simply, it makes the criticism of these practices possible in the first place.

For absent the liberal framework, the most that we can do is notice that the Chinese government adopts different practices from our own, and comment that we, given our preferences, would prefer to live under our system than under theirs, and perhaps even that so would many of the Chinese and colonial subjects of that government. But that fact doesn't allow us, as outsiders, to intervene in that system, or even, with any justification, to criticize it in a way that its practitioners should take seriously any more than our noting culinary differences between us and the Chinese, and our preference for our food would justify criticism of Chinese gastronomy.

For they can respond to us in a parallel fashion: they could note that we liberals have a different system. They could remark that they, the Chinese, would prefer not to live in it, and prefer their own. However, they could remark, they acknowledge that they have no grounds on which to criticize our system, and ask that just as they refrain from doing so, we do likewise with respect to them. What makes moral criticism possible for the liberal is that the discourse of rights presents itself as a universal discourse in an important sense. It makes claims that transcend cultural difference.

The rights posited are not American rights, Tibetan rights, or Buddhist rights, Western rights, or Men's rights, etc....: they are precisely human rights, which are self-evidently possessed by any person. A social structure that abrogates them is not, on this view, simply different from our own in that respect: it is morally wrong in that respect. And to the extent that we can make the liberal framework precise - and that turns out to be a very great extent - we can specify precise ways in which such a system in wrong and in which it must reform or be reformed.

RIGHTS, DUTIES AND PRIVACY

Rights entail duties on the part of others. Where I have a right to something, you have a duty to respect that right. Moreover, duties towards specific persons entail rights on the part of those to whom duties accrue. If you - say as a consequence of a loan - have a duty to pay me a sum of money, I have a right that you do so. If I have a right to practice my religion, you have a duty not to interfere with that practice. Since, as we have noted, rights divide into positive and negative rights, duties similarly divide into positive and negative duties. Negative rights and duties are those liberals regard as universal.

And all of the fundamental rights we have noted are of this character. Positive rights are accorded by particular kinds of institutions, such as government structures, laws, employment contracts or voluntary agreements or associations. These last may be more conventional, less universal, and as such are generally justified on pragmatic grounds or on grounds of mutual agreement, rather than on universal moral grounds.

The important consequence of this mutual entailment between rights and duties for present purposes is that any moral theory that takes rights as foundational ipso facto takes duties as foundational. To the extent that our collective moral landscape is defined by our human rights, our collective moral landscape is equally well defined by our duties. While this may seem like a trivial restatement, it raises a problem: I will argue below that compassion has a defining characteristic an intention and aspiration to benefit even those to whom we have no particular duties, and who have no particular rights against us. We act compassionately, argue, precisely when we act not from duty, and precisely when we do not simply respect the rights of others, but when we positively benefit or refrain from harming where there are no rights and duties.

Moreover, as we shall see, compassion governs our interactions in a private sphere where talk about rights would seem bizarre, for example, relations between parents and children. To the extent that we define the moral landscape by rights and duties, we appear not to define it through compassion. Liberalism and Buddhism are apparently at odds. We can sharpen this point by attending to the deep connection between the liberal conception of the private/public distinction and the liberal discourse of rights and duties, and the consequent centrality of this distinction and of the demarcation of a specifically private sphere to liberal moral theory. This point is conceptual, but can be usefully illuminated through attention to the history of liberal theory.

Modern liberal moral theory has its origins in the work of the Western philosophers Locke and Kant (as well as Hobbes and Rousseau). Each was concerned in his own way to defend the rights of individuals against hegemonic powers that militated against individual liberty - in the case of Locke the British Crown which threatened the development of constitutional democracy and mercantile capitalism, and in the case of Kant ecclesiastical authority that threatened academic freedom and the development of science. Each saw it to be necessary to demarcate that sphere of life in which one's liberty is properly limited by legitimate public authority from that in which one is properly regarded as autonomous, and so to demarcate a private sphere.

For Kant the most important domain to protect as private is that of thought, and as such he is properly seen as the earliest forceful exponent of a fundamental right to freedom of thought and expression. But for Locke, his philosophical predecessor, the original private domain is the home, and the most important right to privacy is the right to property, and to the non-interference with one's use of one's property and conduct in one's home.

Both strains of privacy theory are influential in the contemporary world's most influential articulation of liberal moral and political theory - the Constitution of the United States of America. The constitutional protection of the right to privacy has been forcefully articulated in a series of interpretively important decisions in this century according to which the boundaries of the private sphere are demarcated by rights against self-incrimination, against the intrusion of the state into one's home and documents, against religious coercion, against the abridgment of speech, etc., and against the dictation of one's decisions regarding one's family size and structure. These have been summed up by one Supreme Court Justice in the famous epigram, "The most important right is the right to be let alone."

This epigram in a certain sense simply sums up liberal moral theory. Liberalism is predicated on the demarcation of a private sphere in which one is free to articulate one's ideology, daily life and vision of the good as one sees fit. What one does there may be the subject of comment by others, but not of moral criticism. One's duties concern what one does in the public sphere. Restrictions of one's prerogatives in the private sphere are always prima facie violations of rights. I may be obligated to pay my taxes (a public matter) but I cannot be required to give money to my temple (a private matter) and if I do so it is not out of any duty (unless I have established one through a promise).

Failing to come to work on time is a breach of duty to my employer (a public matter) but failing to go to bed at a reasonable hour is a private matter - perhaps stupid, but nobody's business but my own. Or so liberal theory would have it. Liberal theory, in sum, gets us the goods adumbrated earlier - security of thought and conscience, security in planning our lives, access to the good ideas and beautiful works of others, and a platform for moral criticism - simply by restricting the zone of such criticism to the public, and establishing the sanctity of the private.

Now to a certain degree, I have overstated my case. For liberal moral theory does not in fact ignore moral phenomena other than rights completely, and indeed the most prominent liberal moral theorists often have a great deal to say about character and about virtue. To do justice to all of the nuances of the liberal tradition would take us far beyond the scope of this discussion.

For now, these few remarks will have to suffice to emphasize the contrast to which I wish to draw attention: first, while liberal moral theory is indeed richer than one might believe were one to focus solely on its discussion of rights, liberal political theory is very much concerned to articulate a framework of rights as an exclusive characterization of the moral structure of the public sphere. (Indeed the separation of the moral from the political is another respect in which liberalism diverges from compassion-based moral theory)

Second, even within the moral domain, there is a preoccupation in liberal theory with an articulation of rights which often obscures other moral concerns, and a preoccupation within liberal theory generally with the articulation of the political dimension of our moral lives to the detriment of attention to the private sphere, a preoccupation explained by the demarcation of that sphere within liberalism in the first place. Finally, even when liberal moral theory does turn its attention to matters of character and virtue, the account of these phenomena is often grounded in a primary account of rights and duties.

THE LIMITS OF RIGHTS IN MORAL DISCOURSE

We are now in more of a position to see what is problematic about liberal theory if we want compassion to have an important place in our moral life. When rights are taken to be fundamental, too much comes out morally permissible. Since, for instance, nobody to whom I have no particular contractual arrangement has any right to my generosity in no way obligated to be generous. Since no one has a claim on my concern and need not be concerned for anyone else. Compassion is hence, on this view, strictly optional - one of the many permissible ways to address the world.

This highlights the most important limitation of liberal moral discourse: it is in an important sense silent about character. Since a person's character - his or her fundamental values and set of virtues, vices, dispositions and attitudes - is a private matter, and the first principal of liberal moral theory is to protect individual liberty in the private sphere, liberal theory can in no way by itself recommend or condemn any particular qualities of character. To the extent that we find character to be a morally significant phenomenon, this is deeply problematic. In particular, to the extent that the cultivation of compassion is of genuine moral significance - and for any Buddhist moral theorist it must be - then liberalism is at least deficient in its neglect of this attribute, and at worst wrongheaded in characterizing it as optional.

But there is yet another difficulty afflicting the foundation of liberal theory, one which is indeed acknowledged by the social contract tradition, but which is never satisfactorily resolved: the general duty to respect the rights of others requires a justification. Or, to look at the other side of the coin, the claim that persons have natural rights at all must be justified, antecedent to the task which often occupies most of a liberal's attention, that of specifying exactly what our rights and duties are. And of course one cannot simply appeal to a right to have one's rights respected, or a duty to do one's duty, on pain of infinite regress.

The social contract tradition adopts one of two strategies: theorists in this tradition sometimes argue that the sanction of the rights and duties we recognize lies in an explicit or implicit original agreement to which we are all either tacit parties or heirs. Aside from the odd historical problems this raises, and the problems with the status of implicit or inherited contracts, there is a stunning logical problem with this kind of reasoning. For the original agreement to be in any sense binding there must already by duties to keep one's word and to be bound by agreements presupposed, and correlatively rights that others abide by their agreements. The regress just adumbrated is merely ignored by talk of social contracts as binding.

The second strategy is to argue that it is in each of our self-interests to abide by the hypothesized or hypostasized right-establishing contract - that the alternative is a social disintegration that benefits none of us. There are at least two problems with this form of reasoning, though: first, for most of us most of the time, it is simply false. It is often in fact, in terms of the kind of narrow self-interest to which morality is supposed to be a countervailing force, precisely in our self-interest to shirk our duties, and to violate the rights of others.

This is not surprising. It is one of the reasons for the prevalence of evil. But more deeply, even were this true, it would be the wrong kind of justification for a structure of rights and duties.

For it would then be the case that our having rights and duties would be contingent upon the supposed fact that it is in others' and our own self-interest to respect them. And again, the very point of rights and duties is to restrain action that, while justified from the standpoint of narrow self-interest, is morally wrong. Such restraint clearly demands independent justification. Now of course the demonstration of the inadequacy of these routes to the justification of liberalism as a foundation for morality does not show that no route will succeed. But if some route is to succeed, it will require a lot of argument to show how.

And it does appear that the reasons for the failure to provide a truly adequate foundation for liberalism are principled: valuable as rights are, they are not self-justifying, and broad as their scope is, it is not broad enough to encompass all that is morally significant. It is therefore appropriate to look for a broader foundation for our moral life, and to hope that such a foundation will allow us to preserve what goods rights promise, while giving us moral guidance in those areas where rights fail us. It is with such hopes in mind that we turn to an examination of compassion.

HUMAN RIGHTS AS THE PRODUCT OF REASON

Now there may be those who will object to what I have said up to now on the ground that it is unphilosophical and rather unfair, for, after all, the imperfections in the implementation of the concept of human rights hardly proves that that concept is not a good idea. But my claim is not so much that the concept of human rights is not good, but rather that the peculiar collection of rights set out in the Declaration suggests that that concept is not coherent.

Still there are those of an abstract bent who will undoubtedly argue that one can - and perhaps that one must - conclude on some as yet to be specified ground that human beings do have rights simply by virtue of being human and that the job of an ethicist or a philosopher or the sort of person who takes part in a symposium like this is to explore those grounds, or the logical nature of those rights, without worrying about the individual rights themselves. The fact that a bunch of politicians, aspiring to be statesmen, did a clumsy job of specifying those rights back in San Francisco in 1948, though regrettable, is in this view hardly significant.

It should be noted at this point, however, that even if there were no other objection to this approach, the emphasis on human rights does not seem quite compatible with the Buddha's teachings. A Buddhist would undoubtedly be more comfortable with this argument if one were said to have these rights not by virtue of being human, but by virtue of being sentient, or even just by being. The parochialism of the Western concept of human rights is not limited just to time and geography. The teachings of the Buddha, as I understand them, enjoin me to respect the interests of others - the "rights" of others, if one wants to use that label - without limiting the others to the merely human, or to "agents" or to "persons" or to other limited groups of "right-bearers."

Some Western philosophers who espouse human rights do seem at least partially sensitive to this objection:

It is a mistake, in my view, to make the distinction hinge on the difference between human beings and others: it is not their humanity, a simple biological characteristic having no necessary moral implications, but their personality that makes the crucial difference between right-bearers and other objects. The natural personality of nearly all human beings consists in their having a certain kind of self-awareness, a conception of themselves as initiators of actions that make a difference to the course of events. They are conceptually equipped to envisage alternative possibilities, to prefer one state to another, and to decide on a course of action intended to bring about one in preference to another.

Moreover, each not only knows himself as such a person, but also distinguishes himself and his initiatives from other similar persons and theirs. This characteristic may not be confined to human beings: some chimpanzees educated by human teachers have show a conceptualizing capacity that may extend to this kind of self-conceptualization; it is possible that intelligent dogs or dolphins may have it, or be capable of learning it from human beings. On the other hand, there are some human beings who do not have it; congenital idiocy or brain damage could deprive one of it. Yet it is so nearly universal a feature of human beings that the generalization that human beings are natural persons is pragmatically reasonable, at least as a rule of thumb.

A person knowing himself to be a person in a world of persons is aware that they, like him, have projects important to them, and that his actions may impair theirs as theirs often impair his. This may be no more than a grim fact of life; he may take what evasive action he can, and regret the mess when it fails. On the other hand, he may come to feel that people who understand very well what it is to have their own projects spoiled by the carelessness and unconcern of others ought to have some respect for his - and for him as their author. And he may resent their trampling on these projects without a thought, and, even more, their treating him as a mere impediment or as an instrument for their own projects, as though he had none of his own that mattered.

And if his resentment were grounded in their failure to appreciate what in his view any person ought to be able to grasp in his dealings with another person, he would be supposing a general moral principle - that of respect for natural persons. This amounts to saying that any natural person is also a moral person, a bearer of rights, which constitute for any other person reasons (though not necessarily conclusive reasons) for forbearance in respect of his projects.

From this basic deontological notion of respect for persons, which has nothing whatsoever to do with valuing them, derives a set of very general principles...

It seems to me, however, that the insistence here that one has to be a person in order to have rights, is no more consonant with the Buddha's teachings than the requirement that those who have rights have to be human, especially as the test of being a "person" seems to be that one must have a self-conscious self, a test that is difficult to reconcile with the teaching that all things are empty of self. The teachings of the Buddha give much simpler reasons to respect the desires of other beings:

All beings fear punishment; all fear death. If you take yourself as the measure, you will never harm, you will never kill.

All beings fear punishment; all love life. If you take yourself as the measure, you will never harm, you will never kill. If in seeking happiness you bring harm to others who also seek to be happy, in the future you will never be happy. If in seeking happiness you never harm others who also seek to be happy, in the future happiness will come to you.

The rational deductive approach to human rights assumes, of course, several things: in particular, (i) that the concept of rights, and especially human rights, is meaningful and coherent and (ii) that there is indeed some ground from which such rights can be deduced or upon which such rights are based. It also assumes that one can, once one has found the ground on which human rights are based, deduce by ratiocination the content of the rights themselves and, in some extreme cases, that one can, with recourse to nothing more than one's own rationality, deduce the ground itself. As an example of the latter approach, consider the following passage by Alan Gewirth:

In this book, while trying to profit from the work of my predecessors, I present a new version of rational justification. The chief novelty is the logical derivation of a substantial normative moral principle from the nature of human action. Although the importance of action for morality has been recognized since the ancients, I undertake to show that the connection between them is much closer and more substantive than has hitherto been thought. My main thesis is that every agent, by the fact of engaging in action, is logically committed to the acceptance of certain evaluative and deontic judgments and ultimately of a supreme moral principle, the Principle of Generic Consistency, which requires that he respect his recipients' necessary conditions of action.

To prove this thesis, I have argued that the very possibility of rational interpersonal action depends upon adherence to the morality that is grounded in this principle. Because every agent must accept the principle upon pain of self-contradiction, it has a stringent rational justification that is at the same time practical because its required locus is the context of action. Somehow it does not seem that many persons, or governments, would be persuaded to behave themselves by the "pain of self-contradiction," which must surely be one of the least distasteful forms of *dukkha*, and one that has, I suspect, afflicted every philosopher who has ever written, even Nagarjuna. As Walt Whitman put it:

"Do I contradict myself?

Very well then I contradict myself."

Nor is Gewirth likely to persuade any Buddhist - even a Buddhist philosopher - that he has by pure logic discovered "a supreme moral principle," and one that no one up to now, not even the Buddha, has happened to notice. Pure logic is not the path we are enjoined to follow to reach the truth, is not the middle way. As a student and teacher of the common law I am convinced that its tradition has been perverted by a positivist, and academic, emphasis upon wrongs as opposed to rights, and I suspect, with pretty good reason, that that perversion is a consequence of the sort of philosophical abstraction that requires one to deduce what the law should be - or what it is - from some source outside of itself like a "sovereign" or the "will of the people" postulated by Article 21 of the Universal Declaration of Human Rights or some God-given concept of "natural rights" or even Gewirth's rationality.

On the other hand, the "rights" that arguably make up the major substance of the common law, even as it is today, are quite unlike the nominal entities called "rights" that comprise the intention of the Universal Declaration, even if the latter represent, or disguise, aspirations and interests that fit comfortably within, and to a large part are derived from, the common law tradition. As Justice Holmes once wrote:

The life of the law has not been logic: it has been experience. The felt necessities of the time, the prevalent moral and political theories, intuitions of public policy, avowed or unconscious, even the prejudices which judges share with their fellow-men, have had a good deal more to do than the syllogism in determining the rules by which men should be governed.

From a Buddhist viewpoint, the whole idea of "grounding" the concept of human rights seems pretty problematical, if not downright perverse, especially as the major use of the concept seems to be to supply a justification for ethical, or political, prescriptions that need no justification or grounding. As I understand the Buddha's teachings, one practices right actions because that practice leads to the cessation of suffering - or, better yet, one just practices them. If one "has" right views, then one knows that there is no independent foundation that supports right actions, including the action of respecting the "rights" - or, rather, the interests - of others. Pursuing and clinging to illusory reasons for doing what is right - rather than just doing it - is not following the path to the cessation of suffering. In the arising and cessation of all things that comprises this ocean of birth and death, there is no ground upon which rights could be founded, and there is no ground at all.

The heart - and to me the appeal - of the Buddha's teachings lies in the recognition of the interdependence, the emptiness, of all dharmas, in the recognition that there is, and that there can be found, no fundamental ground, no foundation, for the way that things are - and that no such foundation is needed. To recognize that the concept of human rights is the product of a particular time and place, without any claim to universal validity or to some Platonic other-worldly foundation, is not to justify hunger or the abuses of human rights in Bosnia, or Burma, or Tibet; rather, it is a clarifying of the mind - a seeing of things as they are - and a step, even if it is a small one, toward the cessation the suffering.

Some such recognition is not, of course, limited to those who find themselves within the Buddhist tradition. For example, Richard Rorty has written:

As I see it, one important intellectual advance made in our century is the steady decline in interest in the quarrel between Plato and Nietzsche. There is a growing willingness to neglect the question "What is our nature?" and to substitute the question "What can we make of ourselves?"

One of the shapes that we have recently assumed is that of a human rights culture. I borrow the term "human rights culture" from the Argentinean jurist and philosopher Eduardo Rabossi. In an article called "Human Rights Naturalized," Rabossi argues that philosophers should think of this culture as a new, welcome fact of the post-Holocaust world. They should stop trying to get beyond or beneath this fact, stop trying to detect and defend its so-called "philosophical presuppositions." On Rabossi's view, philosophers like Alan Gewirth are wrong to argue that human rights cannot depend on historical facts. "My basic point," Rabossi says, is that "the world has changed, that the human rights phenomenon renders human rights foundationalism outmoded and irrelevant."

Rabossi's claim that human rights foundationalism is outmoded seems to me both true and important...I shall be enlarging on, and defending, Rabossi's claim that the question whether human beings really have the rights enumerated in the Helsinki Declaration is not worth raising. In particular, I shall be defending the claim that nothing relevant to moral choice separates human beings from animals except historically contingent facts of the world, cultural facts. This claim is sometimes called "cultural relativism" by those who indignantly reject it...

Traditionally, the name of the shared human attribute which supposedly "grounds" morality is "rationality." Cultural relativism is associated with irrationalism because it denies the existence of morally relevant transcultural facts. But one need not be irrationalist in the sense of ceasing to make one's web of belief as coherent, and as perspicuously structured as possible...We see our task as a matter of making our own culture - the human rights culture - more self-conscious and more powerful, rather than demonstrating its superiority to other cultures by an appeal to something transcultural.

Thus one follower, at least, of the rather commonsensical American pragmatic tradition, who places a high value on human rights, does have a clear understanding of the absurdity of attempts to ground those rights on something other than "the historically contingent facts of the world," on something other than the way things are right here, right now. That something is still sadly missing in Rorty's writings, the fact that he seems to sense only flatness where the follower of the Dharma ultimately finds tranquility and joy, does not detract from the validity of his critique, but seems rather to come from the failure to recognize that the consolations of religion can be found by those who recognize the contingency and interdependency of all conditioned things, by those who grasp the fact that: "Form is exactly emptiness, emptiness exactly form."

A SPLIT IN THE WESTERN TRADITION

It is generally accepted that the concept of Human Rights grows out of Western European traditions, not out of Asia, or Africa, or the Americas before the coming of the European colonialists; thus, for example, no one claims that the concept of Human Rights is native to any of the Buddhist traditions. The fact that the Universal Declaration of Human Rights is a "Western" document has led to objections by some who do not find it appropriate as a legal document of universal applicability, but who would not necessarily repudiate the principles that inspired it. It was for this reason that "The Declaration towards a Global Ethic" adopted by the Parliament of the World's Religions in 1993 was carefully drafted so that it would not be a "reduplication of the Declaration on Human Rights."

It is not so often stressed that the concept of Human Rights is the product of two rather different Western traditions: the Continental civil law tradition, with strong ties to the more rationalistic practices of Continental philosophy, on the one hand, and, on the other, the Anglo-American legal and constitutional tradition, which has always seemed to me to be the cousin German to the British empiricist and pragmatic traditions. The Continental tradition is the primary source of the body of "international law" that has come to incorporate, with considerable discomfort, the concept of human rights and it is also the primary source of the of concepts of natural rights and natural law that are often claimed to be the foundation of human rights; the Anglo-American tradition, on the other hand, produced the concept of "inalienable rights" in the British North American Declaration of Independence that is often cited as the *fons et origo* of the concept of human rights.

In this chapter no more than sketch the difference between the two traditions, and this sketch should not be taken as much more than the view of someone so much a product of the Anglo-American that he simply cannot make sense out of the more abstract and "rational" arguments coming out of the Continental tradition. (I suspect, however, that it is exactly my inability to take those "rational" arguments seriously that frees me to hear the Buddha's teachings that there is no independent, persistent self and that all things are interdependent.)

The major differences between the two traditions arise from their having different histories, from their being the product of different causes and conditions. At one time, however, this division did not exist. After the disappearance of the institutions of the Roman Empire in Western Europe there grew up a diverse collection of kingdoms and customs, that, in retrospect, can be seen to have shared a common culture, now known as the feudal system, in which political power and private rights were defined and regulated by customary relations between - not so much "individuals" in the modern, Western sense, as the holders of customary "offices." One key feature of this common feudal culture, and one that has persisted in its Anglo-American descendant, was that its customary relations - its laws - were declared, reinforced, and even established, by the judgments of courts rather than by legislative decrees.

Around the end of the twelfth century, however, on the European continent there was a break in this tradition, and the customary feudal law that had just grown up over the preceding centuries was replaced by the newly rediscovered

"Roman law" of the late Roman empire, a law that had been dead for some six hundred years and that was ill adapted to existing institutions and ill-prepared to deal either with feudal relations or with relations between the emerging nation-states of modem Europe. One unfortunate consequence of this reception of Roman law was that the law became an academic subject studied and taught by professors at the newly instituted universities, rather than by the practitioners and judges of the courts of law.

Another was that the in adopting the law of the late Roman empire as set out in Justinian's *Corpus Juris*, there was strong pressure to also adopt Justinian's fundamental principle that "whatever pleases the prince has the force of law," a doctrine that stands firmly in the way of any effort to protect human rights and other interests from the tender mercies of the state. After all, if law is not the product of the customs of the community, it has to come from somewhere, and the whim of the prince is as "rational" a source as any.

In England, on the other hand, there never was much of a reception of Roman law; as opposed to the continent where the civil law based on *the Corpus Juris* of Justinian replaced the customary feudal law, in England the customary law was never abandoned - rather it gradually evolved into the modern common law. The English resistance to the adoption of Roman law does not have to be explained by some fundamental difference between the English spirit and the continental Geist, nor as a result of initially different word views. The simple, contingent fact was that in at least one significant respect conditions were different in England: during the reign of Henry II the law and custom common to all of England - the common law - had evolved, had been shaped by Henry's judges, into the most sophisticated and fully developed legal system in Europe, a legal system that was quite capable in its own right of dealing with the new problems brought forth by new times.

The differences between the two legal systems have been summarized by a continental scholar of English legal history:

For centuries, in fact until the Judicature Acts of 1873 and 1875, the Common Law of England consisted of a system of actions or legal remedies, each commanding its own procedure, whereas continental law knew general procedural rules which governed all or large classes of causes. English law prefers precedent as a basis for judgments, and moves empirically from case to case, from one reality to another.

Continental law tends to move more theoretically by deductive reasoning, basing judgments on abstract principles; it is more conceptual, more scholastic and works more with definitions and distinctions. In other words it was moulded by the Roman law of the medieval universities. It was this professors' law, marked by exegesis and commentaries on learned books and glosses, which made continental law different from the Germanic and feudal customs and laws of England.

With the exception of Bracton's great law-book, we find none of it in the Common Law, where the Year Books, with their reports of court cases, were typical and utterly different from William Durand's systematic Speculum Judiciale. In England lawyers received their training in the Inns of Court, technical colleges where they learnt their craft like every medieval craftsman, in contact with practicing masters, not in universities at the feet of scholars who were apt to lose themselves in controversy. English law worked essentially within the existing feudal framework, whereas continental law incorporated a vast amount of extraneous elements, mainly of Roman origin. Consequently the feudal idea of relation was central in English and the Roman idea of will in continental law. A final difference is the absence of codification in England. The tradition of case law and empiricism makes very poor soil for codification - the Romans, who were first and foremost practical jurists, never had a codification - but with systematic theory and logical deduction from general premises, codes came naturally on the Continent.

THE CONTINENTAL CIVIL LAW TRADITION

In tracing the history of the concept of human rights, the civil law system of the continent is of peculiar importance because what we today call international law - the law of nations - is a product of the civil law tradition. Even in common law countries, international law is recognized as part of the civil law tradition and is not considered to be part of the common law. Unlike the common law, which just grew like an English garden over the last eight hundred years, the civil law was the product of the deliberate adoption on the continent, though in different regions at different times, of the Roman law as it had been written down and collected in the *Corpus Juris* during the reign of the Eastern Emperor Justinian.

Right through the early middle Ages and up to the mid-twelfth century English and continental law belonged recognisably to one legal family, Germanic and feudal in substance and in procedure. Except for possible linguistic complications, a traveller from the Continent in the days of King Stephen would have had no problem in recognizing the rules, arguments and modes of proof in an English manorial, borough or feudal court. A century later the landscape had changed: Roman law and Roman-canonical procedure were transforming life in many parts of the Continent (and others were to follow), whereas in England a native law, common to the whole kingdom, that was - and remained - free from the substance and the procedure of the new continental fashion, had arisen.

The moment when this dichotomy arose can be pinpointed exactly. It was in the reign of King Henry II, when certain reforms in judicial organisation and procedure were carried out which modernised English law before Roman law entered the scene with such wide and immediate success that no need was felt in later centuries, when the neo-Roman model was available, to give up the native system... On the Continent at this juncture the main modernisation of the law was taking place in the urban world, particularly in northern Italy and Flanders, where local courts of aldermen where the goal was to punish the defendant, were granted liberty to use progressive procedures and rules. Nowhere did these dispersed efforts lead to a new, unified, national or even regional law.

The Church courts, manned henceforth by the learned bishops' officials, began to apply the new law from the

Bolognese textbooks around 1200. About the middle of the thirteenth century the kingdoms began to follow suit...Gradually, under the influence of the universities and following the example of the ecclesiastical courts, Roman law was transforming continental civil and to some extent criminal law, with the active help of governments. But it was the universities that created the new and modern, as opposed to the archaic and feudal law; they provided the books and the men who alone could bring about this new departure on the Continent. In Italy (north and south), southern France and eastern Spain - old Mediterranean lands - this new Roman law was already firmly entrenched in the thirteenth century.

In northern France, Germanic and feudal custom resisted, particularly since it produced some original modernisation of its own, but even there in the thirteenth century the commentators of customary laws were already working with Roman law as their system of reference: they were familiar with its vocabulary, it provided their grammar and it was the universal treasure house where customary lawyers could find answers to the questions left unanswered by local usage. Gradually the courts were manned by people with university degrees. Germany resisted the spread of the civil law even longer, but when it gave in, it went further than France and "received" the "common written laws" in toto.

This law, which was to be found in old books, rather than living practices, was supposedly based upon, and rationally deducible from some foundation outside itself: on the whim of the prince or on the principles of "natural law" (either as revealed by God or developed in the *jus gentium*, that portion of the Roman law that had been developed and applied by the Praetor Peregrinus to disputes to which foreigners were parties.) The civil law was seen as a body of principles, rules, and definitions to be found in the Roman *Corpus Juris*, and in later legislation, which supposedly is capable of resolving all disputes that come before the courts. Unlike the common law system, the judgments of civil law courts are not treated as controlling precedent, or even as being very important; what is controlling are those principles, rules, and definitions, and, if for some reason they are insufficient to resolve a case, the glosses of the law professors. Thus it was almost inevitable that in time most of the major civil law jurisdictions would, starting with the Code Napoleon, codify the civil law, so that today in most civil law countries the law appears to be the product of relatively recent legislation.

One consequence of all this is that civil lawyers do not see their science as being dependent on historical processes; rather the civil law is seen as a rational, deductive system. Another is that the civilians - as civil lawyers are called - tend to see the law as the product of a legislature or other external law-giver, rather than as an open-ended practice that is directed by, but not deducible from, precedents handed down within its own tradition.

Thus civilians tend to be legal "positivists" who find the source of law in "positive" legislation enacted by a "sovereign," or, if they cannot stomach the consequences of such a legal theory, in the commands of a higher sovereign, i.e., in the commands of God, which in turn raised serious problems since the days of the so-called "enlightenment" when God seemed to be, if not dead, at least rather far removed from the immediate world of law courts and politics and battlefields, or, for those who could not believe in God, in the unbelievable theory that civil society and law are founded or a so-called "social contract."

As anyone who recognizes the interdependence of all things would suspect, the civil law did not develop into its modern form unaffected by changes in its cultural, political, and religious environment. Even a hasty and incomplete, and distorted, sketch like the one I am giving here must include some reference to the rise of Protestantism and its bloody consequences in the Thirty Years War, a war whose devastation was not felt to any great degree in England, cut off as it was by the English Channel.

As the Roman law, though it developed the *jus gentium* to deal with the claims of foreigners, never developed a body of law regulating the conduct of politically independent nations, the civil law was not prepared at first to deal with disputes between states, or their rulers, nor were there any courts in which disputes could be heard. Around 1625, however, Hugo Grotius, a Dutch Protestant, published a book entitled *Of the Law of War and Peace* (De Jure Belli ac Pacis), which is today considered to be the first treatise on the Law of Nations, a subject that covered, among other matters, what we now know as International Law (and was once known as the Law of Christian Princes).

De Jure Belli ac Pacis's stature and historical importance lie less in its internal logic or the durability of its normative assertions or associations than in its originality in systematically organizing the entirety of the subject. For specific content, Grotius drew heavily upon the work of earlier writers, employing all manner of legal and moral principles with which, for the most part, his audience was already generally familiar. Before him, however, no one had even attempted to unify these principles so as to establish the authority of their systematic sum, in contrast to that merely of specific principles or limited clusters of principles.

The central thesis of DJBP was the then altogether revolutionary idea that nations, no matter how great their political or military power, are subject to the same principles of law as individuals, in their legal capacity, their contractual undertakings, their social responsibilities, their decisions to resort to war and their conduct of war. All human conduct was rendered measurable by its conformity to a homogeneous, inclusive natural law.

A Protestant bible of international relations, some would later call it - not because it was immediately placed on the papal Index of forbidden works (although the listing is not without significance in this respect), but because it emphasized values with which Protestantism had become closely identified: individuality, personal responsibility and paternal authority within the family as a prototype for the authority of rulers of states, but with the consent of the governed as a basis for the rulers' legitimacy. Capitalist manifesto, precursor of Rousseau's Social Contract, conservator of aristocratic social prejudices - DJBP has represented each of these to one generation of scholars or another.

To legal historians, at any rate, it represents nothing less than an unprecedented effort to establish, both a priori and a posteriori, a regime of universal law independent of church and empire.

This universal law was not, however, independent of Western, and especially Christian, legal and theological concepts, and its universality did not really extend beyond the bounds of Christendom. Grotius was nothing, if not a religious Christian, and his treatise, which covered all of the law, not just the Law of Nations, can be read as an effort to restate the law underlying the greater Christian community that encompassed, and transcended, the various national states of Western Europe that were beginning to replace the earlier feudal communities.

There is much in Grotius's concept of a natural law governing the greater community that would appeal to a Buddhist, but the foundations of that concept are peculiarly Christian and not easily restated in terms comprehensible to a follower of the Buddhist traditions. Even today the strongest supporters of the idea of human rights based on natural law are likely to emphasize that idea's Christian antecedents and to justify it on principles that are not easily reconciled with the traditional teachings of the Buddha. For example, what would one expect a traditional Buddhist - or even a Westerner like myself who tries to follow the Buddha Dharma - to make of this passage from Jacques Maritain's little treatise on The Rights of Man and Natural Law that bears the heading "Natural Law and Human Rights"?

We must now consider the fact that natural law and the light of moral conscience within us do not prescribe merely things to be done and not to be done; they also recognize rights, in particular, rights linked to the very nature of man. The human person possesses rights because of the very fact that it is a person, a whole, a master of itself and of its acts, and which consequently is not merely a means to an end, but an end, an end which must be treated as such. The dignity of the human person? The expression means nothing if it does not signify that by virtue of natural law, the human person has the right to be respected, is the subject of rights, possesses rights. There are things which are owed to man because of the very fact that he is man.

The notion of right and the notion of moral obligation are correlative. They are both founded on the freedom proper to spiritual agents. If man is morally bound to the things which are necessary to the fulfillment of his destiny, obviously, then he has the right to fulfill his destiny; and if he has the right to fulfill his destiny he has the right to the things necessary for this purpose. The notion of right is even more profound than that of moral obligation, for God has sovereign right over creatures and He has no moral obligation towards them (although He owes it to Himself to give them that which is required by their nature).

The true philosophy of the rights of the human person is therefore based upon the idea of natural law. The same natural law which lays down our most fundamental duties, and by virtue of which every law is binding, is the very law which assigns to us our fundamental rights. It is because we are enmeshed in the universal order, in the laws and regulations of the cosmos and of the immense family of created natures (and finally in the order of creative wisdom), and it is because we have at the same time the privilege of sharing in spiritual nature, that we possess rights vis-a-vis other men and all the assemblage of creatures.

In the last analysis, as every creature acts only by virtue of its Principle, which is the Pure Act; as every authority worthy of the name (that is to say, just) is binding in conscience only by virtue of the Principle of beings, which is pure Wisdom; so too every right possessed by man is possessed only by virtue of the right possessed by God, which is pure justice, to see the order of His wisdom in beings respected, obeyed and loved by every intelligence. Despite the efforts of Grotius and other continental scholars to base the civil law on a foundation of natural law the civil law tradition has had a rather spotty record of recognizing and protecting human rights.

One American constitutional scholar has offered us the following description of the failings of the civil law system, a description that he considers to be grossly over-simplified, and rather unfair, but one that does a good job of summarizing the problems that the civil law tradition has had with the concept of human rights (and with the related concept of constitutional democracy).

At the end of World War II, it appeared that creating and maintaining constitutional democracy were arts pretty much monopolized by those cultures that had been cohabitating with the Common Law. History since then has been more checkered. Nevertheless, a critic of the Civil Law might plausibly hypothesize that one basic reason for failures of constitutional democracy lies in that legal system. Not merely does its derivation from efforts to codify the Law of the Roman Empire taint it, but its modern reincarnation was the result of efforts by the Emperor of the French to bring order to his nation and its conquests. However, facilely one transfers the system's concept of "sovereign legislator" from emperor to democratically chosen parliament, the image of sovereign legislator, whether a collective body or a single ruler, ill fits the norms of limited government.

Perhaps even more damaging, the constitutionalist critic might continue, is the Civil Law's hubris: Tempted, like Adam and Eve, by pride and ambition, it tries to fill every void the deity left, eliminate all chaos, impose perfect form, and bottle up the great wind. When what has been called an "obsession for formal rules and procedures" escapes from the courtroom to wider political arenas, what its proponents claim are the system's greatest virtues become mortal sins.

Orderliness, rationality, and comprehensiveness might hone effective intellectual instruments to settle disputes between private citizens or issues of traditional criminal law. When, however, political leaders apply those mental sets to complex problems such as the reach of legislative power, the ambit of rights to privacy and religious freedom, or the quest for compromises among the interests of a dozen competing groups, difficulties multiply, for these sorts of issues are far less amenable, if they are amenable at all, to rule-bound solutions.

The Civil Law, the critic might continue, encourages its people to undertake tasks of constitutional engineering that lie beyond human capability. As the bloody agonies of Iraqi Shi'a and Kurds reminded George Bush in 1991 in the aftermath of Operation Desert Storm, most decisions have consequences that their makers do not, perhaps even cannot, foretell. No single person or group of persons, however brilliant or methodical, can accurately predict the future or provide rules for that future.

Only in the most general and perhaps even a principled way can political leaders hope to conquer unforeseen obstacles. The Civil Law's prompting leaders to attack the unknown with tightly reasoned logic and rigid adherence to formal rules and abstract principles is likely to be counterproductive, if not disastrous; it proliferates rather than eliminates chaos. In sum, the critic might charge, when the Civil Law infects constitutions, its mentality invites rigidity and inspires policies that are principled but impractical.

Worse, the constitutional critic might continue, the Civil Law's tense commitment to order leaves judges no respectable room to maneuver when confronted by authoritarian rule. Unable to reconcile defending constitutional democracy with their role in a fixed legal system, Civil-Law judges have often become panderers to power. Not only did professional German judges form a corps of prostitutes for Naziism, but, during the Occupation, French judges offered similar services at discount prices.

Although the failings of the civil law tradition when it comes to protecting human interests can, at least in part, be blamed on that tradition's dependence on "tightly reasoned logic and rigid adherence to formal rules and abstract principles," that is not solely the fault of the natural law tradition of Grotius and Maritain, a tradition that does, after all, explicitly set out to protect human rights. There was another school of political thought that arouse during the sixteenth and seventeenth centuries that has been influential with the doctors of the civil law: the "realist" tradition of Machiavelli and of Hobbes that leads directly to the "positivist" theories of Bentham, Austin, and Kelsen, a tradition that denies the existence of natural law and that considers law to be nothing more than the positive enactments of a state or sovereign, a tradition that lead ultimately to the conclusion that there is really no such thing as the law of nations or international law, since there is no sovereign to enforce its decrees.

This realist, positivist tradition, which from the beginning of this century to at least the end of the second World War was the dominant influence on the accepted theories of international law, did not have much room for a concept of human rights. Thus it is not surprising that an international lawyer would note:

Apart from other considerations, two theories or attitudes stood in the way of any general recognition by international law in the nineteenth century and first two decades of the twentieth century, of the need to protect human rights. First, there was the so-called 'dualist' theory, according to which only states were the subjects of international law. Individuals, on this theory were objects but not subjects of international law, and without standing to enforce their rights before, or be heard by, an international tribunal.

Accordingly, this theory precluded the recognition at international law of individual human rights. Secondly, there was the doctrine that a state has complete sovereignty over its own nationals to the extent that such sovereignty constitutes a sphere of reserved jurisdiction into which international law is not permitted to reach. This doctrine represented an obstacle to the concept of international protection of human rights, a concept which necessarily involves each state accepting a restriction of its sovereignty in becoming bound by external obligations not to deny protection to the human rights of its own nationals.

THE ANGLO-AMERICAN COMMON LAW TRADITION

What I have said up to now about the development of the civil law is written by someone who cannot claim to know much about the matter. On the other hand, I do - or, at least should - know something about the evolution of the common law. This does not, however, make my task much easier. I am confronted with two problems. One is that knowing perhaps too much about the matter I am likely to get lost in the details. The other is more significant: because the common law is the product, not of logic, but of its own history - because the common law is in my view, the view of a common lawyer, a process, a means of accomplishing something - it is difficult to relate it to timeless, even if recently invented, ahistorical concepts like "human rights."

On the other hand, and this is perhaps the only justification that can give for afflicting you with this chapter, it does seem to me that anyone who tries to fit the concept of human rights into a tradition that recognizes that everything in this ocean of birth and death is arising and fading away - and that places its hope for salvation in the process of following a path to the other shore - is also going to have similar difficulties with such timeless absolutes. One important point about the common law tradition, although this is not often noted in modern academic scholarship, is that, from its inception, the practitioners of the common law have been more concerned with rights than with wrongs.

From the days of Ranulf de Glanville and the book named after him, from the end of the twelfth century of the Common Era to the present day, the important legal issues have almost always concerned the recognition and allocation of rights, not the rectification of wrongs. In fact, in Glanville's time, at the very start of the English common law, with the exception of what today we would classify as criminal actions, the only actions known to the common law were actions based on a right.

All of these actions were commenced by the plaintiff - called the demandant - purchasing a form - known as a writ -

from the chancery, directing the sheriff to summon the defendant - who was often called the "tenant" - to satisfy the plaintiff's claim, and, if he did not do so, to come into court to explain why he had not done it. In none of these actions was there any allegation that the tenant had done anything wrong; all were based on the claimant's right to whatever it was that he claimed: a parcel of land, some cattle, a debt, an accounting from a bailiff, or whatever. In fact, the greatest of these early actions, the action to recover land held by the tenant, was commenced by a writ called the "Writ of Right."

The rights asserted by the claimant in these actions, however, have little in common with the concept of "human rights," a concept that, as we have seen, was not to be invented for several centuries. The rights that were asserted in the original common law actions were always a right to get a particular thing from a particular person who was withholding it. It was not until the thirteenth century that "tort" actions evolved, in which the plaintiff was able to recover the damages for as compensation for a wrong, such as an assault and battery for example, committed by the defendant. In time, for reasons that are intriguing, but simply not relevant to our discussion here, many of the earlier right-based actions were replaced by actions that were in form "tort" actions, but in actuality remained actions to recover something that the plaintiff claimed as of right, not because of a wrong.

Even today, despite the ubiquity of civil actions brought to redistribute losses arising from personal injuries that are, in theory, based on the wrong of "negligence," the significant legal issues under the common law still have to do with rights, not with wrongs. Who has the right to Grandmother's ring, when Grandmother's will does not mention who is to get it? Who is entitled to what, now that the building the contractor was to repair got washed away in the flood? Is the compensation received by an inventor from the sale of a patent taxable as income, or does the inventor have the right to have it treated as capital gains? Is a congregation of soft-shelled Buddhists entitled to a building permit to erect a temple in a residential area where the zoning law permits only single family residences and churches?

It is issues like those, issues involving claims of right, not claims of wrong, that are central to the day to day operation of the common law system, despite the fact - or, rather, because of the fact - that most claims of right do not result in litigation. After all, if the rights are clear - if one can predict with near certainty how a case will be resolved - there is no nothing to litigate. If Grandmother had disposed of the ring in her will or if the contract had an unambiguous clause covering the destruction of the building by flood - or if there had been no flood - then there would be no reason to go to court. Established rights are generally respected; it is wrongs that are anomalous.

Particular rights of this sort are not at all like the generalized abstractions called human rights and they present no problem from a Buddhist's point of view. The precepts may enjoin us not to take what is not given, but it is the local law, not the universal Dharma, that defines how a gift is to be given and who has the power to make it. To the extent that human rights can be analogized to rights of this type, they too will present no difficulties for a Buddhist, who is after all enjoined to respect the claims of others whether they are called "rights" or not. The right to Grandmother's ring or to a building permit is, at this time and at this place, simply facts about the contingent, conditioned world that are not to be ignored, but equally are not to be clung too.

It is not, however, common law rights of this type that have been seen as the source of the modern concept of human rights. As has already been said, the common law, unlike the civil law, is descended directly, without any sharp break, from the feudal law of the middle ages. As one continental scholar said:

During my stay in England I was able to get to know the history of the common law, which is an exciting experience in itself, but has the additional charm, for a continental, of surprise at its utter strangeness. Anyone setting foot in the land of the common law may as well forget his Roman law education; what alone may help him is his knowledge of medieval feudal law.

Now the medieval feudal law was most definitely not a product of legislation nor was it composed of the commands of a sovereign; rather it was a body of custom governing the relations between and among all the members of a community, of a Gemeinschaft. This tradition - or the myth of the tradition - that the law governs the relations between all members of the community and binds even the king, was of great political importance in England during the sixteenth and seventeenth centuries when it was used to counter the absolutist claims of the Stewart Monarchs. It is this tradition that culminates in 1776 in the Virginia Declaration of Rights and the Declaration of Independence of the thirteen united States of America.

The eighteenth century, in Europe and America, drew to its close as the century that had clearly and unequivocally proclaimed the inalienable and imprescriptible rights of man. The proclamations were not, to begin with, the creatures of Gallic enthusiasm, of a revolutionary category of reason run riot in human affairs. They were the product of sober English philosophies, English Puritanism and non conformism, 'respectable' English resistance to absolutism and concern for freedom and toleration. They drew above all on the philosophy of John Locke and the traditions of the Glorious Revolution of 1688...

And beyond that they were the product of the English common law.

Despite the frequent use of Locke's writings as a justification for the recognition of the fundamental rights that were proclaimed at the time of the American revolution and are protected by the constitution of the United States, those rights themselves are - with one possible exception - the result of the legal and political history of England, not of philosophical speculations. Most importantly, those rights were either rights to fair procedures in courts - for example, the right to due process or to the writ of habeas corpus - or simply rights to be left alone without interference by the king or parliament - for example, the rights of freedom of speech and freedom of religion.

Although the recognition of both those types of rights is in the constitution of the United States is very much the parochial product of English legal and political history, they are likely to be looked upon with favor by followers of the various Buddhist traditions. Still, if only because it is a fact - part of the fact of *dukkha* - that the world is often unfair, the concept of "fairness," or of "justice," is not a central concern of those traditions, though, of course, that does not mean that fairness is not something to be desired in a government; on the other hand, it is not likely that many of the procedural rights enshrined in the constitution of the United States, such as the writ of habeas corpus, or the prohibition of bills of attainder, or the right to a jury trial in cases at common law, can meaningfully be translated to other legal systems or other political traditions.

If such procedural rights are not of central concern, the right - the ability - to be left alone, the freedom of religion and speech and thought, is critical if one is to be able to follow the Buddha's teaching that one should rely on oneself. In Buddhism, which is based on the doctrine of the Middle Way, neither the Buddha nor the great Buddhist sages said, "My teachings alone are true." They did not encourage persecution by religious wars, burning at the stake, massacres, or forced conversions for the sake of their own Dharma, nor did they state that all teachings are the same. In the first Suttanta of the *Digha Nikaya*, the Buddha said: "Make a trial, find out what leads to your happiness and freedom - and what does not, reject it. What leads on to greater happiness - follow it."

This practical and sure way of distinguishing truth amid falsehood was meant by the Buddha to be applied to his own teachings as well, for he emphasized that one ought not to believe in the authority of any teachers and masters but should believe and practice the religious truth embodied by them. This is the Middle Way in action - as something practiceable, by means of which one can steer a course between blind dogma and vague eclecticism.

Thus any government that is in turn governed by Buddhist principles would certainly cherish and protect the freedom of thought and expression for all persons, even if it would not see those persons as the autonomous individual rights-bearers of the Western European traditions.

Some of the rights set out in the Universal Declaration of Human Rights - for example, those of articles eight and ten - are procedural rights of the type that can be traced back to the Anglo-American tradition, while others - like those of article eighteen - protect the freedoms of thought and expression and can also be traced back to that tradition.

More problematic is the right to own property that is set out in article seventeen of the Universal Declaration of Human Rights. That right, which arguably can be traced back to the so called "takings clause" of the fifth amendment of the United States constitution, is not a product of the common law tradition, but rather of the philosophical speculations of Locke and Hobbes and other philosophical purveyors of the remarkably naive - at least from a Buddhist point of view - idea that society and government are based on some sort of social contract. Unlike the civil law, and the Roman law before it with their concept of dominium, the common law traditionally has made little use of any concept of "property" or of "ownership;" at common law what is important is possession, and the right to possession, and estates and other interests in land (or in goods and chattels), and there is hardly ever a reason to speak of "property."

Although no Buddhist is likely to object to a legal system that permits one to possess a begging bowel and a set of robes, or even to possess land, the right to own property - with all of its contractarian and anti-communitarian baggage - should be looked upon with great skepticism, for it is the contractarian ideology and its utilitarian offspring, with their emphasis on individuals blindly pursuing their own selfish interests, that are largely responsible for the modern destruction of traditional communities. Moreover the modern glorification of the "right" to own property is hard to reconcile with the

basic teaching that ignorant clinging to things is the cause of
dukkha.

Be that as may be, over time the rights that are the product
of the Anglo-American legal tradition and are enshrined in
the constitution of the United States were transformed into
something much more problematic.

The demand for rights in the seventeenth and eighteenth
centuries was a demand against the existing state and
authorities, against despotism, arbitrariness and the political
disenfranchisement of those who held different opinions. The
demand for rights in the nineteenth and twentieth centuries
becomes increasingly a claim upon the state, a demand that it
provides and guarantees the means of achieving the
individual's happiness and well-being, his welfare. These two
different conceptions of rights...like the opposed conceptions
of "freedom from" and "freedom to," stand in constant danger
of fundamental conflict with each other - a conflict that
dominates our contemporary world.

THE BUDDHA'S TEACHINGS

Whatever may be the sources of the concept of human rights,
one thing is clear: human rights are something that is asserted
against governments, against the people or institutions who
govern others (though sometimes they may be thinly disguised
by references to empty abstractions like the "state" or the
"commonwealth"). There are religions whose primary focus is
on governance, or at least there is one such religion, if it is a
religion: Confucianism; there are religions that have nothing to
say about governance at all, except perhaps to suggest that it is
wise not to attract the attention of the state: Taoism, for example;
there are theistic, theocratic religions like Islam that do not
distinguish between religion and government; and there are
theistic religions, like most of the Western versions of
Christianity, that make a distinction between the governance
of this world and that of the City of God.

Buddhism does not, however, fall into any of these
categories and although in East Asia, Buddhism and

Confucianism have strongly influenced each other, so that it is easy to find statements on political themes from Buddhist sources, but almost inevitably these texts are more Confucian than Buddhist. In its own right Buddhism has never, up to this century at least, developed a political theory, to say nothing of a theory of human rights.

It might have been expected that, with the attention given to the conduct of the laity and the frequency of his advice in social matters, the Buddha would at some time have sketched the political construction of an ideal state: yet no thought of any reform in the existing political set-up is apparent. The warrior class (Khattiyas), priestly class (Brahmanas), householders, Gahapatis, Setthis, Suddas, all occupied a definite status and there is no suggestion in the Buddha's Discourses that this distribution would become modified, except in cases of reference to a general promiscuity resulting from the collapse of morality. Nor does it seem that the Buddha felt the need for any such change since his teaching was designed for, and addressed to, "a householder, or householder's son, or son of some other clan." It seems that he attributed the success of a system to the morals of the people working it rather than to any virtue inherent in the system itself. This, surely, is sound enough, if it is taken that a community develops a system according to its own understanding of life and improves on it as that understanding improves, always assuming that no other system is forced on it from the outside against its will...

The Buddha's teachings are applicable in all circumstances, in hot lands and in cold lands, in the dry season and in the rainy season, in times of plenty and in times of hunger. It is in this sense that they are universal. Do not do anything harmful; do only what is good; discipline your own mind; this is the teaching of the Buddha. The Buddha's teachings have been heard, and have been followed, under myriads of different forms of government, in kingdoms and in republics, under dictatorships and under democracies. Whatever the political form may be, the four noble truths remain true, the eight-fold path remains the path.

Regarding the formulation of a definite scheme of government which would last indefinitely, producing always satisfactory results solely by reason of its own excellence, it seems unlikely that any person of vision, or even any thinking person, would ever have embarked on the task. In the last two thousand years, Western Europe has worked out many types of governments, but, in the main, they present a series of checks and modifications tending towards one side or the other of the principle for which the Greeks of the fifth century BC fought the Persians at Marathon and Salamis, namely, freedom of individual thought versus regimentation of thought. To some extent it might be considered that Plato was advocating the latter, but there is no question that the Buddha entirely advocated the former...

By reason...of the importance assigned to the moral standards and outlook of man in the Buddha's teachings, one must look for a description of the qualities of the people who will operate a scheme rather than for any intrinsic virtue in the scheme itself. If the scheme is one of an autocracy such as prevailed in the Buddha's day, then one must look for political teaching of the nature that will render that autocracy benevolent; this will consist in injunctions to the kings and their proclaimed duties. Of such we have several examples.

But, of course, none of those examples contain any discussion of human rights, or of rights of any sort. The Buddha's ethical teachings are concerned with virtues and right conduct, they are not concerned with rights, and certainly not with rights against the state. Still it is undoubtedly true that the virtuous man - the Brahmin - will respect the rights of others that are recognized by the local laws. Those rights, however, are not going to be the product of any teaching of the Buddha; rather they will be defined by the laws and customs of the particular time and place.

On the other hand, the virtuous man - the Brahmin - is not going to cling to his own rights. The one who takes nothing in this world which is not given - nothing long or short, small or large, good or bad - this one I call a Brahmin. He is free from the very basics of desire for this world or for the next, he is the unfettered one, the desireless one - this one I call a Brahmin.

The concept of human rights is a recent product of the history of Western Europe and of the civil law and common law traditions. To a large extent it has arisen as a response to the religious wars of the sixteenth and seventeenth centuries and to the horrors - the genocide - of the Second World War. The concept of human rights is also to a large extent a product of the modern philosophical and political tendency to replace traditional communities with associations of autonomous individuals pursuing only their individual ends. The teachings of the Buddha, on the other hand, are timeless and adaptable to any legal or political regime. The Buddha, and the successful followers of the Buddha's teachings, having wisdom and compassion, has no need for rights for themselves. And that is why the Buddha has no rights.

Bibliography

Aiyappan, A., and P. R. Srinivasan, *Story of Buddhism with Special Reference to South India*. Madras, India: Government of Madras, 1960.

Auboyer, Jeannine, *Buddha: A Pictorial History of His Life and Legacy*. New York: Crossroad, 1983.

Banerji, Aparna, *Traces of Buddhism in South India*. Calcutta: Scientific Book Agency, 1970

Bapat, P. V., ed., *2500 Years of Buddhism*. New Delhi: Government of India, Publications Division, 1956.

Basham, A. L., *History and Doctrines of the Ajivikas*. London: Luzac, 1951.

Basu, N. N., *Modern Buddhism and Its Followers in Orissa*. Calcutta, 1911.

Bechert, Heinz and Richard Gombrich, eds., *The World of Buddhism: Monks and Nuns in Society and Culture*. London: Thames and Hudson, 1984.

Cabezon, Jose Ignacia, ed., *Buddhism, Sexuality, and Gender*. Albany: SUNY Press, 1992.

Charles S. Prebish, ed., *Buddhism: A Modern Perspective*. University Park: Pennsylvania State University Press, 1975.

Conze, Edward, *Buddhism: Its Essence and Development*. New York: Harper Torchbooks, 1965.

Gellner, David, "Buddhism and Hinduism in the Nepal Valley," in Sutherland, Stewart, et.al., eds., *The World's Religions*. Boston: G. K. Hall, 1988.

Horner, I. B., *The Living Thoughts of Gotama the Buddha*. London: Cassell, 1948.

Jayatilleke, K. N., *Early Buddhist Theory of Knowledge*. London: George Allen & Unwin, 1963.

Joseph M. Kitagawa and Mark D. Cummings, ed., *Buddhism and Asian History*. New York: Macmillan, 1987.

Joshi, Lalmani, *Studies in the Buddhistic Culture of India*, 2nd rev. ed. Delhi: Motilal Banarsidass, 1977.

Karetsky, Patricia Eichenbaum, *The Life of the Buddha: Ancient Scriptural and Pictorial Traditions*. Lanham: University Press of America, 1992.

Keown, Damein et.al., eds. *Buddhism and Human Rights*. London: Curzon, 1998.

Kohn, Michael H., trans., *The Shambhala Dictionary of Buddhism and Zen*. Boston: Shambhala, 1991.

Lamotte, Etienne, *History of Indian Buddhism: From the Origins to the Saka Era*. Louvain-La-Neuve: Institut Orientaliste, 1988.

Lopez, Donald S., Jr, ed., *Buddhist Hermeneutics*. Honolulu: University of Hawaii Press, 1988.

Lopez, Donald S., Jr., ed., *Buddhism in Practice*. Princeton: Princeton University Press, 1995.

Malalasekera, G. P., ed., *Encyclopedia of Buddhism*. Colombo: Government of Sri Lanka, 1961.

Mishra, V. B., *Religious Beliefs and Practices of North India during the Early Mediaeval Period*. Leiden, Netherlands: Brill, 1973.

Morgan, Kenneth W., ed., *The Path of the Buddha*. New York: Ronald Press, 1974.

Nakamura, Hajime, *Gotama Buddha*. Los Angeles: Buddhist Books International, 1977.

Ñanamoli, Bhikkhu, *The Life of the Buddha*. Kandy, Sri

Lanka: Buddhist Publication Society, 1972.

Narada Thera, *The Buddha and His Teachings*. Kandy, Sri Lanka: Buddhist Publication Society, 1988 (reprint).

Prebish, Charles S., ed. *Buddhist Ethics: A Cross-Cultural Approach*. Dubuque: Kendall/Hunt, 1992.

Thomas, E. J., *The Life of the Buddha as Legend and History*. London: Routledge & Kegan Paul, 1927.

Warder, A. K, *Outline of Indian Philosophy*. Delhi: Motilal Banarsidass, 1971.

Warder, A. K., *Indian Buddhism*, 2nd ed. rev. Delhi: Motilal Banarsidass, 1980.

Warren, Henry C., *Buddhism in Translations*. New York: Atheneum, 1963.

INDEX